WEDDING
HANDBOOK

WARD LOCK

A WARD LOCK BOOK

First published in the UK
1993 by Ward Lock
(an imprint of Cassell)
Villiers House
41/47 Strand
London
WC2N 5JE

Copyright © 1993 Ward Lock

Parts of this book have previously appeared in the following
books in the Family Matters series: *The Wedding Planner*,
Wedding Etiquette, *How to be a Bridesmaid*, *The Bridegroom's
Handbook*, *How to Be the Best Man* and *Wedding Speeches and
Toasts*

All rights reserved. No part of this book
may be reproduced or transmitted
in any form or by any means,
electronic or mechanical, including photocopying,
recording or any information storage
and retrieval system, without prior permission
in writing from the copyright holder and Publisher.

Distributed in the United States
by Sterling Publishing Co., Inc.
387 Park Avenue South, New York, NY 10016–8810

Distributed in Australia
by Capricorn Link (Australia) Pty Ltd
P.O. Box 665, Lane Cove, NSW 2066

**British Library Cataloguing-in-Publication Data
A catalogue record for this book is available from
the British Library**

ISBN 0–7063–7083–X

Typeset by Columns of Reading

Printed and bound in Finland by
Werner Söderström Oy

CONTENTS

PART 1   PLANNING THE WEDDING – THE BRIDE AND HER FAMILY

PART 2   THE BRIDEGROOM

PART 3   THE BEST MAN

PART 4   THE BRIDESMAIDS

PART 5   WEDDING SPEECHES

INTRODUCTION

'It will be all right on the day,' they say, and so it will be if you plan your wedding carefully. This book is designed to give practical at-a-glance information that will take the stress out of planning. Checklists and reminders will help you to have everything ready and to be serenely confident on the day. In addition you will find that the book suggests some good ideas you can copy, those little extra touches which convert a conventional wedding into a special occasion you will remember all your life.

BEING WELL ORGANIZED

Keep a large, brightly-coloured, easy-to-find hardback record book for written notes, in a permanent place under your desk phone, or in a bedside table drawer cleared of clutter. This prevents you writing on numerous scraps of paper which would create chaos. To prevent other people giving you bits of paper, use a handbag-size notebook to enable you to keep notes together. Friends can write suggestions in that. A duplicate book is useful for distributing copies of addresses to helpers. Duplicate writing pads enable you to keep copies of handwritten letters. Copy important information into your record book each day, having gathered together notes or business cards in a see-through pocket attached to the back of the book with a clip.

Other useful devices for grouping cards or leaflets permanently are:

For business cards: a card index; a loose-leaf indexed business card holder; see-through pages for a Filofax or similar system.

For leaflets: a loose-leaf folder to hold caterers' brochures, letters, and hotel leaflets.

A wedding album with transparent stick-down pages can display the most amusing business cards and pretty sample wedding invitations you wish to show the family. Later it can display your own wedding invitation, printed wedding menu, and favourite congratulations cards.

Throughout your planning, as you make the major decisions you can enter your important names, addresses and telephone numbers in this book.

COUNTDOWN

A glance at this list will give you a clear idea from the start of what is ahead and will need doing. You can meticulously plan every detail the way you want it. However, if you are short of time you can leave many decisions to the experts who always like to plan happy surprises. The banqueting manager of a large hotel, for example, can arrange for the toastmaster, menu printing, a harpist to play as guests enter and a band. Good hotels can also be relied upon to deal with minor mishaps – the cloakroom attendant being prepared to sew on a button at the wedding reception, or during your honeymoon.

WEDDING CALENDAR

FIRST MONTH AFTER ENGAGEMENT

(First Four To Six Months in Advance)

☆ Tell family
☆ Families meet
☆ Write engagement announcement letters
☆ Buy file or record book of wedding arrangements
☆ Insert engagement announcements in newspaper
☆ Buy engagement and wedding rings
☆ Choose best man, bridesmaids, ushers, pageboys
☆ Hold engagement party

☆ Book church/Meet minister
☆ Collect register office forms
☆ Collect documents to accompany register office forms
☆ Return register office forms
☆ Get caterers' estimates and hotel literature
☆ Meet hotel restaurant banqueting manager
☆ Book caterer, band, toastmaster
☆ Book reception hall or venue
☆ Consult travel agent
☆ Book honeymoon
☆ Order printed invitations, reply cards, serviettes, menus, seating plan
☆ Visit stores to set up wedding lists
☆ Start house hunting by contacting house agents
☆ Contact mortgage brokers and solicitors
☆ Photocopy map of church and reception locations
☆ Appoint solicitor to advise and deal with house exchange and new will
☆ Start making wedding dress if not buying it
☆ Have bridesmaids' dresses made if not buying them

THREE MONTHS BEFORE WEDDING

☆ Choose wedding cake
☆ Select menu
☆ Choose wedding dress if hiring or buying
☆ Choose bridesmaids' dresses if buying
☆ Attend minister's courses for couples
☆ Thank guests who send presents
☆ Order new passport
☆ See doctor or family planning clinic

TWO MONTHS BEFORE WEDDING

☆ Send out invitations
☆ Mother and mother-in-law choose appropriate dresses and hats

✩ Arrange insurance and connection of services at new home
✩ Arrange vaccinations and visas for honeymoon
✩ Visit register office to collect and return forms

MONTH BEFORE WEDDING

✩ Banns are called in church on three successive Sundays
✩ Select photographer/video company
✩ Book wedding cars
✩ Write speech
✩ Deliver notification to registrar
✩ Choose flowers
✩ Choose music
✩ Get order-of-service sheets printed
✩ Get travellers' cheques
✩ Get insurance for bride to drive groom's car
✩ Select going away outfits
✩ Buy attendants' gifts and wrap them
✩ Make sure groom, best man and ushers have booked hired morning dress

TWO WEEKS BEFORE WEDDING

✩ Order new address stationery
✩ Take possession of new house
✩ Get phone connected
✩ Deliver furniture and gifts
✩ Book bride's hairdressing appointment
✩ Make seating plan

WEEK BEFORE WEDDING

✩ Attend wedding rehearsal/Watch another wedding
✩ Notify *The Times* newspaper on Friday for Monday announcement

☆ Collect honeymoon tickets from travel agent
☆ Collect certificates/licence from registrar
☆ Place passports and documents in flight bag/going-away handbag
☆ Wear-in new shoes
☆ Confirm all arrangements including cars
☆ Check route to church
☆ Bride's mother checks guests' RSVP cards, phones those who haven't replied, and confirms numbers with caterer

TWO DAYS BEFORE WEDDING

☆ Families from abroad arrive
☆ Hold stag party/Girls' night out
☆ Guests who cannot attend organize telemessages

DAY BEFORE WEDDING

☆ Families from distant towns arrive
☆ Bride has hairdressing appointment and manicure
☆ Set-up gift display
☆ Deliver luggage to hotel
☆ Collect buttonholes or wedding cake if necessary
☆ Clean family car and fill it with petrol
☆ Clean and tidy house
☆ Bride's mother notifies caterer of late cancellations/final guests' numbers
☆ Put clothes ready, speech in pocket
☆ Clean shoes
☆ Set alarm clock
☆ Deliver schedule to minister (Scotland)

WEDDING DAY

☆ Best man phones groom and ushers to wake them and remedy hitches

☆ Florist delivers bride's bouquet of fresh flowers and bride's mother's corsage to bride's home, other corsages and buttonholes to groom's or best man's home or the church
☆ Flowers are delivered to church and arranged by florist
☆ Best man dresses, then arrives at groom's home, places ring and church fees in pockets
☆ Chief bridesmaid arrives at bride's home
☆ Bride has face made up and is dressed in wedding clothes
☆ Professional photographer arrives to photograph bride at home
☆ Ushers arrive at church and show guests to seats
☆ First car takes groom and best man to church
☆ Second car takes bride's mother and bridesmaids to church
☆ Third, grandest, car brings bride and her father to church

WEDDING CEREMONY AND RECEPTION

☆ Signing register
☆ Best man pays vicar and church fees
☆ Photographs on church steps
☆ Grandest car takes bride and groom to reception
☆ Second car takes host and other parents of bride/groom
☆ Third car takes bridesmaids and/or ushers
☆ Final car takes best man and any guests lacking transport
☆ More photographs
☆ Receiving line
☆ Drinks
☆ Grace by minister
☆ Buffet or dinner

CAKE CUTTING

☆ Sparkling wine served for speeches and toasts by bride's father/family friend, bridegroom, best man
☆ Groom presents bouquet to bride's mother and/or gifts to attendants
☆ Read telemessages
☆ Dancing
☆ Bride and groom change into going-away clothes
☆ Decorate departure car
☆ Departure car departs
☆ Bride's father pays and tips caterers
☆ Clear up hall
☆ Best man takes bridesmaids home

AFTER WEDDING

☆ Return hired wedding clothes
☆ Send off pieces of wedding cake
☆ Thank guests who sent telemessages
☆ Thank guests for presents delivered on wedding day
☆ Select and pay for wedding photographs

THE ENGAGEMENT

In Victorian days a man courting an unmarried girl would have approached the family for permission to marry her and would have only proposed once the consent had been given. Today most couples are living fairly independent lives by the time they agree to marry and family pressure is unlikely to be able to separate them. However, legally, you have to be sixteen before you can marry and in England you need parental consent (or a guardian's consent) when marrying a girl or boy under the age of eighteen. If parental consent is unreasonably withheld, you can apply for a court order.

ENGAGEMENT RINGS

A couple may discuss the possibility of getting married, but when an engagement ring of value has been handed over, the young man has made a commitment, and the bride-to-be and onlookers can see that there is an official engagement. The engagement ring is worn on the third finger of the fiancée's left hand because the Greeks thought this finger was connected to the heart. The Romans introduced engagement rings and after they converted to Christianity a 9th-century Pope stipulated that engagement rings must be worn.

An engagement ring may also demonstrate financial security. Some religious groups (e.g. Jews) require engagement or wedding rings of value to show the husband's ability to support a family. Others accept a ring of no value or no ring at all (e.g. Quakers).

In olden times the groom was supposed to propose in a romantic location on bended knee, presenting his bride-to-be with a ring. The current custom is for the husband-to-be to propose first and then take the bride-to-be to choose her own ring at a jeweller's shop once he has been accepted.

You have a choice of three sources for the ring(s):

a) a jeweller's shop
b) an antique shop
c) a jewellery designer

JEWELLER'S SHOP

Whatever your choice, your first stop should be a reputable jeweller. You will be able to see a wide range of rings, which will help you to identify your likes and dislikes, and obtain some idea of cost which can vary enormously. An assistant will assess the size of ring needed. Size codings are by letter, and the ring(s) you choose may require adjustment to fit.

ANTIQUE SHOPS

Quite a few couples like the idea of buying rings with a little history, and it can be fun to take pot luck and look in antique shops for a second-hand (literally!) ring. Such rings are sometimes significantly cheaper than their brand new equivalents. If it does not fit, a good jeweller will be able to adjust the size. If it is tarnished, again a jeweller will be able to polish it up.

JEWELLERY DESIGNER

For a unique ring, find a jewellery designer to make up

your own special one. Browse round the shops first to get an idea of what you like, then discuss the material, design and price with the designer. Some couples find this process particularly satisfying as they can put a lot of effort and thought into creating a ring which expresses their attachment. Costs are higher than from jeweller's shops, but you can of course set a budget for the designer.

☆ The groom could visit the jeweller in advance and establish the acceptable price range to avoid later embarrassment. If the groom has not done this the bride should avoid opting for an outrageously expensive ring unless she is quite sure that her fiancé can afford it.

The Diamond Information Centre suggests you spend a month's salary on a diamond engagement ring. So that you do not have a harder ring rubbing a softer one, the engagement ring and wedding ring should be the same quality of gold. Matching sets can be bought.

Shop around to compare prices and styles. Illustrated brochures are available from high street jewellers, large suppliers and trade associations such as the National Association of Goldsmiths (Tel. 071–726 4374), London Diamond Centre, or the Diamond Information Centre in London (Tel. 071–404 4444). Individual jewellers make rings to order. When ordering rings by post allow three to four weeks.

☆ *GOLD RINGS* The bride's engagement ring is traditionally gold with a diamond or other precious stone. Solid gold is used because the ring must be of value. Gold plate can wear off and base metals can make the finger go green when the hand perspires. Gold can be nine carat, eighteen carat or 24 carat. The purest gold is soft and less practical as it can be damaged when striking objects or rubbing other rings, so it is mixed with a harder metal. Nine or eighteen carat gold is preferred for practical reasons and economy. European rings are available in eight carat. An eighteen-carat ring is more appropriate for a girl whose other jewellery is eighteen-carat gold, as with much Asian jewellery. Although platinum is silver-coloured it is more expensive than gold. It is a very acceptable alternative. Royalty have rings made of Welsh gold: a natural choice for the Princess of Wales.

☆ *DIAMONDS* Diamonds are called a girl's best friend because of their value. When choosing a diamond consider the 4 Cs: colour, clarity, cut, and carat (weight). Better (and therefore generally more expensive) diamonds have more sparkle. Diamonds are also chosen because they are durable, go with any colour clothing, and are supposed to bring good luck. The diamond is a symbol of innocence and loyalty, and sacred to the month of April, a popular time for marriages.

☆ *CHOOSING A STYLE AND SETTING* Some rings are designed so that extra stones can be added later. If you want a colourful ring, have a central coloured stone encircled by smaller diamonds, or a diamond encircled by coloured stones. You can also have a line of identical stones, a central stone with two stones in contrasting colour of the same size inset in the band, or a raised central stone with two smaller stones in a different colour on the shoulders of the ring.

If you have a second-hand or inherited ring you can alter the ring size and modernize an old ring to make it fashionable. Large stones look impressive twinkling under candle-light. But big flashy rings may snag stockings and hurt your fingers if you knock your hands. Flat styles are practical for everyday wear under gloves. Matching engagement and wedding ring sets are made with interlocking shapes.

OTHER STONES AND THEIR MEANINGS

Birthstones can be used instead of diamonds, or in addition:

☆ *JANUARY*	Garnet (red) for faithfulness
☆ *FEBRUARY*	Amethyst (transparent purple) for peace-making
☆ *MARCH*	Aquamarine or bloodstone for courage and wisdom
☆ *APRIL*	Diamond for innocence or blue sapphire for hope
☆ *MAY*	Emerald green for true love
☆ *JUNE*	Pearl or agate for health and long life
☆ *JULY*	Ruby for friendship or onyx for mutual love
☆ *AUGUST*	Peridot (greenish yellow) or sard-onyx (white onyx layers alternating with yellow or orange sard) for a happy marriage
☆ *SEPTEMBER*	Sapphire or olive green chrysolite for 'freedom from evil'
☆ *OCTOBER*	Opal for hope
☆ *NOVEMBER*	Topaz for friendship
☆ *DECEMBER*	Turquoise for happiness in love.

GROOM'S ENGAGEMENT GIFT/WEDDING RING

The girl can buy her fiancé any gift he likes, such as a gold key ring, watch, cuff links, tie pin, silk tie, clothes or a signet ring. His and Hers rings are available in matching styles and can be romantically engraved with names and dates.

WEDDING RINGS

Wedding rings are usually made in platinum, white gold

(9 or 18 carat) or yellow gold (9, 18 or 22 carat). The lower the carat number, the less pure gold there is, making the ring harder and less lustrous, but costing less. White gold is so soft it is not used in 22-carat form, and over the years it wears away and loses some of its original bright sheen.

It is a good idea to look at wedding rings when you are buying the engagement ring, as your partner will wear them both on the third finger of her left hand and they should complement each other. That does not mean you have to buy them at the same time, but you may be able to form some idea of what you want the wedding ring to be like when you purchase the engagement ring.

A groom's ring can match the bride's. His ring will be pricier because it is larger. Both rings can be engraved with date and name. The groom might prefer a signet ring, or a practical gift such as a watch.

SAFETY AND INSURANCE OF RINGS

Jewellers supply pretty ring boxes with cushioned linings. When washing your hands return the ring to its protective box within an inside zipped pocket or a securely fastened handbag. If you are not wearing your ring on honeymoon, avoid losing it by securing it, for

example, to a necklace, bracelet, or soft watchstrap. Replace the ring before travelling in crowds. Keep the receipt for insurance purposes.

ANNOUNCING THE ENGAGEMENT

Once you are engaged, you want to share the good news with everyone you know.

TELLING THE FAMILY

Nowadays, whether the groom asks the bride's father for permission or merely informs him of the engagement depends on various factors, including the bride's age. A young man without his own home and a reasonable income would do well to discuss the matter with his own parents. Their advice or offers of finance may help him approach her parents successfully.

An older man would probably get the girl's agreement first. Then she tells her parents the good news. Having established that his offer is accepted, he can confidently inform his parents.

Both families may want to meet quickly. His family could invite hers home for a general celebration and her family may reciprocate to start discussing wedding arrangements. Or her family can take the initiative.

After the family, close friends are informed by phone or letter before the general newspaper announcement.

TELLING AN EX-GIRLFRIEND OR BOYFRIEND

Very personal communications such as this are supposed to be delivered in person, if you can trust yourself and your former loved one to remain polite and dignified. When phoning to explain avoid opening by saying, 'I've decided to get married.' A girlfriend who doesn't know there is someone else in your life might think you are proposing to her!

If you write, avoid sending a negative letter explaining in detail why you do not want to marry the person you are writing to. Your letter should convey warm, positive feelings about your past relationship and express the view that you wish to remain friends.

You may all meet later in life, so try to remain cordial for everyone's sake. When you write you could include an invitation to the engagement party. The ex might bring along a new love, or find romance amongst your single friends. Sample letter:

> *Dear Bob,*
>
> *You have been such a close friend of mine that you are the first person I must tell that Romeo Montagu and I have decided to get engaged. I know that you care for me very much, as I do for you, so I do hope that you will be pleased for me…*

NEWSPAPER ANNOUNCEMENTS

The bride's family usually pays for the announcements in their area and in national secular or religious newspapers, but the families of the bride and groom could split the bill, the groom's family placing announcements in their local papers. Formal newspaper announcements in national newspapers such as *The Times*, *The Daily Telegraph* or *The Independent* follow a similar set style which can be brief. *The Times* is read all over the world and carries announcements for weddings in the UK and abroad of all religions. The following will appear in the section called 'Forthcoming Marriage Announcements':

**Mr A. B. Smith
and Mrs Y. Brown**
The marriage will take place shortly between Mr Alfred Ben Smith of Harrow, Middlesex, and Mrs Yolanda Brown of Reading, Berkshire.

**Mr B. C. Smith
and Miss B. A. Brown**
The engagement is announced between Brian Christopher, son of Mr and Mrs John Smith, of Wiltshire, and Brenda Anne, daughter of Mr A. Brown, MSc, and Mrs Brown, of Bristol. The wedding will take place in February in Bristol.

**Mr A. B. Smith
and Miss Y. Z. Brown**
The engagement is announced between Albert, younger son of the late Sir Albert Smith, and of the Lady Grey, Lancashire, and Yolanda, youngest daughter of Dr Jim Brown, of Australia, and Mrs Anne Wise of Virginia, United States.

You can phone *The Times'* Court and Social advertising department for details of prices and advice on wording. But they must receive notification in writing with the signature of bride or groom or one of the parents and the address to which the bill will be sent.

'Son of' or 'daughter of' usually means the only son or the only daughter, though you can state 'only son of'. 'Younger' means younger of two. 'Youngest' means youngest of three or more, while 'elder' means elder of two, 'eldest' of three or more. 'Third son/daughter' can be inserted if there are several.

ENGAGEMENT OF STEPCHILDREN

If the groom's father is dead and his mother remarried, state 'Peter, son of the late Mr John Brown, stepson of Mr Graham Jones'. If Peter's mother was still married to Mr John Brown at the time of John's death you say, 'son of the late Mr John Brown and Mrs Brown'. If she was already divorced from John when he died say 'Peter, son of the late Mr John Brown and Mrs Anne Brown'. If Anne had remarried Graham Jones before John Brown died you say 'Peter, son of the late Mr John Brown and Mrs Graham Jones'.

LETTER OF CONGRATULATION

After reading newspaper announcements.

12 Artillery Avenue,
Edinburgh,
Scotland.

Dear Juliet,
I opened the Times newspaper today and was
delighted to hear that you are getting married.
We seem to have lost touch in the past few
months while I have been abroad/taking exams/
living up north/but I have often thought about you.
If you can spare a moment I would love to know
how you met Romeo, and about your plans.
Wishing you a long and happy married life,

Anne

The bride-to-be can reply by phone and send an invitation to the engagement party or wedding.

THE ENGAGEMENT PARTY

Quite often one or two gatherings are held to celebrate your engagement. Such parties were once the occasion on which the engagement was officially announced, but today's guests are tipped off in advance on the cause for jubilation. The bride's parents have traditionally borne the cost of the event, but this habit is changing as the engaged couple themselves tend to take over the financing.

The engagement party takes place when the ring has been bought, as soon as possible so everyone can meet the proposed other half.

Some couples use the engagement party as an opportunity to entertain people who may not be able to come to the wedding itself, or who, because of restrictions on numbers, will not be invited to attend. Do make lists and consult your family about whom to invite – some relatives may be upset about being neglected in favour of friends from outside the family circle. Invitations are verbal, not written or printed.

The engagement party may be the first time that the bridegroom meets some of his fiancée's extended family. As when meeting his future in-laws, this can be a little intimidating and it is well worth making an extra effort with such people who will be part of his life from now on.

CHECKLIST: the engagement party

☆ Decide on venue
☆ Agree the date
☆ Prepare a list of guests
☆ Issue invitations
☆ Order/prepare food and drink
☆ Welcome guests
☆ Make engagement announcement/speech
☆ Ensure guests who require it have transport

ENGAGEMENT PARTY INVITATIONS

For a large formal seated dinner party cards look better and save time. Stationery shops and printers have examples of typefaces. For formal occasions wording is in the third person as if a secretary is writing on behalf of the hostess. For an informal party you can buy pre-printed invitation cards and fill in the blanks. Invitations read:

> *Mr & Mrs Mark Capulet*
> *request the pleasure of the company of*
>
> ....
>
> *at an engagement party*
> *to celebrate the engagement of*
> *Juliet Capulet and Romeo Montagu*
> *on Saturday January 1st at 8pm at*
> *The Cottage, Little Village, Surrey.*
>
> *Mrs M Capulet*
> *1 Mansion House*
> *High Street*
> *London SW1*
> *Tel: 01-123 4567*   *RSVP*

Newsagents and stationers stock pads of colourful illustrated engagement party invitations suitable for a young person's party or a buffet.

These invitations are usually in the first person. A typical form of wording is:

> *To* ....
> *Please join us to celebrate our engagement*
> *Time* ....
> *Place* ....
> *From* ....
> *RSVP*

You fill in the blanks.

A hand-written note from the couple can be in the first or third person and begins:

> *Juliet Capulet and Romeo Montagu*
> *invite you/John Brown to a party*
> *to celebrate their engagement*
> *on July.........*

Include the home address for the RSVP if it is different from the party location.

REPLY TO AN ENGAGEMENT PARTY INVITATION

If no reply card is included, reply in the first or third person following the style of the invitation. In the first person you begin 'Thank you very much for your ...' If the invitation is in the third person, you should reply in the third person:

> *John Brown thanks Mr and Mrs Capulet for their*
> *kind invitation to the engagement party of Juliet*
> *Capulet and Romeo Montagu to be held on*
> *Saturday January 1st at 8pm at The Cottage,*
> *Little Village, Surrey, which he has much pleasure*
> *in accepting.*

To decline, you say, for example, 'which he regrets he is unable to accept owing to absence abroad'.

State the time, place and date. The hosts are unlikely to

be holding two engagement parties, but they might hold two parties in the same month, and if they wrote the wrong date on your invitation or you misread their writing they will be able to warn you.

PARTY VENUE

The engagement party can be held at the girl's parents' home, or a hall, and there may be another party for the young people at her flat.

Guests take gifts which will be useful in a new home. No speeches are necessary though at large gatherings with seated dinners somebody usually stands at the end to toast the VIPs – the happy couple – and thank the hosts. The hosts stand near the door at the end of the party to say goodbye and be thanked.

INTRODUCTIONS

You will be introducing many people to each other at such events, and it is worth remembering a few rules of etiquette on how to do this. Men are introduced to women, not the other way round, so you say 'Richard Boyle, meet Marian Foot'. Men generally stand up when being introduced to a woman. If one person is clearly older than the other, the rule to follow is that the younger one is introduced to the senior person. You may find it helpful to repeat the introduction the other way round to help your guests remember names, and perhaps add a little information about them. So you might say 'Peter Brittan, please meet my sister, Libby Diamond. Libby, this is Peter, my old school friend.' Try to use full names, not 'Mr' and 'Mrs'.

These gatherings are quite informal and might consist of drinks, or a light, buffet-style meal. The bride's father may make a short speech ending with a toast to the happy couple. The bridegroom replies by proposing the health of both sets of parents.

Even if you do not hold an engagement party, you should bring both sets of parents together as soon as is practical. If they have not met before, it might be worth keeping the meeting quite private away from other relations. These initial meetings can be a little tense as people who hardly know each other are under some pressure to get on. Their common ground is the bride and bridegroom, so be prepared to make a lot of the conversation and be the subject of much of the talk.

CHANGED RELATIONSHIPS

Once you are engaged, many things in your life will change. Friends who previously saw only one of you will begin to assume that the pair of you will be coming along for a drink, or to dinner. Of course people may have treated you both as an established couple for years, but you might notice your engagement has some effect on these friendships – you really are a 'couple' now.

IN-LAWS

It is one thing to meet the parents of a girlfriend or boyfriend, but quite another to meet your future in-laws. With luck, you will have seen them many times already and have established a friendly relationship. That should become even warmer as they welcome you fully into their family circle. If you have had less contact, or have not always hit it off, now is the time to make a lot of effort. When you visit them, be sure to take a gift – flowers or a bottle of wine – anything which they will appreciate and which shows that you are trying to be friendly.

As time goes on, try to keep that effort going. For instance, if you are writing to your parents, your fiancé could pop in a note, perhaps to tell them whom he has chosen to be best man, or some other item of news which will interest them. Little gestures like this amount to more than one big gesture later on – you are building up a stock of goodwill.

If your fiancé has had little contact with your parents (perhaps you live long distances apart, or your engagement has happened quickly, or there is some rift between you), he should be as open as he can. You will be able to brief him on what to expect. Don't take it for granted that he will remember the names of all your relations, write them out, possibly in family chart form.

The bride's parents will naturally wish to know as much as possible about their future son-in-law: where you were born, your parent's occupations, the size of your family, your job, where you plan to live, and so on. However intrusive or irrelevant the questions, try to be tolerant. It never feels comfortable to be 'vetted', but in this case it is inevitable and your behaviour now is the foundation for an important future relationship.

If your relationship with your fiancé(e)'s parents has previously been uncomfortable, there is all the more reason to try to bury the hatchet now. Fathers are notoriously possessive of their daughters, and no boyfriend of hers seems able to win their approval. Try to understand this – if you have a daughter one day, you might end up feeling much the same! However, there is no harm in being quite blunt and saying 'I know we haven't really seen eye to eye before, but I hope we can learn to understand each other in the future.' Of course you will not use those exact words, and you may merely imply them by inviting your future father-in-law out for a drink, but if a rift worsens now, everyone will suffer – your fiancée and everyone connected with the wedding.

Most reasonable parents will respond to such overtures, and whatever the tensions of the past, they will want their daughter to be happy. If you make her this, her parents can ask for no more. Contrary to popular myth, fathers-in-law can be harder for a bridegroom to deal with than the frequently abused mother-in-law. Your fiancée may well find the opposite to be the case, hitting it off instantly with your delighted father while your mother sizes her up and decides whether she is the right woman to care for her son.

RELATIONSHIPS WITH EACH OTHER

Being aware of the various new pressures your relationship is now under, is essential at this time. When you attend family gatherings, you are often expected to behave as new lovers. You may not be new lovers in reality (you could have been lovers for years) but people like to see engaged couples in this light. Try to voice any disagreements in private, and present a united front in public.

CANCELLING THE ENGAGEMENT

Jitters and doubts can occur and the chief bridesmaid and best man should offer moral support when the volume of organization and family diplomacy required seems overwhelming. Ministers of religion, doctors and other advisers often use phrases such as, 'Don't worry, it's such a huge step, affecting your whole life, that most people occasionally wonder if they're doing the right thing.'

Avoid arguments within your family and between the two sides. Conflicts occur if she insists on living in the centre of town when he can only afford a suburban house, or his parents complain that a buffet will not be enough for their relatives travelling across the country. A Midlands wedding went ahead despite the boy's parents' refusal to attend because they thought that the girl wasn't good enough for him. There is always hope that the couple's parents may be reconciled when their first grandchild is born.

WORDING OF CANCELLED ENGAGEMENT ANNOUNCEMENT

Newspaper announcements simply state the names and say that the wedding will not take place. Strictly speaking, it should be implied that the girl has broken off the engagement. She might have had second thoughts after being persuaded to accept a flattering proposal immediately. It would reflect badly on him if it seemed that he rashly proposed to every girlfriend, then heartlessly changed his mind. It would also be uncivil of him to imply that on knowing the girl better he decided she was unsuitable to be his wife.

An announcement by letter could go as follows:

> *Alice and I are very fond of each other but after serious heart-searching she/we decided that our aims in life are so different that it would not be right for us to get married at this time. We are sorry if changing our plans has disappointed those close to us, but feel that by separating for a while/by staying just good friends, in the long run we will both be happier.*

RETURN OF RING

The Church originally demanded that a man or woman who broke their promise forfeited the ring. Grand-parents may tell you the Victorian ruling that if he cancelled the engagement she was entitled to keep the ring. He was lucky if the girl's father did not sue him for breach of promise and the hurt girl was content with a pretty ring as consolation. It is not done to give somebody a present and ask for it back, but if the boy has cancelled, many girls will not want to keep a ring which reminds them of a broken engagement and often return it anyway.

If she cancels the engagement she returns the ring, which he can – if he so chooses – give to a future fiancée. The general rule nowadays is return the ring because engagements are shorter than they used to be. Obviously if the girl is given a ring and the next morning she changes her mind she must return the ring. However, if she wears the ring for years and has grown used to it the situation is different.

RETURNING WEDDING GIFTS

After an engagement is broken, gifts for a new home are not needed. Gifts sent in advance by wedding guests must be returned, preferably in person. This gives relatives the chance to express dismay or relief and offer consolation along the lines of, 'Never mind. It seems hard now, but you may end up marrying someone even nicer. I hope you do.'

☆ Resist the temptation to say, 'I never liked him/her. I always thought he/she was an ugly, stuck-up, ... !' You never know, they might get back together next week!
☆ If the wedding goes ahead or the young man quickly finds another bride, the stored present might be given to him again. However, the second bride-to-be may have a different wedding list.

PART 1

PLANNING THE WEDDING

—

THE BRIDE AND HER FAMILY

WEDDING DECISIONS

WHAT KIND OF WEDDING DO YOU WANT?

The first decisions to be made are whether you wish to have a religious or a civil ceremony, and what sort of reception you both want. Most church and register office weddings take place on a Saturday, although they can take place on any other day of the week except a Sunday. Jewish weddings are held on a Sunday or a weekday, not on the Sabbath (Saturday).

CHURCH WEDDINGS

Getting married in church means you are taking part in a religious ceremony. It also generally implies a grand occasion attended by many friends and relations with the bride dressed in white and accompanied by several bridesmaids. Church weddings require a number of formalities (see pages 73–6), and are usually held either at the bride's local church, or, if she now lives a long way from where she grew up, at her parents' local church, which would normally be the church of her parish. In addition to the religious implications, church weddings are generally much more of an 'event'.

REGISTER OFFICE WEDDINGS

Register offices are often located in local civic offices, and are therefore a good deal less aesthetically attractive than a church. Register office weddings are usually on a smaller scale, with fewer guests and a fairly short ceremony. If you have a choice of register offices to marry in (through your both living in different districts) you might like to visit both first to see how they fit in with your plans. You may find the rooms are too small for the number of guests you would like to invite, or that the building would look awful in photographs.

SECOND MARRIAGES

If one or both of you are divorced you may have a little difficulty arranging a church wedding. The first thing to do is talk to the minister of the church of your choice. With luck, he will be perfectly happy to conduct a full service, provided that the decree absolutes can be produced. If he is not, there may be another local church where the minister has no such reservations. If this is not the case, or you do not wish to have a full church service, you could marry at a register office and then have a short service of blessing in a church. This type of wedding is usually fairly informal, with a relatively small number of guests.

RECEPTIONS

In any case you will want to think about what kind of reception to hold after the wedding. This is in many ways the major part of the wedding, in the sense that it is where guests will spend most time, and will see most of the bride and bridegroom. Factors to consider include:

1 Number of guests.
2 Venues available within easy reach of the wedding ceremony (hotels, other establishments with banqueting facilities such as museums or zoos; one popular

option is a marquée in the grounds of or near the bride's parents' home)

3 Whether you want a formal sit-down meal or informal buffet

4 The time of the wedding ceremony. If the service starts at noon, the guests will be hungry. If the wedding is in mid-afternoon, they will have had lunch and can wait longer for the next meal

Many couples choose to host an evening party after the reception, for close friends, young relations and perhaps some guests who could not be invited to the wedding service.

Whatever kind of wedding day you would prefer it may be affected by what others want, how much time you have for organizing the event, and how much you want to spend.

CHOOSING A DATE FOR THE WEDDING

The best time of year for a wedding depends on the length of your engagement, when you can get time off work, and seasonal weather here and for a honeymoon abroad. Check when you can obtain a booking at the church, reception venue, and honeymoon destination, and take possession of your new home. Commitments such as examinations taken by the best man or brides-maids, or sister-in-law's pregnancies, should also be considered.

MARRIAGE SEASON

Late spring was previously popular for weddings because there were tax advantages. The weather should not be too cold, long light days are pleasant for bride and groom to travel abroad, and you can pay low- or mid-season prices for the honeymoon.

SUMMER WEDDINGS

Summer is also popular, allowing guests from abroad or far away to combine the wedding with a summer holiday. Resort hotels are busiest in summer and country hotels tend to be booked for weddings on Saturdays. But many city hotels are less full because business people are away on holiday and conferences which normally fill city hotels are held in autumn and winter. This applies to London, certain inland UK cities, Paris, and New York.

AUTUMN AND WINTER WEDDINGS

July to September is another popular time for weddings. If you get engaged in the spring and take three to six months to organize the wedding you can marry in late summer, without waiting a whole year for a spring wedding. If one of you is a teacher you might honeymoon in the autumn half-term, when the weather is still reasonable.

Late winter weddings are not ideal for big church weddings because on colder days guests might be delayed by bad weather. The bride and bridesmaids need coats, and you are less sure of getting sunshine for photographs. However, winter is a good time for small weddings in register offices, or marrying abroad, with a skiing honeymoon. Winter honeymoons in the sun are superb if you can afford exotic honeymoon destinations.

STUDENT MARRIAGES

If you get engaged while studying, time your wedding for after the examinations. Weddings require organization which should not coincide with revision. Marrying while studying does not necessarily interfere with studies. One survey showed that married students did better in examinations because single students looking for a date were expending more time on social life! If you do not want to delay the wedding until studies finish, consider switching to evening study courses.

Exam dates ....
....
....

WEEKDAY VERSUS WEEKEND WEDDINGS

Register office weddings take place from Monday to Friday and on Saturday mornings. You can marry in church on Saturday, but not Sunday because that would interfere with church services. Avoid religious festivals, processions, and events such as football matches which result in traffic jams.

Forthcoming events ....
....
....
....
....
....
....
....

On weekdays it is easier and cheaper to book reception halls and honeymoon hotels. However, at weekends most guests can get off work more easily. The day of the wedding might also be influenced by the departure day of the honeymoon package tour.

Honeymoon departure day ....

FINDING A NEW HOME

First agree the location of the new home in city, suburb or country. Proximity to work is one factor. Finance and mortgage are others. If you both work in the city and rely on public transport, draw a line around your two work locations. Where they overlap identify railway stations or bus routes. Pick the good or cheap areas. Then start house hunting using estate agents or newspapers in that area. You may also want to stay near where you live now, or move near parents.

☆ *HOUSE AGENTS*

Name ....

Address ....

.... Tel. ....

Property to see: Address ....

.... Tel. ....

Family informed No/Yes. Appointment made by phone No/Yes.   Offer made   No/Yes. By (name) ....

.... Date ....

To (name) .... Written acceptance received

No/Yes (date) .... from (name) ....

....

Deposit date ....   Contract exchange date ....

Surveyor name ....

Address ....

.... Tel. ....

Building Society name ....

Address ....

.... Tel. ....

Mortgage ....

Insurance Company name ....

Address ....

.... Tel. ....

Premium paid for building/contents ....

From date .... Renewal due ....

Long engagements can be spent redecorating a property 'needing improvement'. Rebuilding, rewiring, plumbing, glazing and decorating are time-consuming. If the new home is near the register office or church you can hold the wedding reception there, and spend the first night of the honeymoon in it. Ensure the new home is ready before the wedding. If time is running out invite attendants to a painting party, supplying paint and brushes, cassette music, sandwiches and soft drinks.

WHO PAYS FOR WHAT?

Traditionally the bride's family pays for the wedding and does most of the planning. As a result the bride's family's church is often chosen for the ceremony, and the bride's mother arranges the church flowers. For a first marriage they pay for the wedding reception, the bride's dress and trousseau, and the car from her home to church.

☆ The groom chooses his best man and ushers, and traditionally he and/or his parents pay for: transporting the groom and best man to church, the church service, best man's and ushers' matching accessories (ties and matching pocket handkerchiefs, gloves), buttonholes for the best man, ushers, fathers of bride and groom, the bride's bouquet, church flowers, corsages or flowers for bride's mother, groom's mother's corsage, the car from the church to the reception, the departure car, the honeymoon, and the home the bridal couple move into.

☆ The best man and ushers buy or hire their own clothes.

WHO DOES WHAT

☆ *THE BRIDE*

The bride chooses her bridesmaids, her own dress, the colours of the bridesmaids' dresses, and the flower colours. All her work is done in advance. On the day she is 'Queen for the day' and is not obliged to do much except look decorative, repeat the vows, sign her name, throw her bouquet and chat to her guests. The chief bridesmaid may help her to dress, the chauffeur opens the car door, her father leads her up the aisle, and her husband makes the speech.

☆ *THE BRIDE'S MOTHER*

She organizes the catering for a young bride and advises on everything else too. She dresses elegantly, and is given a corsage to distinguish her.

☆ *THE BRIDE'S FATHER*

He escorts the bride in the procession and the bride's mother-in-law in the recession. He pays for the reception, and often makes a speech, usually the first speech. He is in clothing co-ordinated with the groom. He may be doing behind-the-scenes managing such as paying caterers. Being host and most senior he invisibly settles queries immediately or postpones disputes with staff until later. Therefore neither bride nor groom, nor bride's mother should have their day spoilt by uncertainty, and the guests, too, are undisturbed.

☆ *THE GROOM'S MOTHER*
The groom's mother advises if asked, dresses in smart fashion similar to the bride's mother, taking care to choose a different colour, wears a corsage for identification, and is an honoured guest.

☆ *THE GROOM'S FATHER*
He wears similar attire to the groom and groom's family, because he, too, is an honoured guest.

☆ *THE BEST MAN*
He may help the groom dress. He is responsible for arranging transport of the groom to the church, carrying the ring, paying church fees, possibly signing as witness, escorting the chief bridesmaid in the recession, arranging transport for everyone from the church to the reception, making a speech, and handing over honeymoon documents.

☆ *THE USHERS*
They seat guests at church, help the best man with transport and are generally helpful to the groom and

best man. Ushers also hand out order-of-service sheets and organize transport and parking for guests. They wear formal wedding party clothes and button-hole flowers for identification.

☆ *THE CHIEF BRIDESMAID*

She may help the bride to dress and soothe her nerves on the morning of the wedding. At the wedding she holds the bride's bouquet, and organizes younger bridesmaids and pageboys. She may also assist the bride by holding the bride's gloves, prayerbook, handbag, signing the register as witness, and partnering the best man in the recession. Younger bridesmaids assist the bride, sometimes carrying her train. The chief bridesmaid may take charge of wedding clothes when the bride changes.

☆ *THE TOAST-MASTER*

He announces the names of guests approaching the receiving line, asks for silence for the minister to say grace before the meal, introduces speechmakers who will make toasts, reads telemessages, calls for the cake-cutting, and the first dance.

COLOUR SCHEMES

As the bride, you will be the centre of attention so select dress colours to complement your complexion. Accessories should match your hair and eyes or contrast with your dress. When planning the flowers and dresses, pick a predominant colour or two contrasting colours. Old favourites are pink or baby blue and white. Pastel pink and silver is pretty; deep Italian pink with black is sophisticated.

Everything starts to fall into place once you have chosen a colour scheme and wedding theme. For example, for a spring wedding the bouquet was yellow and white with green leaves, the colour scheme following that decision. If your theme is yellow flowers, plant daffodils in windowboxes for a spring wedding, or yellow roses for a summer wedding reception in your parents' garden. Choose a yellow bouquet and hair ribbons, and buy bridesmaids yellow dresses, belts or sashes. Yellow roses decorating the wedding cake can be co-ordinated with yellow serviettes. For a yellow kitchen in the new home put yellow crockery on the wedding present list.

CHOOSING THE BRIDESMAIDS

The hosts who are paying decide whether to hold a big or small wedding. A first-time bride marrying in a church often likes to have bridesmaids, especially if she has younger sisters, or nieces. The bridesmaid, chief bridesmaid, or maid of honour assists the bride.

WHO CAN BE CHOSEN

The religion of the bridesmaid may be different from that of the bride and groom, especially if the bride and groom are of different faiths, and are perhaps considering a register office wedding. At an orthodox wedding check that the authorities accept the bridesmaid for the ceremony and that she knows whether she must pray and sing in public. Non-Jews cannot be attendants at orthodox Jewish weddings but they can be attendants at Conservative (USA) or Reform (UK) weddings.

WHO SHOULD BE CHOSEN

It is diplomatic to choose bridesmaids from both families, just as the groom will include the bride's brother or brothers amongst his ushers.

Family take precedence over friends. Usually the bride's oldest sister is her chief bridesmaid and young sisters the other bridesmaids. After that come cousins or nieces, especially if they live nearby, the bride knows them well and sees them often. If the bride has no sisters the groom's sister can be chief bridesmaid and his other sisters, nieces or cousins or her cousins and nieces will be the other bridesmaids. Finally, friends are chosen. If no family or friends are available the bride may choose children she knows well through her employment, especially if she is a teacher or nanny. Tiny tots who adore the bride and are seen regularly, even daily in the months leading up to the wedding, can still be given an important role even though members of her own family are available and already selected as bridesmaids.

If the bride wants a bridesmaid to help her organize the wedding – as would an older bride less dependent on her own mother, she may choose someone living nearby.

COST CONSTRAINTS

Since the bride or her family traditionally pays bridesmaids' expenses, she may limit the number of bridesmaids or have none if she has insufficient budget for finding their accommodation, paying for clothes and choosing a gift for each one (although the groom usually covers the latter).

PREGNANT ATTENDANTS

A pregnant attendant is perfectly acceptable. If she is married, as a matron of honour she can dress differently from the bridesmaids. If the wedding is a long distance away, remember that airlines will not accept passengers in advanced stages of pregnancy. Stress and air pressure might cause miscarriage or premature birth in mid-air risking diverting the plane to hospital. You wouldn't reach the wedding anyway!

DIFFERENT ATTENDANTS' ROLES

CHIEF BRIDESMAID

When there are two or more bridesmaids with a big age gap the older one is the chief bridesmaid. If two friends of similar ages are chosen the one who knows the bride better, or who lives nearer and therefore has a bigger helping role, is accorded this honour. Americans tend to favour having joint chief bridesmaids who walk together at the ceremony.

MAID OF HONOUR

As the bride is 'queen for the day' it is fitting that she should be attended by maids of honour. A sole bridesmaid cannot be chief bridesmaid. She is maid of honour. The bride can choose to have two maids of honour. For example, the bride's sister can take turns with the groom's sister so that they share the role. Alternatively the bride might pair a friend as maid of honour with her existing sister-in-law. Or if her brother is single and he has a live-in girlfriend she could be called maid of honour or the less specific American term honour attendant.

MATRON OF HONOUR

A divorcee, widow or older bride is likely to choose a married friend to be an attendant. You can have two matrons of honour if the bride's older sister and best friend are both married. A matron is a married woman, perhaps the bride's older sister. An older helper such as the bride's mother or a substitute for the bride's mother (such as a married aunt) may take on the role. She acts as a secretary, companion and expert on everything! Certainly if she is older or has been married a long time she can offer the benefit of her experience of married life as well as her own wedding. It is considered lucky to have a matron of honour.

BRIDESMAIDS AS WITNESSES

Bridesmaids and groomsmen can all sign the register. If you plan to do this tell the vicar or priest in advance so that they can add extra lines so it looks neat. Of course you shouldn't sign unless you have been invited to do so. A junior/child bridesmaid can have the thrill of signing after two legal witnesses have signed.

As only two witnesses are required often the chief bridesmaid is the only one of several bridesmaids to carry out this role, the other witness being the best man.

WITNESS WITHOUT BRIDESMAIDS

When circumstances prevent bridesmaids being appointed, a favoured female friend of the bride might be chosen as witness.

The witness does not join in the church procession and recession nor wear distinctive clothes. The role of witness might be offered to a friend at a register office wedding.

APPOINTING A WITNESS IN ADDITION TO BRIDESMAIDS

This is a good solution for the bride who wishes to satisfy a sister who is unsuitable or unwilling to be a bridesmaid, or older sister-in-law with an important role. The advantage to the witness is that this means less cost and less fuss than being a bridesmaid. Perhaps an important female friend from abroad unexpectedly becomes able to attend the wedding and surprises the bride after bridesmaids and their dresses have been chosen; she too could be a witness.

ACTING WITNESS INSTEAD OF BRIDESMAID

The girl who declines to be a bridesmaid despite the bride's protest might please the bride by volunteering to be witness, although the reluctant bridesmaid should not insist on this role if another person has already been selected.

MOVING THE DIFFICULT BRIDESMAID

Sometimes one bridesmaid cannot agree on the dress style, shoe colour, or anything that the bride and other bridesmaids are happy with. Maybe she dislikes the other bridesmaid and is annoyed at having a rival, can't make up her mind about dress style, knows exactly what suits her and won't accept anything else, or can't afford the clothes but is too embarrassed to say so. The bride, who must decide when there is no agreement, can speed progress and please other bridesmaids by transferring the girl to the role of witness, and with luck, everyone will be happy.

WITNESS AT RENEWAL OF VOWS

At a second marriage or renewal of vows, when bridesmaids are not appropriate, female attendants can be honoured as witnesses. A couple in their forties renewed their vows 24 years after their first small wedding, this time as a grand occasion setting out stylishly in two stretch limousines with their four adult children as witnesses.

JUNIOR BRIDESMAID

The junior bridesmaid is a term applied to describe a bridesmaid age 8–14. The bride might have two or a group but there has to be a limit in numbers. More than twelve bridesmaids looks absurd but a class of school-girls could form a guard of honour at the church exit instead, pairs of girls holding clean hockey sticks or long-stemmed flowers to form an archway.

Bridesmaids aged under 8 can be either train-bearers or flower girls. The smallest girl has the least responsibility and merely carries a posy.

RING-BEARER

The ring-bearer is often a small boy carrying the ring, which is tied or loosely sewn onto a cushion with two ribbons. Tiny children who cannot be entrusted with a gold ring carry a symbolic substitute which is not used during the ceremony. The ring-bearer walks ahead of the bride in the procession but need not stand during the ceremony. Being ring-bearer gives him a job which makes him feel important – and keeps his hands respectably occupied. The ring-bearer could be a little girl – the choice depends on the numbers of children of each sex who are allotted roles.

FLOWER GIRL OR BOY

The flower girl or boy carries flower petals, whole flowers or confetti. She gives flowers to guests on either side of the aisle before or during the procession.

The flower girl dresses differently from bridesmaids. She might be the daughter of the bride's sister or best friend. If the bride chooses a small niece she needs to have an older bridesmaid who can take charge of the young child.

In the recession the flower girl walks before the bride, unlike bridesmaids, in order to scatter flower petals at the church door as the bride exits, throwing more while walking ahead of the bride along the churchyard path. Check in advance how far she should progress and that the church does not object. There may be a ban on petals inside the church on carpets in case people slip on them, a stipulation about the type of material that can be thrown, or a charge for sweeping up.

PRESENTER OF LUCKY HORSESHOE

A lucky horseshoe can be handed to the bride in her recession down the church aisle or on the steps of the church afterwards. The bride may be given several lucky horseshoes, by her mother, the chief bridesmaid, a small niece, and other well-wishers. Write a goodwill message on the back of the gift and sign it so she knows who her lucky horseshoes are from. The lucky horseshoe is silvery, or padded white satin, lace-edged and held over the bride's arm by a silk ribbon. Small rolling pins, Welsh love spoons and other favours produced commercially are sold in bridal shops. They are also sold by specialized cookware shops for decorating wedding cakes. Or make your own cardboard lucky black cat or chimney sweep picture for a child to present.

BABY BRIDESMAID

The baby bridesmaid can be a general nuisance, crawling up the aisle, cooing at guests, or peeping under the bride's dress. Usually the bride's daughter, sister, or niece has to be carried by the bride's mother, father, granny, or nanny even if she is nominally a bridesmaid. During the marriage ceremony and church service babies should be kept at the back so that if they cry or need changing they can be taken out quickly and unobtrusively. The church or cathedral may ban push-chairs or allow them only partway into the building, not near the steps leading to the altar.

As the baby cannot walk she/he does not do much except be photographed sitting on the bride's lap (perhaps on a cushion over a piece of waterproof cloth to prevent unpleasant accidents!) or beside the bride in the carriage.

Somebody must be in charge of changing the baby, not the bride in her white dress, nor bridesmaids wearing their expensive gowns. Spare nappies and a second baby's dress are advisable.

Babies are likely to fall asleep. A very prettily decorated white pushchair with white sunshade at a summer wedding reception shows thoughtfulness and practicality. A rocking cradle on wheels with white canopy can be brought along, assuming the bride agrees, providing you can get the cradle up steps into the building. This saves going home early to babysit or deliver to a babysitter.

BEST GIRL

Just as the bride can have a male pageboy as well as bridesmaids, the groom can choose a female attendant. The best girl is the closest female relative (such as his twin sister, sister, mother or aunt) or closest friend (such as his flatmate or business partner). It is still rather unusual.

CHECKLIST: Names and roles

Attendants' Names:
Best Man ....
Chief Usher ....
Ushers/Groomsmen ....
Matron of Honour ....
Chief Bridesmaid or Maid of Honour ....
Adult Bridesmaids ....
Junior Bridesmaids ....
Pageboy(s) ....
Flower Girl ....
Presenter of horseshoe to bride ....
Presenter of bouquet to bride's mother ....

Reader(s) during service:
  minister ..../ second minister .... /bridesmaid(s) ..../
  other ....

Singers during service: church choir/
  bridesmaid(s)/other ....

Guard of Honour ....

Witnesses ....

Roles for: bride's sisters ....; bride's brothers ....;
  groom's brothers ....; groom's sisters ....;
  groom's cousins ....; bride's cousins ....;
  groom's nieces and nephews .... , bride's nieces
  and nephews ...., bride's adult friends ....,
  bride's pupils ...., bride's married relatives and
  friends ...., matron of honour's child; best man's
  child ....; step-sisters ....; step-children ....

Roles: carrying train, carrying bouquet, carrying bride's
  ring, carrying bride's prayerbook, witnesses, flower
  girls, holding hen party, entertaining visiting guests,
  hosting and serving at reception.

Total number of attendants .... Are they paired? Yes/No

---

CHOOSING THE BEST MAN

The choice of best man is crucial to your – and other
people's – enjoyment of the wedding. In many ways he
will be more prominent at the reception than the
bridegroom, what with making speeches, helping people
find their seats, acting as master of ceremonies, and so
on. He will be the groom's fellow-organizer, troubleshooter, friend, and will ensure he survives the stag
party! It is therefore wise to decide who is to be the best
man when you first begin to consider possible dates for
your wedding. He can then also be involved in the
preliminary arrangements.

The best man is usually a single man who is the groom's brother or closest friend. On some rare occasions the 'best man' has been a woman; this adds a whole new element to the proceedings and will certainly surprise (and possibly delight) many of the wedding guests. This is the exception rather than the rule, however.

Like it or not, a brother or closest friend may not be the perfect choice as best man. Perhaps he stutters terribly when asked to speak to a group of people, or is very forgetful and might not bring everything he needs on the day. Think your choice through carefully, for it will reflect on you – guests at a wedding do not base their judgements of the bridegroom solely on what they see of him; they also have a good look at his representative, the best man.

The following list notes the qualities required, in a rough order of importance:

☆ Capable of making a speech
☆ Reliable
☆ Well organized
☆ Unflappable
☆ Acceptable to the bride's family
☆ Good with people

The speech is at the top of the list because it is the most public of his duties and the one the best man will be remembered for. Groom and best man can, if they choose, work together on their speeches (see Part 5) but you must be confident that your best man will not 'freeze' on the day.

The other qualities are required because the best man plays an important role in behind-the-scenes organization, and is central to the smooth running of proceedings on the big day.

The checklist below clearly shows that in addition to being the bridegroom's minder, the best man has a number of organizational duties. Once you have selected the person you feel is best equipped to handle the job, sound him out. He might reel in terror at the very idea, or have been best man so many times that he is thoroughly fed up with the role, and would prefer to have less responsibility by being an usher.

Don't be offended if he refuses — think whether you would do the job yourself, and what reservations might enter your head. Have a second choice in mind and be honest with him: 'I asked Mike first because I've known him since we were kids, but he just doesn't feel he can do it, and I think you would be brilliant.'

When he has accepted the honour, the best man should be introduced to the chief bridesmaid as soon as possible, since they will work together quite a lot in their duties, each performing a similar role for the bridegroom and the bride respectively.

JEWISH CEREMONIES

The best man at a Jewish ceremony is usually of the same faith, and often one of the bridegroom's brothers. If he has none, a close male relative is generally chosen. In addition to the duties at other types of religious ceremony, the best man may help the bridegroom to practise reciting in Hebrew. If top hats are not being worn, skullcaps must be worn in the synagogue. After the ceremony, the best man hands any fees including travelling expenses to the rabbi and the cantor (singer), in sealed envelopes.

NON-CONFORMIST CEREMONIES

Non-conformist, such as Quaker, ceremonies are much more informal, and a best man (or bridesmaid) is rarely chosen.

THE BEST MAN'S RESPONSIBILITIES

According to the size of the wedding, the initiative of the groom, and other members of the wedding party, the best man does some or all of the following:

☆ Helps select ushers and instructs them on clothing required and church seating plan.

☆ Agrees on clothes style, buys own, or visits hire company with groom and ushers for fitting.

☆ Meets chief bridesmaid/maid-/matron-of-honour to arrange co-ordination.

☆ Writes speech.

☆ Organizes stag party venue, transport, food and drink.

☆ Checks route to church.

☆ Attends church rehearsal.

☆ On the day phones and wakes the groom. Phones and wakes ushers.

☆ Dresses in wedding clothes. Puts speech notes in pocket.

☆ Travels to groom's house. Collects from groom the ring, church fees, and travel documents.

☆ Helps groom dress.

☆ Phones car hire company to confirm they are coming or checks that car starts.

☆ Gets groom to church on time.

☆ Looks after wedding ring and hands it over at marriage ceremony.

☆ Handles licences or documents required for wedding.

☆ Makes payment of church fees.

☆ Acts as witness signing register.

☆ Escorts chief bridesmaid in recession.

☆ With aid of ushers gets guests onto church steps for group photograph.

☆ Stands in group photograph on church steps. Then ushers bride and groom into first car.

☆ Arranges transport of entire wedding party, groom and bride, bride's and groom's parents, bridesmaids, and stray guests, from church or register office to reception.

☆ Acts as toastmaster, announcing guests at receiving line at reception.

☆ Announces that minister or bride's father will say grace.

☆ Calls for silence for the cake cutting.

☆ Delivers speech. Reads telemessages. Keeps the telemessages and gives them to the bride's mother after reading them, at the end of the evening, or next day.

☆ Announces first dance and last dance, if any. Dances with bride, bridesmaids.

☆ Looks after groom's accessories such as top hat, and luggage.

☆ Helps groom change into departure clothes while ushers decorate departure car, or, together with the ushers and friends, decorates departure car while groom is changing.

☆ Keeps travel documents and hands them over to groom – or bride.

☆ Drives couple to departure point and returns car and hired wedding clothes.

☆ Supervises clearing of reception hall, collecting lost property.

☆ Sees that bridesmaids and stray guests get home safely.

☆ Returns own and groom's hire clothes to hire company, collecting deposits.

☆ Buys spare copies of local paper containing wedding pictures.

CHOOSING THE USHERS

One of the first things the bridegroom and his best man will decide is the choice of ushers (if there are to be any). Their chief role is to show guests to their seats in church, hand out service sheets or hymn books, and help to organize transport to the reception. One may be put in charge of overseeing car parking at the reception venue. Since they will be directing guests, it is clearly an advantage if they know many of them (as ushers drawn from your families are bound to) so that they do not constantly have to ask 'bride or groom' at the church entrance.

The ushers traditionally escort the bridesmaids from the church, so you will need to check with your fiancée on how many bridesmaids there are to be. For most reasonably large church weddings, six or eight ushers are required. They should be unmarried men chosen from among your friends, and both families – it is important that suitable men in your bride's family are offered the honour of the role.

Sometimes one man is appointed chief usher and leads the team. This is particularly usual when the best man is based a long way away and will only be free to take up his duties the day before the wedding. In this case, the bridegroom may select another good friend to take on some of the best man's preliminary duties, and ask him to accept the role of chief usher. The chief usher escorts the bride's mother and the bridegroom's parents to their seats.

A general rule is one usher for every fifty guests, up to four ushers.

THE USHERS' RESPONSIBILITIES

☆ Meet groom and best man to agree on clothing.
☆ Visit hire company for fitting.
☆ Buy clothing accessories, or collect tie and handkerchief from groom or best man.
☆ Be guests at stag party.
☆ Be first to arrive in church. Collect buttonhole flowers from florist decorating church.

☆ See that car park attendant has removed barrier. Or appoint one usher to stay at entrance to car park, directing guests, turning away or redirecting lost passers-by.

☆ Greet guests arriving in church.

☆ Hand out order-of-service sheets.

☆ Ask guests whether they are friends of 'the bride or the groom'.

☆ Direct guests to seats, bride's family and friends on the left of the altar, the groom's on the right.

☆ Walk VIPs to their seats, i.e. groom's parents, bride's mother. One usher should be delegated to wait and escort the bride's mother, giving her his arm, preferably the chief usher if he is her oldest son. But if he is best man, her second son is the choice.

☆ After the bride enters, close the church door.

☆ As bridal party sets off down aisle for recession, open church door.

☆ Organize one usher to go to house where reception is being held to direct parking.

☆ Hand out drinks.

☆ Be photographed with groom and best man.

☆ Pay compliments to bridesmaids and dance with them if they do not have other escorts.

☆ Escort bridesmaids, grannies and other stray guests home.

THE BRIDE'S DRESS

The popular style is ankle length. When the wedding takes place in a church (or synagogue) the dress often follows old-fashioned convention, covering the bride up to the neck and down to the ankles and wrists, though the dress may have see-through net areas from bust to collar.

Summer dresses may have shorter sleeves and lower

necklines. Colours can be white or off-white or pastel colours such as creamy yellow, baby pink, pale blue, or lavender. The bride can wear ribbons in her hair and on her dress echoing the colours of the bridesmaids' dresses.

Some churches object to brides wearing bright red, which is unconventional and can look garish. In olden days red had associations with the devil and prostitution. Few people nowadays remember or care about such symbolism because fashionable colours change every season.

The tradition of wearing a white dress is, contrary to popular belief, a relatively recent one. Before the invention of the sewing machine in the mid-nineteenth century, all clothes were considered too expensive to be worn only once, so brides tended to marry in everyday best clothes. Although white is now the favourite colour for first-timers, second-time brides or those closer to forty than twenty, tend to marry in a more expensive version of a day-dress in a pastel colour.

DRESS MATERIAL

Lace is favoured because it is pretty, delicate, decorative, and expensive. Nottingham lace is obviously what you should wear if you live in that area and have close relatives working in the industry.

Evening dress material is shiny and elaborate so that it can be seen under dim lighting. Ordinary cotton is lightweight and cool for a summer afternoon dress, but a more glamorous material is better for grand weddings. Bridal dress shops sell white satin flat or heeled shoes.

☆ The bride's dress is kept a secret for good luck, and is not seen before the wedding. This ensures that everyone has a lovely surprise. For the same reason the bride is not seen by the groom on the day of the wedding until she appears at church.

THE BRIDE'S VEIL

The veil dates back to biblical times in the Middle East. The bride wore a veil for modesty. She walks up the aisle with her face modestly concealed. When the veil is removed by her groom, herself, or her bridesmaid, at the altar before signing the register, the groom is the first to see her. She returns down the aisle with the veil thrown back and all the guests can see her smiling. The veil is usually attached to a circlet made of similar material to the dress, with pearls, flowers, lace or other decoration. A bride can also wear her hair up, secured with a lattice of white ribbons or flowers. This looks particularly effective against dark hair.

BRIDE'S MAKE-UP

Professional make-up artists can be employed for a wedding. They often go for a more subtle effect than the bride might like. The bride may feel tempted to exaggerate her eyes with centipede false black eyelashes, or wear heavy red lipstick or lashings of crimson blusher. Professional make-up may be disappointing at the time, but it produces a more elegant, natural effect in photographs, and looks less dated in years to come.

BRIDE'S ACCESSORIES

The belt of a day dress can match the dress material or the accessories. A neater appearance is gained by matching accessories. Shoes and handbag can be dyed the same colour.

If the dress has small false pearls sewn on it, ear-rings or pearl droplets can be worn to match, and pearls on the shoes. Pearls are said to resemble tears and therefore to be unlucky. But if you are not superstitious and you like pearls, by all means wear them. Jewellery and watches should be in similar styles and of like metals – such as all gold or all silver. Don't wear a watch with a plastic or mangled brown leather strap and a scratched watchface. Even if you are on a low budget you can find smart, reasonably priced evening-style watches with white, black or metal straps, and imitation diamonds around the watchface. Sometimes father or mother can lend a spare analogue watch which looks suitable with period clothes.

☆ Wear: 'Something Old, Something New, Something Borrowed, Something Blue, and a Sixpence in your Shoe'. The borrowed item represents friendship, and the blue is for faithfulness. The sixpence (or fivepence) in the shoe symbolizes never being without money.

BRIDE'S JEWELLERY

The minimum of jewellery is worn, perhaps because the puritanical tradition of the Reformation says you do not glitter too much in an Anglican church. Besides, you do not want to distract attention from the ring.

The engagement ring is worn on the left hand to go with the wedding ring. You can simply leave it off for the day if you like.

☆ A divorcee removes her previous wedding ring. She might wear the old wedding ring before acquiring the new one because she is used to wearing a ring or doesn't want people to think she is an unmarried mother. But it looks odd to wear two wedding rings and may remind her new husband on the day that he is number two. A wedding ring can be remodelled with a stone to make a dress ring.

BRIDE'S INFORMAL CLOTHES

Marrying in a register office allows a greater freedom of dress than a church wedding where revealing low necks or very bright colours would seem irreverent at a place of worship.

A bride at a register office wedding usually wears a smart day-dress, or a suit with a hat, or even a trouser suit, but there is no reason why she cannot wear the traditional long white dress if she wants to.

☆ Some register offices have a room where the bride can change her outfit. A bride who marries in a long white dress with a heavy train will need a going-away outfit if she is departing to the airport or on public transport the same day.

WIDOW'S WEDDING CLOTHES

Widows may well be merry about getting married again, but they are not supposed to look gleefully triumphant, as if the first husband has at last passed away and the real fun has begun. So a matron-of-honour is acceptable, but no crowds of angelic bridesmaids. The bride might have a neat corsage, rather than a showy bouquet.

CORRECT DRESS FOR THE GROOM AND ATTENDANTS

All attendants should be clear and liaise about what to wear: it's easy if you know the rules.

☆ *THE GROOM*

In theory, for a formal wedding the groom should wear morning dress. This means a grey or black swallow-tail coat, striped trousers and a grey silk hat. If he does wear this outfit the rest of the groom's party, including the best man, bride's father, groom's father and ushers, should also be in morning dress. In reality this can be a very costly business since most men do not have a morning suit in their wardrobe and so have to hire one. Although morning dress does make the occasion extra special, many people opt instead for a smart dark suit which they will be able to wear again.

☆ *THE BEST MAN*

The best man's accessories – such as his carnation – should distinguish him from the groom (he doesn't want the bride's distant cousins congratulating him) and from the ushers.

☆ *THE USHERS*

If you decide to hire morning suits you might prefer that all the ushers look identical. Grey is a safe colour. To create a co-ordinated look the groom might buy the ushers matching ties and handkerchiefs. Their buttonhole flowers should all be the same colour.

☆ *THE BRIDES-MAIDS*

The chief bridesmaid, especially if she is of similar age to the bride, must be dressed so that strangers can tell which is the bride. She can wear a more sophisticated style than younger bridesmaids, but in the same or similar colour. The matron-of-honour's clothes are more suited to an older married woman, e.g. a smart suit and hat, with a corsage co-ordinating with the bride's bouquet colour perhaps, showing her role as a member of the wedding party.

Bridesmaids should all wear the same colour material for a co-ordinated look, with matching or contrasting shoes. Accessories can be in a colour that matches the ushers' buttonhole flowers, ties, pocket handkerchiefs, or that cummerbunds can echo.

GUESTS' CLOTHES FOR A FORMAL WEDDING

The time and location of the wedding as well as the size decides how formally you should dress. Religious weddings are more formal than those in a register office.

The invitation wording generally gives an indication of correct dress. A reception after six can mean evening dress. 'Black tie', written on the invitation means men wear a bow tie and black dinner jacket. When men wear black tie the women wear long dresses or evening dresses of current fashion. Guests who find themselves under-dressed can pop home to change if they live nearby. However, the bride may wish to put guests at their ease by saying that clothes are not important. 'I invited you, (guest's name), not your suit!'.

FLOWERS

FLOWERS FOR THE WOMEN

The bride's bouquet is paid for by the groom's family. It can co-ordinate with flowers decorating the church. Two families with weddings at the same place can arrange to share the cost of flowers. The bride may choose the same flowers to decorate the wedding tables. Corsages for the mother and mother-in-law are bought by the groom, and may echo the bride's bouquet, and of course must not clash with the colour of the dresses.

FLOWERS FOR THE MEN

The buttonhole decorations for the ushers are bought by the groom. Usually carnations are worn. The groom might wear a white carnation to echo the bride's dress. Other members of the wedding party might all wear another colour echoing the bridesmaids' dresses, e.g. pink, yellow, cream, or red. One system is for the bride's family to wear white carnations, while the groom's wears red. The men's buttonhole flowers are worn on the left. You cannot go wrong. The man's jacket will have the buttonhole slit on the left.

FLOWER SYMBOLISM

Daffodils mean welcome, orange blossoms signify happiness in marriage, red roses represent love, white roses mean worthy of love, and white carnations are for purity.

THE LEGAL SIDE

The bride and bridegroom must take care of a number of legal formalities well in advance of the wedding ceremony whether this is to be a religious or civil one. Some of these require several weeks' notice so it is prudent to plan ahead and ensure that all necessary steps have been taken before the busy last month or two.

ENGLAND AND WALES

In these countries a marriage can take place at a civil ceremony, a Church of England ceremony, or in accordance with the rites of any other religious denomination.

CHURCH OF ENGLAND

Marriage here can be authorized in any of four ways:

a) Publication of banns
b) Common (ordinary) licence
c) Special licence
d) With a licence issued by a superintendent registrar

PUBLICATION OF BANNS

This is the most popular method, and involves the notice of your impending marriage being read out in a church in both the bridegroom's and bride's parishes. You must first contact the minister of the church where you would like the marriage to take place and ask for his permission to hold the service. If you both live within that parish, that is all you need to do. If not, you should both also visit the minister of the church in the parish where the other one of you lives.

Each minister arranges for your marriage banns to be read aloud in the relevant church on three successive Sundays before the wedding ceremony. A small charge is made for doing this. It is customary for the engaged couple to attend at least one of the services when the banns are read.

If you live in different parishes, the minister in whose church you are not getting married will sign a certificate confirming that the banns have been called. Without it, his counterpart cannot perform the wedding service, so make sure you pick the certificate up in good time.

If one of the couple is a serving member of the Royal Navy at sea, the banns can be read by the chaplain or ship's captain, and a certificate stating that no objection has been raised must be provided.

Incidentally, check your birth certificates before visiting the minister, and make sure you know what your full legal name is. You may find to your surprise that you have one or two middle names you were never aware of, or even that the name you are known by is not your official first name. This is important as the banns should include all the names shown on your birth certificate, and if appropriate, any other name by which you are usually known. If you discover an embarrassing middle name now, you must get used to it, because your full name has to be read out at the marriage ceremony. If you think it is going to cause sniggering in the congregation, tell people about it beforehand – it will be easier to handle all round!

COMMON LICENCE

This is a much quicker procedure in which the residential requirement is that one of you must have lived in the area served by the church to be used for the ceremony for at least 15 days prior to the application. Banns are not read and the licence is issued the next day. This is a good standby if there has been a slip-up and it is too late to read the banns.

These licences can be obtained from the local surrogate (who may be the minister himself, and if not he can advise whom you should contact) or by visiting the Faculty Office, 1 The Sanctuary, Westminster, London SW1. The applicant must sign a declaration that there is no legal reason for the marriage not to take place, and that either party fulfils the residential requirements.

SPECIAL LICENCE

There is an unusual method in which a licence is issued from the Faculty Office by the Archbishop of Canterbury, but only when there is some special, urgent reason why other methods cannot be used.

SUPERINTENDENT REGISTRAR'S CERTIFICATE

Another rarity, this certificate is issued by the superintendent registrar for the district in which the marriage will take place, and must be applied for at least 21 days ahead of the wedding date.

OTHER DENOMINATIONS

If one partner is a Roman Catholic and the service is to be held in an Anglican (or other) church, the marriage is called a 'mixed marriage'. Such marriages can only take place in one church, not both. The Roman Catholic church used to excommunicate its members for marrying in a non-Roman Catholic church, but the rules today are more relaxed. A bride and bridegroom of differing religions are expected to meet a priest or minister of both faiths and learn something of the other's beliefs. Some Catholic priests may expect a series of informal discussions in which the Catholic partner promises to guard his or her faith and bring any children up in it.

Marriages between two people of differing Protestant and non-conformist denominations are less complicated, although obviously the minister will wish to be informed of both parties' beliefs. The real problems start when one partner is a declared non-Christian – in which case it would be very difficult to persuade a minister or priest to allow the ceremony to be held in an Anglican or Catholic church.

If you both hold strong, but different beliefs, you will probably have discussed these together many times before. Although you may well be able to tolerate each other's beliefs, it can be much harder to agree in what faith any children you have should be brought up. If it becomes an issue between you, you could seek counselling from representatives of either (or both) faiths, but do allow time to consider this important point.

JEWISH WEDDING

A marriage within Jewish rites can only take place between two Jews, and some documentation proving their faith may be required. Under Civil Law, all marriages must take place before a Superintendent Registrar of Marriages. For Jews, this marriage can be held ahead of the Jewish religious service, or directly after it, at the synagogue. The latter is only possible when the synagogue's Minister or Secretary is recognized as a Registrar's representative.

REGISTER OFFICE WEDDINGS

If you opt to marry in a register office you will need to contact the local superintendent registrar. His address can be found in the telephone directory under the heading 'Registrar of Births, Deaths and Marriages'. The superintendent registrar will arrange the marriage in one of three ways:

a) Certificate
b) Certificate and Licence
c) Registrar General's Licence

CERTIFICATE

This is arranged from a form giving the names, addresses and ages of those who wish to be married, together with where the wedding is to take place. If either party is under 18, a declaration that the parents' consent has been given is also required. The official then makes an entry in his notice book, and issues the certificate 21 days later – valid for three months from the original notice book entry.

If the couple have lived in the district controlled by the registrar for at least seven days, only one of them need appear to make the declaration. If not, each must visit their respective district registrars, and be able to show that they have lived in that district for seven days prior to the visit.

CERTIFICATE AND LICENCE

This follows a similar procedure, except the residential qualifications are different. One person must have lived in the district for 15 days prior to the application. Their partner must normally reside in England or Wales, and does not need to visit a registrar.

The licence is issued one clear day after the application.

REGISTRAR GENERAL'S LICENCE

This is an unusual method used when one party is seriously ill and cannot be moved. The other party must visit the local superintendent registrar to obtain a certificate or licence, but residential conditions and waiting periods are waived.

SCOTLAND

The days of couples eloping to Gretna Green in Scotland to get married with two witnesses taken from the street are over, but the rules in Scotland are still different from England and Wales. Banns are not required to be read, and both parties must obtain a marriage notice form from a registrar of births, deaths and marriages, and inform the registrar for the district in which the ceremony is to take place. The minimum notice period is 15 days.

The following documents are required in addition to the marriage notice:

1 Birth certificate
2 If the marriage is not the bride's or groom's first, a copy of the divorce decree or annulment, or the death certificate of the former spouse
3 If either party lives outside the United Kingdom, a certificate of no impediment to marriage.

If any of this paperwork is not written in English, a certified translation is required.

After this, a date can be confirmed for either a civil or religious marriage.

NORTHERN IRELAND

In Northern Ireland notice to marry should be made to the District Registrar of Marriages, and the residence qualification is seven days. Marriage may take place by: licence, special licence, banns, certificate from a registrar or licence from a district registrar of marriage.

MARRYING ABROAD

Some couples choose to marry far from their own country, and spend their honeymoon in some possibly exotic location. The number of guests would obviously be very restricted, as it would be expensive for them to attend such a wedding. Requirements are different in every country, so you must find out what documentation will be required to ensure the marriage is legal. The minimum is probably your birth certificates, proof of residence, and a certificate showing that there is no impediment to the marriage. Make an early visit to the foreign consul of the country concerned to find out what you have to do.

SECOND MARRIAGES

Second marriages are fairly common today, reflecting the high divorce rate. Remember that neither party can re-marry until the decree absolute has been granted. Widows and widowers can marry in a church or synagogue. Divorcees may find the church of their choice declines to marry them (this applies particularly to Anglican churches and invariably in Catholic churches).

WHO CAN MARRY WHOM?

Her Majesty's Stationery Office prints leaflets detailing the rules and these are available from your nearest Registrar of Births, Marriages and Deaths. In England the minimum age for marriage is eighteen, sixteen with parental consent. Rules in Scotland are different. Write to your nearest Scottish Register Office for details.

When marrying a foreigner you need documentary confirmation that your marriage would not be illegal in their home country.

For a special licence to marry outside your Anglican parish (because you have sentimental attachment to another church, or have recently arrived from abroad) apply to the Archbishop's Registrar at Lambeth Palace, London.

WHO CANNOT MARRY?

CONSANGUINITY

Certain marriages are forbidden as con-sanguineous or incestuous, because blood relations may increase the risk of medical problems. These are people who are related in a direct line. A man may not marry his mother, daughter, grand-mother, grand-daughter, or aunt. Simi-larly, a woman may not marry her son, father, grandson, grandfather, uncle and so on. You can marry a first cousin or a second cousin, though most people check their family health history first.

AFFINITY

You cannot marry anyone to whom you are closely related through marriage – your ex-wife's or ex-husband's direct relatives. It would create family conflict. A man cannot marry his ex-wife's mother, daughter, and so on. A woman cannot marry her ex-husband's father or son, and so on.

Laws have been relaxed to allow a man to marry the niece of his ex-wife even if the ex-wife is alive. The minister may still refuse to marry you, but might permit you to be married in his church if another clergyman agrees to officiate.

ADOPTION

Marriage to your adopted children is banned. Further details can be found by applying to the registrar's offices. For-bidden marriages are listed in the prayer book.

ARRANGING THE CEREMONY

Full details of procedure for marriages in England and Wales can be obtained from your local Register Office. Or write to General Register Office, St Catherine's House, 10 Kingsway, London WC2B 6JP, tel. 071–242 0262. Their literature covers most things you might think of asking, plus a few more you never thought of. For example, it tells you what to do if you are marrying abroad because you are in the family of a serviceman stationed overseas or want to legitimize a child born before you got married.

REGISTER OFFICE MARRIAGE STATEMENT

In a register office the groom speaks first, repeating after the superintendent registrar, 'I do solemnly declare that I know not of any lawful impediment why I (groom's name) may not be joined in matrimony to (bride's name)'. Then the bride makes a similar statement. Afterwards the registrar says the words which the groom repeats, 'I call upon these persons here present to witness that I (groom's name) do take thee (bride's name) to be my lawful wedded wife.' The bride says the same thing. The superintendent says, 'You are now man and wife together'. The wording is prescribed by law.

The wording in a register office for the declaration and contract is standard but may be said in English or Welsh.

The two witnesses must be aged over 18. The register office procedure only takes about five to ten minutes.

The bride has to give her name, age and occupation and her father's name and occupation. Work out the terminology, so you don't hesitate over whether you should be writing clerk or civil servant. In both register office and churches the bride should not be more than ten minutes late, because she could be delaying another wedding.

REGISTER OFFICE MARRIAGE, SCOTLAND

You could marry at a register office anywhere in Scotland. For forms, write to General Register Office, New Register House, Edinburgh EH1 3YT, tel. 031–556 3952.

MARRIAGE ON SHIPS

You cannot be married on the high seas on British ships. Royal Navy personnel can give notice of intention to marry on ships and later marry on shore. You can marry on some foreign ships under foreign marriage laws. If the ship is moored on a river or in a port in Britain this can make a difference. Consult the local registrar's office.

RELIGIOUS CEREMONIES

MARRYING A WIDOW/WIDOWER

Traditionally a grieving widow or widower mourns a year before recovering and remarrying. Major stresses in life, a funeral, moving house, and getting married, are a lot to cope with in quick succession, or to inflict on children and relatives not feeling like a jolly wedding. Three months is the minimum decent time. Wedding announcements are made six weeks ahead – barely a month after funeral and memorial services! Besides, you need about six weeks to prepare documentation for the new marriages.

A son can give the bride away, or her future father-in-law, uncle, friend, or a woman. Daughters and grand-children can be bridesmaids. Widows and widowers may marry in church.

REMARRYING IN CHURCH

A marriage which is declared void or annulled may enable a second wife or husband to marry in church or other religious premises. Marriages can be declared void if one party was under the age of sixteen, had VD, or the woman was pregnant by another man. The objection must be raised within three years by the aggrieved party who was deceived at the time of marriage.

OUTSIDE CHURCH

Marriages can take place outside a church in special circumstances, e.g. when one of the partners is imprisoned, housebound or confined to hospital. Catholics and Anglicans must marry in a register office or church. If you are a member of another religion you may need a registrar present, or a register office ceremony first. See below.

SECOND MARRIAGE FOR A DIVORCEE

Discuss with the minister what is acceptable to him. A service of blessing can be held with an address by the vicar, hymns and prayers and candles in church, and the men wearing morning suits. The bride's dress is usually not ankle-length white (the vicar may say this is inappropriate because the ceremony is not a wedding) but can be something equally pretty such as pale blue satin. One couple had a beautifully decorated church with flares along the country church path in midwinter. This can be followed by a reception as romantic and elaborate as you like.

CHURCH OF ENGLAND STANDARD RELIGIOUS CEREMONY

In the Church of England you are married by a vicar. Banns are called in advance, and the vicar takes care of all documentation. No registrar's certificate is needed. At your own parish church you do not necessarily need a birth certificate if evidence of your age is on the parish register from your baptism.

CHURCH ETIQUETTE AND PUNCTUALITY

Ushers should arrive an hour in advance to show guests to their seats and hand out order-of-service sheets. Guests should arrive at least fifteen minutes in advance. Guests should not arrive at church drunk, walk in laughing, nor walk in or out during the wedding ceremony. It is usual for the bride's friends and relatives to sit on the left-hand side of the church and for the groom's family and friends to sit on the right. Close family sit nearest the front.

The groom must be there, be on time, and be sober. The best man is responsible for this. The groom and best man wait by the altar at least half an hour in advance. The bridesmaids wait by the church door. (It is also possible to have the chief usher or best man by the church door. He goes inside to nod to the groom and vicar that the bride has arrived.) In many churches the vicar waits by the church door and precedes the bride in the procession.

The bride's mother arrives just before the bride and sits in the front pew on the left of the aisle. (After this nobody else enters.) Latecomers wait in the hallway or go upstairs to the gallery.

The bride's car may arrive five minutes early to allow time for photographs. The chauffeur opens the door for her father to alight in the road and her father goes round the back of the car to the kerb to help out the bride.

The bridegroom is waiting with the best man in the front right-hand pew. The vicar is at the altar rail.

A signal is given to the organist to start playing the music. On hearing the music the groom, best man and anyone else who was seated must stand upright.

PROCESSION ORDER

The bride with her father on her left proceeds up the left aisle, or the centre aisle if there is one. Tiny bridesmaids holding the train follow, then the chief bridesmaid. The bride's family are seated on the left of the aisle. (NB. Orthodox Jewish weddings are slightly different. See below.)

The father escorts his daughter in the procession up the aisle, followed by the bridesmaids. The bride stops facing the altar, next to the groom who is now on her right. The chief bridesmaid stands behind the bride, and takes the bouquet and gloves, so that the bride is free to hold out her hand to receive the ring. The bride's father gives her away then steps back to sit with the bride's mother in the front pew.

The groom says his vows with his hand on the bride's. They release hands so that she can place hers above his when she makes her vows. In many churches the bride's veil is lifted immediately after the vows and exchange of rings when the vicar says to the groom, 'You may now kiss the bride'. Alternatively the veil can be lifted during the hymn, before the prayers or in the vestry.

The Russian and Greek Orthodox bind hands. So do the Anglo-Catholics who are high church, favouring statues, incense, and vestments.

TRADITIONAL AND MODERN CHURCH OF ENGLAND WEDDINGS

During the conventional church wedding you are required to disclaim knowledge of any impediment to marriage, and declare your consent. The marriage must take place between the hours of 8 am and 6 pm, with open doors, and two witnesses.

It is worthwhile for the couple to look at the choice of wording before meeting the minister, to avoid arguing with each other in front of him. Ministers, however, are usually diplomatic and may help you reach agreement.

The traditional wedding service is in the Book of Common Prayer, available from bookshops, churches, cathedral bookshops, etc. The familiar service is in archaic language, 'Wilt thou have' . . . 'thy' wife, 'ye', etc.

The replies being 'I will', and 'I take thee' . . .

The priest asks who 'giveth . . .' and the father or friend steps forward to hand his daughter to the minister who sees that the groom's hand is placed on the bride's.

The ring is placed on the prayerbook, then the priest hands the ring to the groom. On placing the ring on the third finger of the bride's left hand the groom keeps his hand on the ring while he makes his statement and again archaic language is used, 'I thee wed', 'thee worship', and 'thee endow' . . . etc.

More significant is the fact that the bride's response includes the word 'obey'. The couple kneel and a prayer is said while the rest of the congregation remain standing. Then the priest joins their hands and pronounces them married.

The bride and groom decide whether they are happy with the older language and find it more beautiful and meaningful. It is less important whether the congregation understand the vows.

The *Alternative Service Book* of 1980 contains the modern version, and inexpensive reprints of the marriage service alone can be obtained from bookshops such as Mowbrays near Oxford Circus, London, by mail order, and from SPCK, 112 Marylebone Road, London NW1.

The groom is asked 'will you' (take this woman) . . . to be 'your wife?' and he replies, 'I will'. The bride follows the same procedure.

Other differences include using the word 'share' instead of 'endow'. The bride may omit the word 'obey'. The giving away is optional. The couple are pronounced married.

The signing may take place at this point or after an optional number of further hymns, psalms, prayers and blessings. Some couples also opt for an address.

RECESSION ORDER

For the recession, or return down the aisle, the bride is on the groom's left, so he has to move before leading her down the aisle, followed by the bridesmaids.

The bride returns down the right or centre aisle. Her husband is holding her right arm. Small bridesmaids hold the bride's train. The best man and chief bridesmaid follow behind. Finally come the bride's mother with the groom's father, then the bride's father with the groom's mother.

HYMNS, READINGS AND PRAYERS

For committed believers, hymns such as 'Jesus shall reign where'er the sun ...' can be very moving, adding significance to the occasion. If you have invited many non-Christians, they will be puzzled by a choice of hymns such as 'Stand Up, Stand Up For Jesus'. It is tactful to choose innocuous hymns such as 'All Things Bright and Beautiful' so that everyone can join in the singing. Old Testament readings and prayers will similarly be more familiar and acceptable to a mixed-faith congregation.

CHOOSING CHURCH MUSIC

The traditional music 'Here Comes the Bride' is Wagner's *Wedding March* or *Bridal Chorus* from the opera *Lohengrin*. The wedding march for the recession down the aisle is from Mendelssohn's *Midsummer Night's Dream*. The pieces were chosen by Queen Victoria's eldest daughter for her wedding and have been popular ever since. An alternative to 'Here Comes the Bride' is Handel's *Arrival of the Queen of Sheba*.

Suitable hymns include 'Amazing Grace'. For the recession Clarke's *Trumpet Voluntary* can be played. You may need music while waiting for the bride's arrival, and during the signing of the register (e.g. *Ave Maria*). The organist can offer suggestions and a hymn book to look at. (The organist is probably rather tired of playing 'Here Comes the Bride' and may try to encourage you to make a more original choice of music.)

Sheet music is obtainable from music shops. The *Alternative Service Book* contains the titles and words for many popular hymns, and psalms such as the 23rd psalm 'The Lord is my shepherd ...'.

GUARD OF HONOUR

On emerging from the church the couple can be greeted by an avenue of well-wishers wearing uniform, often raising arms and symbols to form an arch. Army, Navy or Air Force officers raise ceremonial swords. Police raise truncheons. A cricket team raises bats. Adult school-friends wear the old school tie. Students raise scarves aloft. Schoolchildren, Boy Scouts and Cubs hold up hats or caps.

CONFETTI AND BELLS

Well-wishers throw confetti over the bride and groom as they make their way to the car, especially at country churches with a walk from the church door to the church gate. Get permission from the church to throw confetti because some regard it as litter. If confetti is allowed, the chief bridesmaid and best man should agree who will be delegated to supply confetti to guests, so that the bride is not disappointed. If confetti is not allowed in the churchyard it is thrown as the couple emerge outside the church gate, using confetti made of a substance which can be eaten by birds.

Wedding bells are rung to announce that the bride is married. (Bell-ringers require payment.) In city centres crowds in the street will stop to see the bride being photographed on the church steps before she gets into the car.

PHOTOGRAPHS AND VIDEOS

Permission is required for photographs or video-recordings in churches and religious establishments. The minister may feel that the video camera will distract or detract from the religious atmosphere. He may permit photographs in church before and after the ceremony but not during the service.

Photographs before the service could include the bride getting out of the car, on the arm of whoever is giving her away, or with her bridesmaids who are waiting for her at the church door.

☆ *GROUP PHOTOGRAPHS*	The majority of photographs will include the bride. She will be photographed on her own, with the groom, and with all the wedding group and various members of the wedding party such as her mother, her parents, the chief bridesmaid, or the matron-of-honour.
☆ *WHOM TO PHOTOGRAPH*	The groom may wish to be photographed with the ushers. Other VIPs or guests of honour can have individual portraits and photographs with bride and groom or both. For example, the bride's mother, the bride's parents, the groom's parents, and both sets of parents. Don't forget VIPs outside the family – the friend who loaned the car photographed with the car, the person who made the cake photographed with the cake, and nanny.
	Photograph the speechmakers, the cake cutting, throwing the bouquet, raising glasses for toasts, and waving from the car with Just Married signs.
☆ *PHOTOGRAPHS WITH CHILDREN*	Pretty photographs can be taken of junior bridesmaids and pages with the bride and groom, on their own, and with their parents. Don't let

children jump into every photograph. Have bride and groom
photographed separately before or
after the wedding reception, and
take photographs in different parts
of the garden. While children pose
with the bride, photograph the
groom alone.

WRITING FOR INFORMATION

When writing to the Dean or Provost of a cathedral
address him as The Very Revd. For more information
check *The Book of Common Prayer* or contact the
Church of England Enquiry Centre, Church House, Great
Smith Street, Westminster, London SW1P 3NZ, tel.
071–222 9011.

CHURCH OF SCOTLAND,
WEDDINGS IN SCOTLAND, AND
SCOTTISH WEDDING RECEPTIONS

Four weeks in advance of the wedding (six weeks if you
were previously married), take the money for the fees
and your documents (birth certificates and any divorce
decree or death certificate of former spouse) and deliver
your marriage notices to the registrar. You must go to the
Office of the Registrar fifteen days prior to the marriage
(not more than three months prior). Return to collect the
Marriage Schedule in the week before the wedding. (It
cannot be given to you more than seven days earlier.) It
must be handed to the minister before the marriage
service starts. The minister cannot proceed without the

Marriage Schedule because it is a criminal offence to do so. (You could deliver it the day before in case you forget it on the day.)

The minister's fee is not always set; it is usually up to you. You may make a voluntary contribution to the church heating or lighting, or there may be a set fee. The organist and church officer usually receive a set fee.

The bridesmaid might journey to church with the bride or be taken there by the best man (after he has delivered the groom).

The Church of Scotland, the established or national Church, is Presbyterian. Unlike the Church of England it is independent from the state. (Other Presbyterian Churches include the United Free Church.) You can be married by a man or woman minister, in a church or other building such as a home or hotel, at any time – late afternoon such as 4 pm or 5 pm being popular.

The groom may wait at the church door or by the communion table (there is no altar), at the minister's discretion. Ministers are described as The Reverend, not as Reverend which is an Americanism.

For more details about church weddings contact the Church of Scotland, 121 George Street, Edinburgh EH2 4YN, tel. 031–225 5722; or the Scottish Episcopal Church, tel. 031–225 6357.

You can marry in Scotland according to other faiths (e.g. Bahai) and in a register office. Scotland is considered romantic, especially the nearest point to the border, Gretna Green, formerly the destination of eloping couples. About one thousand five hundred marriages still

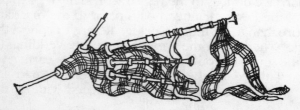

take place every year at Gretna Green, although it is so small that the post is routed via Carlisle, just across the border in England. There is a long waiting list, so write to Gretna Green Register Office well in advance for details.

Scottish couples often choose to wear formal Scottish clothes even in daytime. A Scottish groom and other Scotsmen wear dress tartan kilts, an English best man or groom wear a morning coat, and Scottish bridesmaids wear plaid sashes. Girls in kilts wear black patent leather shoes with silver buckles. As the car leaves the church, traditionally the couple throw coins and sweets to the local village children. Do not throw coins, sweets, bridal bouquets or anything else near a roadway where children will scramble, push and run near traffic.

A Scottish piper in a kilt can be at the reception hotel playing outside the front door, in a courtyard, or on a balcony to welcome guests on arrival. Photographs should include the piper. During the reception the same piper can play reels. Scottish food such as haggis is served and malt whisky is popular.

A Scottish bagpipers' agency in London can supply a piper to play bagpipes in church during the signing of the register and recession (in England get the vicar's permission).

The receiving line starts with the bride's parents, then the groom's parents, then the bridal couple, then the bridesmaid and finally the best man (ladies first all along the line).

Toasts and cake cutting precede the meal. Guests go to the tables first and bride and groom arrive last.

At the reception the minister sits on the bride's left, between the bride and the bride's mother. The bride's father is left of the bride's mother. Next comes the groom's mother, with the groom's father on the bride's far left. The bridegroom has a bridesmaid on his right with a best man at the end of the table.

The meal is followed by reading telemessages, then

another toast to the bridal couple, the groom's reply ending with toast to the bridesmaids, the best man's reply, and then maybe toasts to the couple's parents and/or speeches by them.

Some Scottish towns are dry (ban alcohol). In any case you should offer non-alcoholic drinks at the same time as alcoholic drinks so that for toasts and other occasions guests have a choice.

For details contact Church of Scotland, Enquiry Department, 121 George Street, Edinburgh EH2 4YN (phone no. as before).

WELSH WEDDINGS

The ceremony will take place in Welsh if the bride and groom speak Welsh. The Church of Wales, and Welsh Congregational Churches in Wales or London can supply ceremony details which are similar to the English equivalents.

At the reception there are numerous speeches and then the floor is open to guests to make speeches, 'Would anyone else like to say a few words?' Dancing may include Welsh folk dancing, reels such as the Llanover Reel, harpists, choirs singing songs such as *The Ashgrove*, and bards reciting poems composed in the Welsh language mentioning the bride and groom.

METHODIST WEDDINGS

The Methodist Church is the largest of the Free Churches. You do not have to be a Methodist or even a Christian to marry in a Methodist church. Christians marrying Christians from other churches or marrying Sikhs, Jews or Muslims might ask Methodist ministers to marry them. Discuss it with the minister. Methodists will marry divorced people but each minister may use their own discretion. Some ministers will marry a divorced person in church if they are the one deemed 'innocent'.

In the Free Churches you address the minister as 'Mr.' When speaking about him you refer to him in the third person as The Reverend. Address an envelope to him as The Reverend, but begin the letter with Dear Mr Smith, or whatever his name is. However, the minister is unlikely to be fussy about whether you get it right.

In a Methodist church you are married by a minister who explains what you have to do. You have your back to the congregation, and the minister is close enough to whisper instructions so it is almost impossible to make a mistake. Kneeling is optional, and your decision may depend on your wedding clothes. You could kneel for blessing at the end of the ceremony.

Brides wear white as is the custom. Bridesmaids may stand or sit, depending on their age. You can decide this at the rehearsal. No hats are necessary.

The administrator of one United Reformed Methodist church explained that although traditionally the bride did not remove her veil until the end of the service, nowadays they ask the bride to remove her veil at the beginning. So check with your local church.

A registrar is not needed. The minister acts as registrar. The minister will explain everything to you. He will want to see you two or three times and talk about marriage. At many churches classes are held where you meet other couples.

Historically, the foundation of the Methodists was linked to the temperance movement and no alcohol is allowed on the premises – a law which the minister cannot waive. Since most people like to serve alcohol at wedding receptions it is not common to hold receptions on Methodist premises.

QUAKER WEDDINGS

Sunday is not considered a particularly holy day though meetings are often held on Sunday for convenience. 'Friends' marriages are exempt from certain provisions of the Marriage Act (1949) such as registering the premises for marriage and you can marry in the bride's home if no Quaker Meeting House or regular meeting place is nearby. Quaker meetings are essentially democratic, with long periods of silent reflection broken when someone feels inspired to speak, read, or after due consideration to respond to another's thoughts or offer support. For example, on the occasion of a wedding an Elder might rise to reflect upon the blessings of marriage or ask for a blessing upon the couple. To create the right atmosphere they arrange for sufficient numbers of regular attenders to be present at a wedding so that guests unfamiliar with the ambience do not outnumber the others.

An application to the Registering Officer of the monthly meeting to be held in the bride's home area must be made at least six weeks in advance. If the couple to be married are not Friends they must have attended meetings or be in sympathy with Quaker philosophy and two Friends must write in support of their application. A certificate has to be obtained from the Superintendent Registrar. The forthcoming marriage is then announced at a meeting, in the same way as banns are read in the Church of England. Assuming that there are no objections, those at the meeting set a date for a meeting when the marriage will be solemnized.

The bridal couple usually arrive in their own car since a Rolls-Royce is considered ostentatious. The bride wears no veil and need not dress in white. Best man and bridesmaids are not necessary. Morning coats are not usually worn by the men, just grey or dark suits and carnations. There is no procession or music. The bride's mother may have decorated the room with vases of flowers, possibly employing the help of a professional florist.

The bride and groom sit facing the meeting. The best man and bridesmaids, if any, sit beside them and the immediate family sit close to them. After a period of quiet, when a sense of harmony prevails, the couple hold hands. Both stand and recite promises. He speaks first. They promise to be 'loving and faithful'. There is a slight choice of wording – 'with God's help' or 'with divine assistance'. The form they both use is decided in advance in consultation with the Elders. A wedding ring is not necessary, but is often placed on the finger immediately after making the promises.

There is then a time of silent communion during which those attending may occasionally be inspired to express their thoughts and prayers. Meetings do not end after somebody has spoken but following a period of about half an hour's silence when an atmosphere of calm prevails. The meeting ends with two of the Elders of the Meeting shaking hands.

A marriage certificate is signed by the couple and two witnesses and read aloud. It is kept by the couple. Then the register is signed by all four and the Registering Officer.

If the reception is held in an adjoining room all the worshippers join the bride and groom to share food the bride's family has provided. No alcohol is served. If the reception is held elsewhere only those specifically invited attend.

For more details contact the Religious Society of Friends, Friends House, Euston Road, London NW1 2BJ, tel. 071–387 3601, or their Registering Officer. A leaflet called *Your First Time at a Quaker Meeting* is available from Quaker Home Service in London. Send guests a leaflet explaining Quaker meetings with invitations, so that they know what to expect. Different regulations apply in Scotland.

ROMAN CATHOLIC WEDDINGS

The Catholic Church requires a minimum of six months' notice to prepare the couple and prepare documents. The couple can be married by a bishop, priest, or deacon.

No head covering is required for bride or guests. Latin is no longer obligatory and mostly is not used, except in the mass where Latin is optional.

☆ *PRELIMINARY QUESTIONS*

Three preliminary questions are asked including one about whether you are ready to bring up children according to the law of Christ and his Church (the response being, 'I am').

☆ *MARRIAGE IMPEDIMENT DISCLAIMER*

You may say the words after the priest or read that you do not know of any impediment.

☆ *DECLARATION OF CONSENT*

The bride and groom declare consent ('I will').

☆ *VOWS BEFORE WITNESSES*

The couple join right hands (father placing bride's hand on groom's). The priest says the formulae which are repeated by the groom or bride, or vows may be read from the book.

The traditional 'For better for worse' formulae is the same as that laid down for Church of England. The groom calls on the congregation to witness, and says the few words ending, 'till death do us part'. The couple separate their hands and rejoin them, and the bride says the words ending, 'till death do us part'.

☆ *GIVING OF RINGS*

The priest blesses the ring before it is placed on the bride's finger, or two rings are blessed before being exchanged. Traditionally the groom placed the wedding ring on the bride's thumb, saying, 'in the name of the father,' on the second finger saying, '... in the name of the son,' on the middle finger saying, 'and of the holy ghost,' finally on the third finger saying, 'Amen'. If two rings were used the bride then placed his ring on his fingers, following the same practice of placing it on one finger after the other, saying the same words. The groom may do this or place the ring directly on the bride's third finger, saying the above words.

After the solemnization of the marriage, i.e. the vows, there may be a nuptial mass during which either or both of the couple receive holy communion, consecrated wine and bread given only to baptized Catholics. A blessing is said over the newlyweds and they are sprinkled with holy water.

After the ceremony the bride and groom go to a table at one side to sign the register so they are still in view (or in the sacristy), and then stand so that the bride is on the groom's left for the recession.

You can read the exact wording in *The Rite of Marriage for use of congregations in The Diocese of England and Wales* which you can obtain by mail order from Mowbray's Bookshop in London, or from your local Catholic church. *The Rite of the Sacrament of Marriage* is published by the Catholic Truth Society.

If your family books are old, see the Roman Catholic mass revised in the 1960s (before that mass was in Latin). Check if there are later changes. The Code of Canon Law lists which marriages are forbidden, not necessarily the same as those disallowed by British or European law. Currently marriages between first cousins are not allowed but you should check the latest rulings.

The priest may be invited to the wedding reception in which case he will say grace before the meal. A priest named John Brown would be addressed as Father Brown or Father John or simply Father. When you know him very well you might just call him John.

The wedding service and nuptial mass may take over an hour. A copy of the wedding service and nuptial mass can be obtained from Mowbrays bookshop in London. For more details contact The Catholic Marriage Advisory Council, London Centre, 23 Kensington Square, London W8 5HN, tel. 071–937 3781. You may wish to place a wedding announcement in a Catholic newspaper.

EUROPEAN CATHOLIC WEDDINGS

In Catholic countries such as Spain and Italy the engagement ring is worn on the right hand during the engagement, and moved to the left hand on marriage. The same applies to Catholics in some non-Catholic countries such as Holland.

In France and most European countries the marriage contract is signed at the town hall before the church wedding.

In France and Italy divorcees and pregnant brides wear cream or pastel colour dresses. The groom enters the church accompanied by his mother.

In Spain one parent of the bride accompanies one parent of the groom in the procession.

EASTERN OR GREEK ORTHODOX

Eastern Orthodox is a term used by the Greek Orthodox, and Ukrainians (from Russia), also Syrian, and Coptic (from Egypt), who have varying practices. You will find current addresses of the Serbian (Yugoslavian), Russian Orthodox and other churches in the London yellow pages under Places of Worship and Religious Organizations.

☆ *GREEK ORTHODOX WEDDINGS*

Remember that the head of their Church is not the Pope but the Patriarch. The Greek bride, her father, and maid-of-honour may travel to church in the same car, the best man giving the bride her bouquet at the door. The bride usually wears white although this is not compulsory. The priest places crowns on the heads of bride and groom, and the ceremony is called crowning. The 'Father' – not the bride's father but a holy man, might marry them in a Greek Orthodox cathedral. Guests need not cover their heads.

At Greek Orthodox weddings there are many best men and best women or bridesmaids according to the couple's status. Attendants pay for the bride's dress and lead the first dance.

At the reception, it is a Greek/Cypriot custom to pin money on the bride.

☆ *GREEK-CYPRIOT WEDDINGS*

On a Greek island wedding the whole village would be invited, so a London wedding with 500 guests is not uncommon. There are no bridesmaids but instead female representatives from different families called first lady, second lady, and so on, and each family decides who represents them. The wedding invitation goes to the head of the household and he decides who should attend.

☆ *UKRAINIAN WEDDINGS*

You could have three bridesmaids and three best men. The singing is in Ukrainian. The couple wear a green wreath of myrtle on their heads. The couple's hands are tied together. The Guard of Honour could wear Cossack green and red.

At the reception the bride's mother greets the married couple with bread and salt. Your menu might include Chicken Kiev, honouring the Ukrainian capital city in Russia. (For those who don't eat garlic offer an alternative dish.)

JEWISH WEDDINGS

Jewish weddings are often large with many guests – and increasingly non-Jewish guests.

WHEN AND WHERE

Jewish weddings are held on Sunday or weekdays, not on the Sabbath (Saturday) which would interfere with religious services, nor on major holy days such as Yom Kippur, an autumn day of fasting. Extremely orthodox Jews do not travel on the Sabbath which starts and ends at dusk, affecting the timing of the wedding on Friday night in winter, and Saturday night in summer.

Unlike Christian church weddings which should be in daylight, Jewish tradition favours weddings late in the day with a view of the sky. In the UK, Jewish weddings are often held late in the day followed by a seated evening dinner-dance at a large hotel.

One couple whose families lived near each other, but who attended different synagogues, chose a third synagogue and invited the rabbis from the other two synagogues to attend.

In Israel, evening weddings take place in the open air under the stars. They may be in hotels with a canopy for the ceremony on the terrace. If marrying or honeymooning in Israel note that El Al does not fly on the Sabbath.

BEFOREHAND

Before a wedding, an orthodox rabbi might require the bride to take a *mikva*, a ritual bath involving total immersion, rather like baptism, for symbolic purification. A bride who is reluctant might be asked to go away and think about it. Another rabbi might be less insistent on this.

Orthodox brides and grooms fast until the ceremony, to start marriage afresh. The groom must not be intoxicated or the marriage ceremony is invalid.

JEWISH SECOND MARRIAGE

The secular divorce allows a Jewish woman to remarry in a register office. A Jewish divorcee wishing to remarry and have her second marriage recognized under Jewish law needs a *Get* or divorce document, issued by rabbinical authorities if the husband agrees to divorce. The *Get* enables her second marriage to be recognized and the children to be legitimate under Jewish law.

The Reform synagogues allow men and women to sit together, and use English language for about half the service. The Liberals are even more Anglicized and modernized, eating pork and appointing women rabbis.

Debate continues about the status of the children of non-orthodox Jews, and children of a Cohen (the name means priest), who is not supposed to marry a divorcee. More information can be obtained from The Chief Rabbi who has written a booklet about the marriage service, from your local Rabbi, synagogue office secretary, or the *Jewish Wedding Book*.

The orthodox Jewish bride and her mother and mother-in-law arrive at the synagogue in the same car because the two women accompany her up the aisle. A Liberal or Reform synagogue's bride who advances up the aisle with her father arrives at the synagogue with him.

☆ *THE JEWISH MARRIAGE SERVICE*

At orthodox Jewish weddings men and women sit separately. Head covering is required in the synagogue. The groom might wear a white satin cap. Usually a small paper skull cap will be provided for men who don't have velvet or silk skullcaps. Ladies wear hats. The bride is led in by both her mother and mother-in-law in the orthodox synagogue, by her father in the Reform synagogue. The groom lifts her veil momentarily to check he is getting the right girl!

The prayer book has Hebrew on one side, English opposite, with instructions about when to stand. If you cannot follow, simply stand and sit when everybody else does. The ceremony takes place under a canopy representing the new home. The couple recite in Hebrew. The ring is placed on the bride's pointing finger of her right hand so everyone can see it. Later she transfers it to her left hand.

The groom breaks a glass under his foot. Everybody claps and shouts 'Mazel tov!' (good luck). Orthodox synagogues do not allow videos; some Reform synagogues do.

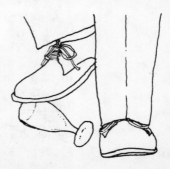

The couple and the witnesses sign the register and are given a marriage certificate in Hebrew. After the ceremony the bride and groom are left alone together in a synagogue room, no longer for consummating the marriage, just for a quick cuddle in private. Most couples do not wait but rush to the reception. One couple waited expectantly to be summoned, eventually locating the adjoining hall where the reception was proceeding merrily without them!

☆ *WEDDING RECEPTIONS*

At the reception the rabbi says grace in Hebrew before and after the meal. Extended grace and songs with jolly choruses follow the meal. At ultra-orthodox wedding receptions men dance around the room in a big circle between courses, holding handkerchiefs so that one person does not touch another. Rousing music is played and the bride and groom are carried aloft on chairs.

At a large seated Jewish wedding a loyal toast is made to HM The Queen. This is because such toasts were common on formal occasions in past times. It also demonstrates that despite playing the national anthem of another country (Israel) later, the hosts and guests are loyal British subjects.

☆ *KOSHER FOOD*

Provide Kosher food for guests. Meat and milk are not served at the same meal. Coffee is served black, or with a non-milk product, until several hours after meat. Following fish dinners you can have ice cream or cream desserts and coffee with cream.

AMERICAN WEDDINGS AND RECEPTIONS

Many states will not grant permission for marriage until supplied with documentation showing that both parties have had a medical test proving their blood is free of VD or AIDS symptoms, to protect children of the marriage.

Weddings feature small bridesmaids strewing rose petals in front of the bride and little children as ring-bearers with the rings on cushions. Ushers or grooms-men, and bridesmaids are paired off in the recession. Home weddings are permitted. Jewish couples can marry on the Sabbath (Saturday) in winter after dusk.

MUSLIM WEDDINGS

The day before the wedding the Muslim girl has her hair and body prepared to look as attractive as possible, and her hands are decorated with red patterns. Orthodox weddings take place on an auspicious day such as the birthday of the prophet, at night, e.g. 8.30 pm. You can hold a wedding on a Friday, but not on a sad day commemorating martyrdom or the first month of the Islamic year. Two witnesses are appointed from each family – four in all. The groom's side provides the bride's white or red saree, lots of jewellery, perfumes, and fresh flower garlands. Her family provides his clothes.

Guests should remember that they will be removing their shoes and sitting on the floor in the mosque, so dress accordingly. The Islamic wedding is not necessarily held in the mosque but perhaps in the bride's house. Men and women, including the bride and groom are in separate rooms. The religious leader who supervises goes to the bride who is asked if she accepts the groom and she nods three times.

Under Islamic law a man must wait until his first wife has had three menstrual periods before he embarks on a divorce. This is in order to ensure that the first wife is not bearing another child.

More details on Sunni weddings can be obtained from the Regents Park Mosque in London. A Shia centre is based in Stanmore, Middlesex.

The bride will be dressed with many jewels and an elaborate heavy dress which may be any colour, perhaps a white sari and a garland. The bride can have a gold wedding ring. (Among some communities the groom's must be silver, not gold.)

The couple are seated in different rooms in the mosque, but symbolically sitting back to back. Two priests conduct the ceremony, beginning with a sermon on marriage and then the vows. Lady guests should cover their head, e.g. with a scarf, and their legs. Face and hands may be visible. Non-Muslims may enter the mosque.

When a wedding takes place in a mosque there will be an hour or two spent at a reception there and then the ladies go to one house, the men to another.

Afterwards, sweets are given. Muslim guests eat Halal meat or vegetarian food, no pork. Rice and curry are popular. Orthodox Muslims do not drink alcohol so hosts should ensure a plentiful supply of non-alcoholic drinks, Coke, juices, etc. The groom's family gives presents to the bride's mother and the bride's family gives presents to the groom's mother. The gifts you give the wedding pair are the same as for any bridal couple, something for the home such as a clock or bedlinen.

Coins are thrown at the departing couple – make sure that coins do not damage the departure car.

HINDU WEDDINGS

Marriage takes place at a register office, then a Hindu temple where the priest officiates. He chooses an auspicious day depending on the couple's horoscopes.

A wedding car takes the groom with his sisters. The bride might wear red or pink, not usually white which is the colour of mourning and would be worn by a widow. The bride covers her head but guests need not. The engagement ceremony may take place on the first of the seven days of ceremonies, or the rings may have been exchanged earlier. Brothers and sisters have roles in the ceremonies. The couple walk around a fire in a basket seven times. Garlands are exchanged.

The reception is on the last day. Gifts of money end with the number one, e.g. £21 or £31. Customs of people from South India differ from those originating in North India. Not all Hindus are vegetarian but many are, so vegetarian food will be required at the reception held in the bride's mother's house or hotel.

SIKH WEDDINGS

Sikhs have arranged marriages. After the register office marriage the Sikh wedding is held at a weekend or on a bank holiday at a Sikh temple.

Lady guests should cover their heads. Sikh women wear saris with the ends over their heads or a Punjabi outfit with a knee-length dress, trousers and a long scarf to go over the head. Men may use a handkerchief or a hat. The orthodox Sikh observes five rules, wearing long hair, boxer shorts, a bangle, a comb in his hair and a dagger. Sikh men wear turbans over their long hair. A clean-shaven man will grow a beard before the wedding and wear a turban.

A Sikh is married by a Garanthi or priest at a Sikh temple. The groom and male congregation gather in a forecourt or indoors in bad weather at 9 am or 10 am. The priest says a prayer of blessing. Equivalent members of each family meet and exchange garlands of tinsel, starting with the groom's father and bride's father (or uncle). Her brother meets his brother or cousin, and so on.

Guests are welcomed into the hall where they receive tea and vegetarian samosas (no meat is allowed in the temple), and sweets. Then everybody removes their shoes, and covers their head to move into the holy area, bowing their head on entering and putting money into a box for the temple, advancing to kneel and bow towards the book.

The groom sits on a blanket facing the holy book. The groom's father-in-law presents nuts and sweets to the groom and a gold bangle.

The bride wears a red or pink sari edged with gold thread embroidery, and has gold jewellery in her nose and on her forehead. Others remain seated while close female relatives lead in the bride who kneels and bows her head to the holy book and sits on the floor by the groom. The bride is expected to cry because she is leaving her parents' home forever to live in her mother-in-law's house. A familiar sister-in-law from her household (her brother's wife) or a married sister sits alongside to help and comfort her. The marriage promises are sung, accompanied by the music of small drums beaten with the hands. The priest sings hymns and musicians play a little drum and a kind of harmonium.

The bride's father gives the groom a long scarf

symbolizing giving away the bride. Then the bride and groom rise and walk clockwise around the holy book four times, the groom leading the bride by the scarf which is draped over his shoulder. After standing for prayer, guests give sweets and money to the bride, about £5, in addition to wedding presents given previously. The money goes to the bride's mother-in-law. Elderly people put a hand on the head of the bride and groom to bless them after giving them money. Guests bow their heads to the holy book.

The couple sign the Sikh wedding book while guests depart for the reception held in a hall. The food for as many as 400 people may be made by family and friends and consists of chapatis, vegetable samosas, puris, curries and so on. Alcohol is served. The bride returns to her parents' home, from which the groom and his immediate family collect her.

BAHAI WEDDINGS

When marrying a Bahai, you can have a Bahai wedding and then a church wedding, as the Bahais have no objection. Anyone who believes in one God can marry in the Bahai faith. They accept the founders of all the monotheistic religions, Moses, Jesus, Mohammed, and their own leader.

The Bahai national centre is in London but Bahais are scattered throughout Britain. There is a House of Worship on each continent – the main one being in Haifa, Israel, but few people are near one and most weddings take place in a home or hotel. The wedding is presided over by a member or elected officer of the local spiritual assembly.

You need a register office certificate. In Scotland the Bahai wedding is recognized and no extra civil ceremony is necessary, so Bahai officers officiate. But in England a register office marriage takes place first. The Bahai organization in London can supply a book called *Marriage: A fortress for well-being*.

There are no arranged marriages. The bride and groom must get the consent of all living parents, because weddings are considered to be uniting families. Parents who do not consent may be persuaded to change their minds. But having given consent they cannot withdraw it afterwards.

There are no ritual requirements, except reciting, 'Verily we are content with the will of God'. The bride and groom can read poetry or play music. There are no rules about dress – except that clothing tends to be fairly modest. The bride can wear white, which is popular, but a red sari would be equally acceptable or any other suitable attire, and a best man and bridesmaids can take part. There are no rules about food except that no alcohol is drunk.

BUDDHIST WEDDINGS (SRI LANKA)

Sri Lankan Buddhist weddings take place in the home, not related to religious ceremonies, though a few prayers might be said. An auspicious day and auspicious time of day is chosen.

The bride wears a white dress or sari, worn draped over the opposite shoulder to the Indian sari, with frills at waist level, and seven necklace chains.

ORIENTAL WEDDINGS

Chinese wedding cars are decorated with a doll dressed in bridal costume on the bonnet and balloons.

The Japanese may hold the traditional Japanese wedding with the bride and groom both wearing kimonos, the bride having her face made up chalk white, or a Western-style wedding. The Japanese bride is expected to wear up to five outfits for the wedding day, where a display of the family's wealth is customary. The Japanese bride is likely to marry in a hotel under low lighting so wedding dresses decorated with elaborate beads would be appropriate. The Japanese wrap money, including tips, in fancy envelopes. Shoes should be removed on entering a Japanese home.

DOUBLE WEDDINGS

When you have a double wedding, both couples should be treated equally. But walking up the aisle in the procession, somebody has to go first, so that is the elder groom, and in most cases he is with the elder bride as well.

At the reception held by the bride's parents, if the two brides are sisters, generally the elder bride takes precedence.

MIXED-FAITH MARRIAGES

(See notes above on Register Office, Free Church, and Bahai ceremonies. Non-conformist weddings are an advantage to those of mixed religion.)

People of liberal views often marry with the blessing of both families, but the orthodox may require conversion before you can be married on their premises. Technically some religious premises are licensed to marry only people of their own religion, therefore one or both of you must say that you follow that religion. This sometimes requires merely a nod as the secretary fills out an application form for you, your signature on the form and a non-committal declaration of belief in one God during the ceremony.

Rules vary with the allegiance of the congregation, and the liberality of the minister. Ask before committing yourself to a particular church or minister. If you are shy about offending the Head of the Church or the Chief Rabbi by raising difficulties, speak to their secretary.

ROMAN CATHOLIC RULES

Traditionally the spouse of a Catholic was required to convert but this is no longer the case. Roman Catholics in the UK do not require children to be brought up in the Roman Catholic faith, but they require the Roman Catholic partner to be strongly committed to seeing that the children have an opportunity to be Catholic. You may be required to state your intention to do so before you can get married. Discuss whether you are happy for one or both parties to agree to this. Some mixed-marriage couples bring children up learning about both faiths. Check by sending for the available literature. You may be able to have a ceremony with Christian ministers of Catholic and Protestant beliefs present.

JEWISH RULES

The non-Jewish bride-to-be is expected to convert to Judaism because the children are only considered Jewish if they have a Jewish mother. She spends time learning how to run a Jewish home so that she can buy and cook kosher meat, light candles and say the Hebrew prayers over them for the Friday night family meal welcoming the start of the Sabbath. It is easier to convert into the liberal synagogue than into the orthodox one, and it is easier to convert in the US. It is easier to marry in a liberal synagogue than in an orthodox one. To be married in an orthodox synagogue in the UK you have to prove that your parents were married in an orthodox Jewish manner, e.g. by presenting a document showing that they married in an orthodox synagogue, not a liberal one. Converts may prefer to marry in an orthodox synagogue to protect their children from doubts raised later because one parent was a convert. Rules may change, so check with the Chief Rabbi's office in London.

ISLAMIC RULES

Under Islamic rules Muslim women may not marry a man from another faith but this is not the case for Muslim men. Muslim males can marry women from other monotheistic religions, Christian and Jewish. Sunni and Shiite Muslims have different rulings on morganatic marriages which prevent the children of morganatic wives inheriting (morganatic means morning, i.e. without full rights). Shiites accept morganatic marriages, which would affect a man who has up to four wives (in another country). A Muslim cannot marry a mother and daughter simultaneously. An agreement to refrain from polygamy can be written into a marriage contract. Check with the Regents Park Mosque in London or your local authorities.

Register office address ....

.... Tel. ....

Forms collected ....

Documents ordered ....

Forms returned ....

Date of wedding .... Arrival time ....

Starting time .... End time ....

Minister's name and title ....

....

His/Her home address ....

.... Fee ....

Other minister's name and title ....

Address ....

....

Church/other premises address ....

.... Tel. ....

Fee to join congregation ....

Annual fee ....

Payment/donation for wedding ....

Date ....

Timing

Groom's car arrives at ....

Bride's car arrives at ....

Ceremony starts at ....

Ceremony ends at ....

Bride's car departs at ....

Last guest leaves at ....

Organist's name ....

Address ....

Tel.

Fee ....

INVITING THE WEDDING GUESTS

HOW MANY?

List all those people you would both like to invite: relatives, friends, schoolfriends, workmates, people you know from social clubs, neighbours, and those who invited you to their wedding. Your address book is the first prompter. If you held a large engagement party you may want to refer back to your previous guest list (though you may then need to pare the numbers down to keep within your budget).

COSTS

Discuss with whoever is paying the maximum number they envisage entertaining. The bride's father might be willing to tell his daughter the limit of the budget. Decide whether you would prefer to have a smaller number of guests at the ideal venue enjoying an extensive menu, or more guests at a less glossy location. Greater numbers mean higher costs. For costly weddings you may have to leave a deposit, and insure against cancellation, which would involve loss of the catering deposit.

SAMPLE COSTS

☆ *TWENTY GUESTS* Food at £5 per head would cost £100, food costing £10 per head = £200, food at £20 per head = £400.

☆ *FIFTY GUESTS* Food at £5 per head = £250, at £10 per head = £500, at £20 per head = £1,000.

☆ *ONE HUNDRED GUESTS* Food at £5 per head = £500, food at £10 per head = £1,000, food at £20 per head = £2,000.

☆ *MORE THAN ONE HUNDRED GUESTS* A £10 meal for two hundred means £2,000, for three hundred, £3,000, and so on.

As numbers of guests increase, allow for a proportionally extra cost for a larger wedding cake, more drinks, service, VAT, hire of hall, toastmaster, entertainer or band, flowers, balloons and favours.

CHILDREN

You might exclude children because you must limit numbers, or because the celebration will continue until late at night. If the problem is cost, you might exclude teenagers from a dinner, but invite them to come along later for the dancing.

EQUAL NUMBERS OF RELATIVES FROM EACH SIDE

The host should allow for the groom's family to require an equal number of guests. If the groom's family is larger, a compromise might be reached if the groom's family want to contribute to the cost, providing that the bride's family don't mind being outnumbered.

ADDITIONS AND DELETIONS

You will probably find that a few extra people have to be invited. Somebody gets engaged or married and cannot come without their partner. You realize that you have forgotten to include the minister and his wife. You have not listed yourself or the immediate wedding party. The family in Canada whom you thought would not come have arranged their holiday specially to make it possible.

If your numbers are large the extras may be balanced out by a few late cancellations. Guests are too sick with colds or flu or too pregnant to travel distances. They are abroad because of work or holidays. They suffer minor mishaps like pulled muscles, broken limbs or lost teeth.

Number of party guests ....

Number of guests at seated dinner ....

Number of children ....

Number to arrive after dinner ....

Numbers at separate disco/other party ....

ORDERING PRINTED INVITATIONS

High street stationers have books of sample invitations showing wording and printing styles on different quality paper and card. For a large formal wedding engraving on thick card with silver or gold edges is appropriate. The same printer can usually print order-of-service sheets, and menus with a list of toasts. You can also order placecards and printed items such as matchbooks and balloons.

TYPICAL WORDINGS

Mr and Mrs John Brown request the pleasure of the company of ....
at a reception to celebrate the marriage of their daughter Anne Marie to Mr Michael Hastings at ....
on ....

The widowed mother who has remarried and is acting host with her second husband informs you that:

Mr and Mrs Peter Green .... to the marriage of her daughter ....

The bride and groom, acting hosts:

Miss Anne Marie Brown and Mr Michael Hastings request the pleasure of your company at a reception to celebrate their marriage ....

or

The pleasure of the company of .... is requested at the marriage of Miss Anne Marie Brown to Mr Michael Hastings.

or

Anne Marie Brown and Michael Hastings request ....

SECOND MARRIAGE

If the bride is divorced or widowed she is usually paying for her own wedding without assistance from her father. She keeps her prefix Mrs (especially if she has children), and could use her married surname. Her invitation might read: 'Mrs Anne Matthews invites you to a reception to celebrate . . .' or more usually 'Mr David Brown and Mrs Anne Matthews . . .'.

The invitation goes out before the marriage and reception so if the bride-to-be is widowed she is still Mrs John Matthews. (This tells guests whom her child Jimmy Matthews belongs to.) She may change her name after the marriage.

OTHER STATIONERY

☆ Order-of-service folded card with words on the cover: Wedding Service/The Wedding Service/Our wedding service.

☆ Placecards for tables: Anne and Stephen, January 26th, 19—.

☆ Serviettes: Thank you for sharing our happiness/joy; Thank you for being with us today and for all your good wishes.

☆ Balloons, matchbooks, cards for wedding cake sent to those who cannot attend: With the compliments of Anne and Stephen, January 26th, 19—.

Cards can be printed in silver or gold, with borders of bells or bell-shaped flowers, or cut with oval holes or hearts projecting above the top edge, and matching white envelopes lined with shiny gold paper.

Stationer's/Printer's name ....

Address ....

.... Tel. ....

Acceptable/Not acceptable (reason ....

...........................). Family informed   No/Yes.   Order made by phone   No/Yes.   Confirmed   in   writing   No/Yes.

By (name) ....

Date ....   To (name) ....

Written confirmation received   No/Yes (date) ....

From (name) ....   Deposit ....

Paid for ....   Delivered ....

ARRANGING ACCOMMODATION FOR GUESTS

Send hotel lists or brochures to guests who might be staying overnight. The bride's mother can make bookings for guests who live far away. Block bookings in hotels may qualify for a discount, or a free room. If the reception is held in a hotel guests may wish to stay there. Talk to family about accommodation in their homes for close relatives and guests who are on a budget, especially if no reasonable commercial accommodation is nearby.

Arrange to meet VIP relatives at airport or railway station. If you live in a remote country area, tell guests which train to catch and send a car, minicab or coach to meet it. A small van can run a shuttle service.

Local hotel name ....

Address ....

....

....   Reservation tel. ....

Local car hire company name ....

Address ....

....   Tel. ....

Price station to home ....

Price station to hotel ....

GUEST LIST

GUEST NAME	ADDRESS/ PHONE	INVITED ACCEPTED/ REFUSED
....	....	....
....	....	....
....	....	....
....	....	....
....	....	....
....	....	....
....	....	....
....	....	....
....	....	....
....	....	....
....	....	....
....	....	....
....	....	....
....	....	....
....	....	....
....	....	....
....	....	....
....	....	....
....	....	....
....	....	....
....	....	....
....	....	....
....	....	....
....	....	....
....	....	....
....	....	....
....	....	....
....	....	....

GUEST LIST

HAS TRANSPORT/ ACCOM- MODATION	SENT GIFT	WAS THANKED
....	....	....
....	....	....
....	....	....
....	....	....
....	....	....
....	....	....
....	....	....
....	....	....
....	....	....
....	....	....
....	....	....
....	....	....
....	....	....
....	....	....
....	....	....
....	....	....
....	....	....
....	....	....
....	....	....
....	....	....
....	....	....
....	....	....
....	....	....
....	....	....
....	....	....
....	....	....
....	....	....

TRANSPORT

GUESTS' ARRIVAL

For out-of-town guests, photocopy a map marking the route into town from your guests' direction of arrival.

If you anticipate 100 or so cars arriving simultaneously at the hotel reception ask if the hotel can provide two doormen to open both car doors and speed up the exit of guests from cars.

TRANSPORT TO CHURCH/REGISTER OFFICE

Alternatives to the traditional Rolls are a Daimler or a Bentley. It is not unknown for the hire company to say that the car has broken down and send another colour and model. Check in advance how many vehicles they have, what substitution would be made in the event of a breakdown, and whether they will give a discount if they cannot supply the exact car booked. Confirm in writing. Most companies put white ribbon on the car; some additionally place silk flowers on the parcel shelf.

If you are using the groom or best man's car, arrange the following: Clean the car outside and inside. Fill the car up with petrol. Have the boot sufficiently clean for transporting wedding clothes. Keep a second set of car keys in a designated place in case the first set gets locked in the car boot or falls down a drain. Buy white ribbon and decide where to tie it. (A Rolls-Royce has the Silver Lady on the front of the bonnet; streamlined cars have fewer places for tying ribbons.) Put items such as a shaving foam canister for decorating the car in a box in the car boot.

If the best man is driving the groom's car he should take the car along the route and find out where he can park if there is a double yellow line outside the church. Calculate the time required for the journey in traffic. Learn how to operate reverse gear, unlock the car boot, remove the petrol cap, set and stop the car's burglar alarm. Obtain any needed car park ticket, parking disc or permit. Borrow the groom's garage key, or block of flats' security barrier card for returning the groom's car. Make a map for the guests.

TRANSPORT TO RECEPTION

White is the popular wedding car colour but the bride's white dress and the car's white ribbons look more dramatic against royal blue or a dark colour. Using your own car means you have a chance to practise taking photos of the couple and the car. If the best man and groom do not have smart cars, review which friends own fancy cars, for example the bride's father's neighbour, or the groom's boss. For even more panache hire a horse and carriage, or make a novelty of an original vehicle you have available. Decoration required includes a white ribbon on the second wedding car.

OTHER OPTIONS: TAXI/BUS

Black vintage taxis or white taxis can be hired.

To avoid parking problems in London a couple hired a red London bus from London Transport, complete with driver. They were not allowed to add white ribbons, but the photographs were amusing and distinctive anyway. The bus took the guests to the register office and on to a restaurant. Afterwards it collected everybody and took them back to the couple's home where their cars were parked.

DECORATING THE DEPARTURE VEHICLE

Best man and ushers should stock up with car decoration equipment. Make a 'Just Married' sign. Get old shoes or boots and ribbon. Buy spray-on foam.

Bridesmaids can remove flowers from bouquets, attaching them to the car with wires. Lipstick can be used to write slogans on windows (not chemicals on car paint!) such as: 'It's Legal', 'Off To Get A Little Sun And Air', 'Wave If She's Pretty'.

Foam signs can be removed with window cleaner, or petrol if all else fails. Have a cloth handy in the boot for wiping off 'Just Married' signs which might obscure vision.

The newlyweds might depart with cans tied onto a hired motorcaravan used for their honeymoon, visiting distant family, taking champagne and cake to those who could not attend the wedding.

GOING-AWAY CAR

Check that the bride's going-away outfit is suitably stylish or amusing, appropriate for the going-away vehicle, especially if it is unusual. Astride a tandem or motorbike she should avoid wearing a tight skirt. A hat needs an anchor slip or ribbons. Without a hand free for her clutch bag or handbag she needs a shoulder bag. If the couple are riding off on a motorbike, they should decide who is transporting the luggage.

When the bride and groom are not changing into going-away outfits the car must be decorated quickly. Paint a 'Just Married' card in advance. Sellotape on a balloon or two – perhaps borrowed from the reception decorations.

COPING WITH PRACTICAL JOKES

If the groom's friends include many jokers planning such tricks as spreading flour over the car handles they should drop heavy hints before the wedding, 'you will be surprised . . .'. Then the best man can help the groom to avoid damage to his new car by borrowing an obliging friend's beat-up crock for the going-away car.

Jokers may spray the car with shaving foam, and padlock chains and bells onto the bumper – you will need to find a garage with a hacksaw to remove these. If you use the best man's car, he can take the padlock key and remove the chains later. Drive to a nearby house in the decorated car. Let the best man explain to the clothes hire company why the clothes are daubed with flour (serves him right) while the laughing bride and calm, unflappable groom transfer to a smart car or hire car. (Best man, or groom, must ensure all luggage and vital documents go into the second car!)

FOREIGN WEDDING CUSTOMS TO COPY

You might copy some ideas from Europe. On the continent a Mercedes, a VW, or a vintage car is popular as a wedding car. The bride's bouquet might be placed on the bonnet.

EUROPEAN DECORATION

In Europe cars are decorated differently. A small car would be decorated with bows made from strips of white ribbon, net, lace, or muslin. Bows are tied to the two upright sections on the front bumper. The main ribbon crosses from the windscreen wipers to the front head-lights, making an X or upside V. A bow is tied in the middle between the windscreen wipers, and more bows where the ends are attached to the headlights. Bows can be tied to the car aerial.

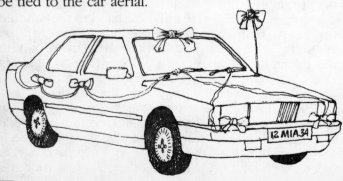

In France and Italy, flowers are put around the inside of the window frames so they are visible from outside, as well as on the back parcel shelf.

In the country in Switzerland they make arches over the village street hung with items relating to the bride and groom, e.g. baby clothes for a nurse, whisks and wooden spoons for a chef. The bride and groom might roll-up to the reception dining room door on a restaurant kitchen trolley, or the hotel's luggage trolley. Usually they arrive local style, in winter on skis, by helicopter borrowed from helicopter-ski schools, in sledges covered with fur rugs, or horse-drawn sleighs with sleighbells.

TRANSPORT AND DECORATION IN ISRAEL

Fresh flowers in geometric patterns decorate wedding cars in Israel. White balloons can be tied to the bumpers and roof. Bridal couples drive around Jerusalem in a horse and carriage being photographed at picturesque holy sites before reaching the reception. You could do the same in English cities or seaside towns.

MUSLIM TRANSPORT DECORATION

The groom's car is decorated to take him to the mosque, and the same car takes the bride and groom from the ceremony to the reception.

HINDU TRANSPORT DECORATION

The priest places a painted coconut, symbol of life, before the car, which is colourfully decorated with red ribbons, balloons, or commercial giftwrap bows.

TRANSPORT CHECKLIST

Check that you know all of the following details about your transport: Vehicle/chauffeur/driver/owner or hire company name/address/tel.

For bride/groom/family/guests/collect from address/ time/deliver to address/decoration/charge/period of hire/ extra charges/insurance/petrol/tips.

HIRE COMPANY

Name ....

Address ....

.... Tel. ....

Acceptable/Not acceptable (reason) ....

.... Family informed   No/Yes.

Booking made by phone   No/Yes. Booking in writing No/Yes. By (name) ....

Date .... To (name) ....

Written confirmation received   No/Yes (date) ....

From (name) ....

Insurance ....

PLANNING THE WEDDING RECEPTION

WHERE TO HOLD THE RECEPTION

Home or away? Marquees in city gardens or country fields offer you the option of seated meals or buffets. Halls and hotels are ideal for sit-down meals. So are barns, stately homes, and baronial halls. The first thing to do is make an early booking of the hall.

PROFESSIONAL CATERING

The size of the wedding reception affects the time spent selecting a caterer. Agree the menu including alternatives for dieters and vegetarians. Confirm everything in writing, including whether waiters serve buffet only or all drinks and food at tables, service charge, expected additional tipping, and VAT.

SCOTLAND

You can order heart-shaped cakes at Gretna Chase Hotel on the English side of the border for Valentine's Day when five or six marriages take place with hotel receptions, and couples book four-poster beds or bridal suites.

The minister is master of ceremonies/compère. The

minister and his wife sit at either end of the top table normally but at a Scottish wedding the minister sits centrally next to the bride. A ceilidh band with a fiddle and accordion play Scottish dances, no disco music or waltzes. Food will be cock-a-leekie soup or Cullen skink (Scottish fish soup), haggis or Aberdeen Angus beef, dessert of Atholl brose or cranachan – whisky, cream, honey and oats.

IRISH RECEPTION

Irish whiskey can be served at the start of the reception and at the end, neat or mixed with Guinness to make 'Black Velvet'.

JEWISH RECEPTION

Kosher food requires supervision of the products by rabbinical authorities, and preparation in a kosher kitchen, where neither crockery nor food are contaminated by non-kosher food (pork and shellfish). Large hotels have arrangements with kosher caterers who will either steam-clean the kitchen or cover surfaces with cloth for the day.

A typical meal might include smoked salmon or melon, kosher chicken or meat, dessert without lard (avoid pork products). Several London restaurants provide kosher catering.

Fish (not shellfish) and fruit, with pretty paper plates and cups could be used to supplement a meal catered at home if you have guests requiring ethnic food.

MUSLIM RECEPTION

No pork is served, only halal meat, and no alcohol. Western-style wedding cake with the cake-cutting ceremony is popular. There are no toasts but a speech may be made by the groom's family, welcoming guests who have made the effort to travel from afar; the groom may speak, complimenting the bride. Guests should dress prepared to sit on a carpeted floor.

HINDU RECEPTION

There may be hundreds of guests so a video enables hosts to enjoy seeing who was there. Hindu brides live with the mother-in-law. Non-Hindu brides whose vegetarian mother-in-law comes to stay from overseas need cooking pans which have not been used for meat. Salt is used to scrub fat off a frying pan used for bacon, or new pans are bought.

DRINKS

A trade rule is half a bottle of wine per person. However, the amount of alcohol consumed varies according to the reception's length and quantity of food. Offer aperitifs such as sherry, and later drinks such as white wine with the food. Include different brands of beer, mixers, rosé and sweet wines, low-alcohol drinks like Kaliber from Guinness, a 1% alcohol from Bass, and Diet Coke. Champagne or sparkling wine is needed for the toasts. Children can be given Perrier, fruit juice or soda water. Provide ice buckets.

CATERERS

Name ....

Address ....

.... Tel. ....

Meal prices ....

Drink prices ....

Other extras ....

Notes ....

Acceptable/Not acceptable (reason ....

....). Family informed   No/Yes.

Booking made by phone   No/Yes.   Booking in writing

No/Yes.   By (name) ....

Date .... To (name) ....

Written confirmation received   No/Yes (date) ....

From (name) ....

Insurance ....

BUDGET CELEBRATION

If you have no budget at all, follow your register office wedding with a restaurant meal. Send your small number of guests a handwritten note in advance saying, 'Mary and I will be celebrating by having a meal at Antonio's Italian Restaurant in the High Street at 7 pm. The cost will be about £10 per head and if you would care to join us we shall be delighted to see you.'

If you feel it is an imposition to ask friends to pay for their own meal and want a quiet wedding, you can have a register office wedding somewhere remote and far from where you live. Then celebrate on your own in a hotel with a four-poster bed and order yourselves a super restaurant meal with a bottle of champagne.

SELF-CATERING

Home-made cake can be iced professionally, or a bought cake can be decorated at home. Organize sufficient space for freezer storage – perhaps using neighbours' help. You can hire equipment, coat racks, seats, drinking glasses, etc. Plan the timing of making food, calculate time for laying tables, and whether serving staff are required.

RECEPTIONS HELD AT HOME

If you are planning a marquee you need a large enough garden for the marquee suitable for the number of guests you are inviting. Have a wet weather plan and a fine weather plan for a home wedding reception. You may want an awning from the house to the marquee.

Ensure you have enough chairs and crockery, cutlery and drinking glasses. Glasses can be borrowed from off-licences. Collect glasses in advance so you don't find suppliers have run out on the day because other customers borrowed the lot. You need enough freezer or larder space for the cake and all the food. You may have to enlist the aid of neighbours, friends or relatives. Alternatively book a catering company who will turn up with the food on the day. If you are providing the tablecloths, fresh flowers or silk flower arrangements these should be in place well in advance of the caterers' arrival.

House guests can help with catering and preparing the home for a home wedding reception. Work out a rota for the use of the bathroom so that on the day the bride or groom has precedence. Everybody should keep their clothes, hairdriers, and toothbrushes in their bedrooms.

Make provision for the guests' clothes, a clear bed, an

empty cupboard with spare hangers, or a borrowed or hired clothes rail (advertised in national newspapers).

Signs indicating locations within the house are useful, for example, coats upstairs (arrow pointing to staircase), toilet/gentlemen's toilet (arrow to downstairs cloakroom), ladies' coats and powder room (arrow to bedroom), second toilet/ladies' toilet (arrow to upstairs bathroom), drinks this way (arrow to kitchen), food this way (arrow to living room), photographer at end of garden by roses (arrow to French windows), marquee this way (arrow to side gate).

On a kitchen pinboard place a typed list of useful phone numbers such as the railway station, nearby hotel, car hire and so on. Or stick business cards from local taxi firms on a pinboard by the phone.

SELECTING THE WEDDING CAKE

Traditional cakes have three tiers, five tiers with column supports, or simply each layer resting on the one below. Shapes include circular, square or heart-shaped. A miniature bride and groom can be placed on top, or a vase of fresh flowers. Sample the cake to check quality. Vegetarian wedding cakes without animal fats can be made to order at Harrods.

EUROPEAN-STYLE RECEPTIONS

Wedding cakes are tiered white iced cakes but usually sponge cakes, not the heavy rich fruit cake which is used in Britain.

In France the centrepiece is a *pièce montée* (a mountainous piece), a pyramid of choux buns. Other reception food might include a tier of iced white trays on white columns, bearing different gateaux and pastries on each level.

In Italy guests are given small sweets, usually white and pink sugar-covered almonds in little muslim bags tied with ribbons or in porcelain boxes.

The Swiss reception might be decorated with candles, Christmas fairy lights, sparklers, and bubble blowing. The lights are turned out for the bride to enter to 'Here Comes the Bride', and ultra-violet light illuminates her white dress.

Cake supplier

Name ....

Address ....

.... Tel. ....

Prices ....

Dates and times ....

Notes ....

....

Acceptable/Not acceptable (reason ....

....). Family informed   No/Yes.

Booking made by phone   No/Yes.   Booking in writing

No/Yes.   By (name) ....

Date ....   To (name) ....

Written confirmation received   No/Yes (date) ....

From (name) ....

Insurance ....

TABLE DECORATION

You can have candles, printed menus, placecards, serviettes, crackers, matchbooks or balloons printed with names and dates, and fancy paper plates. Partial buffet or full service may be provided. Check what will happen to leftover food and the tables' flower displays. Can guests take the flower displays, or will flowers be saved for the bride, bride's mother, and mother-in-law?

SEATING PLANS

Order at the top table is as follows. Bride and groom are seated in the centre with the groom on the bride's right. It is easier to identify who's who if his parents are next to him and hers are next to her. This is ideal for ethnic minority families where husband and wife are inseparable, or mixed-race marriages where his side can't talk to hers because of language or other cultural differences.

Alternatively follow traditional etiquette dividing the parents. Put the groom's mother-in-law on his right, and the bride's father on the bride's mother's right. This is thought to make conversation more interesting, since you can talk to your own family at home.

The caterer or stationer can draw up a seating plan with a printed edge and names written on by someone with good handwriting. If you have many guests display two copies of the plan.

Children over seven can be seated, under-sevens provided with a crèche. Hiring a childminder/communal babysitter for a couple of hours and getting pizzas delivered could be cheaper than ordering ten seated dinners which probably won't be eaten.

SEATING

☆ *TOP TABLE*

1 ....
2 ....
3 ....
4 ....
Bride ....
Groom ....
1 ....
2 ....
3 ....
4 ....

☆ *HER FAMILY TABLE*

1 ....
2 ....
3 ....
4 ....
5 ....
6 ....
7 ....
8 ....
9 ....
10 ....

☆ *HIS FAMILY TABLE*

1 ....
2 ....
3 ....
4 ....
5 ....
6 ....
7 ....
8 ....
9 ....
10 ....

☆ *HER FRIENDS' TABLE*

1 ....
2 ....
3 ....
4 ....
5 ....
6 ....
7 ....
8 ....
9 ....
10 ....

☆ *HIS FRIENDS' TABLE*

1 ....
2 ....
3 ....
4 ....
5 ....
6 ....
7 ....
8 ....
9 ....
10 ....

TOASTMASTERS

Hotels and caterers can put you in touch with toast-masters, some of whom are part-timers. The Guild of Professional Toastmasters has over a dozen members who are trained or experienced full-time toastmasters with references. Their headquarters is in London, listed under Toastmasters in commercial telephone directories, but they may travel.

Toastmaster's name ....

Address ....

.... Tel. ....

Fee .... Special instructions given ....

....

....

CAKE-CUTTING

After the meal people may be too full to eat cake but if you leave cake-cutting until later everyone may have disappeared from the tables. Cutting the cake before the speeches gives the caterer time to cut the cake neatly while speeches are being made and serve it to fill the lull after speeches. If the meal is at lunchtime the wedding cake can be served with coffee at tea-time.

An engagement party or stag party held at home can be a dry run for the wedding reception. Work out where you have room for the receiving line. Be inventive. If the hall is tiny you could have the receiving line on the lawn alongside the front garden path. You can have it on the stairs if the house has a wide staircase. Alternatively have a maid in starched apron at the front door to show the guests where to put their coats, and the family standing in a receiving line on the back garden path, perhaps in front of the marquee. In addition to a marquee, you might use ribbons and stands to mark off a pathway.

PHOTOGRAPHS

AMATEUR PHOTOGRAPHY

Ensure amateurs have equipment including tripod, flashgun, spare batteries, and plenty of film. You should probably reimburse the photographer for the cost of the film or provide it yourself. Have at least two cameras in case one jams.

Camera .... New batteries ....

Flash .... Tripod ....

Film .... Cost ....

The best man can send an usher to the high street one-hour photograph developers and get photographs back in time to show the couple and guests. Retake the poorer shots and order duplicates of the successful ones.

Developing and printing service company

Name ....

Address ....

.... Tel. ....

Date and time for collecting prints ....

Wedding album cost .... Duplicate cost ....

You can order duplicate sets of colour prints by post. Envelopes are displayed at post offices and airports. Colour slides which include processing can be posted on the wedding day or by the best man the next day in time for the slides to be on the doormat when the bride and groom return from their honeymoon.

SELECTING PROFESSIONAL PHOTOGRAPHERS

Look at friends' wedding albums. See two or three photographers and their sample books and get written estimates of cost before deciding. Some photographers operate on an hourly basis. Others make a minimum charge, plus a charge for the number of photographs ordered. They might offer a leather album filled with a certain number of prints. There could be no obligation, just a choice of packages, with the option of deciding which to accept after you have seen the photographs. Check whether you are getting a specific photographer or one of the company's team.

PHOTOGRAPH SUBJECT CHECKLIST

☆ Photographs of bride alone and with parents at her home.
☆ Bride (and father) in wedding car outside their house.
☆ Bride arriving at church/register office.
☆ Procession.
☆ Altar.
☆ Signing register.
☆ Recession.
☆ On church steps with minister and all the guests.
☆ Bride and groom kissing or hugging in car.
☆ Bridal party in garden of reception venue.
☆ Bridal party at top table.

☆ Cake cutting.
☆ Speechmakers.
☆ Selected guests. (Tell photographer about VIPs such as granny.)
☆ Bride and groom at top of stairs with bride's dress and train draped down stairs.
☆ Bride and groom with both sets of parents.
☆ Bride and female attendants.
☆ Groom with best man and ushers.
☆ Wedding present display (useful for insurance).
☆ Bride and groom in going away outfits standing with new luggage by wedding car.
☆ Bride and groom waving from wedding car through open doors or windows.

Ask if the photographer will stay right to the end. If the hotel room is nearby he can photograph bride and groom in the four-poster bed or jacuzzi with the champagne, or in the bedroom or living room of the new home. Studio pictures can be taken of the bride in her wedding dress before or after the wedding.

Some photographers develop the films on the wedding day and cheaply reprint group photographs in bulk for all the guests. Pictures can be enlarged to poster-size for framing and hanging on the wall. Photographs can be printed to look like oil paintings, or transferred onto souvenir plates, tablemats, keyrings, and jigsaws (for the junior bridesmaid and pageboy). You can also have stills made from a video film.

VIDEOTAPING

Choose the hire company after viewing their film and comparing the cost of videotape with and without a soundtrack. Specify the order of main scenes. Decide how leftover film will be finished, by taking randomly selected dancing guests, or more photos of bride and groom. Find out the cost of a duplicate film for parents.

Photography/Video firm name ....

Address ....

....

Tel. ....

Special instructions ....

....

Acceptable/Not acceptable (reason) ....

.... Family informed   No/Yes.

Booking made by phone   No/Yes.   Booking in writing

No/Yes.   By (name) ....

Date .... To (name) ....

Written confirmation received   No/Yes (date) ....

From (name) ....

Alternative company ....

ENTERTAINMENT

LIVE MUSIC

You might ask a relative with a lovely voice to sing, or engage a band specializing in local music, or an unusual instrument to play a solo at the wedding reception. Some possibilities are: a pianist, harpist, string quartet or clarinettist, guitar or accordion player, choirboy, church choir, a school or university group, a Scottish piper, a Welsh male voice choir, Irish piper and fiddler, Caribbean or Greek band, band with trumpet player. Specialist firms supply musical groups.

Musicians should be asked to play quietly so guests can talk during the greeting of guests at the receiving line. Guests take their places at table or wait by the buffet until the bride enters last, often announced by the playing of 'Here Comes the Bride'. During the meal, mood music can be played.

WEDDING THEME SONGS

Wedding theme songs are *Congratulations* (Cliff Richard), *Love And Marriage* (Sammy Cahn), *Going To The Chapel*, *Get Me To The Church On Time* (My Fair Lady), *The Wedding Song* (Peter, Paul & Mary), *Kiss The Bride* (Elton John), *Hawaiian Wedding Song* (Elvis, Andy Williams and others) and *I'm A Believer* (The Monkees).

PERSONAL SONGS

Caribbean Calypso singers and Welsh singers can make up songs including the bride's name or groom's characteristics. Many songs already exist, e.g. for the bride *Annie's Song* (John Denver), *Michelle* (The Beatles), *Diana* (Paul Anka), *Sara* (Fleetwood Mac), *Looking For Linda* (Hue and Cry). For the groom the singer, disc jockey or best man can make a jokey compendium: *He's My Blue Eyed Boy* (Piaf), *You're So Vain* (Carly Simon). If the bride and groom cannot already say 'they're playing our song', find them a happy song like *Beautiful Day*, or one fitting the wedding day weather such as *Sunshine Of My Life*, *Singing In The Rain*, or *White Christmas*.

SENTIMENTAL MUSIC

Include songs everyone knows so they can join in choruses. Romantic slow music is obtainable on record collections of love songs such as *Endless Love*. Include nostalgic snatches of songs from the wedding period of the bride's and groom's parents and grandparents, such as Victorian *Daisy Daisy, Give Me Your Answer Do*.

BRITISH ISLES REGIONAL

Pick regional music from the wedding location. For example, English songs include *Maybe It's Because I'm A Londoner* or *You'll Never Walk Alone*. Scottish favourites include *A Gordon For Me*, *Gay Gordons*, *Mull of Kintyre*, and *Skye Boat Song*. For Welsh guests select a mixture of Welsh harp music or traditional songs such as *Men Of Harlech* and *The Ashgrove*. Irish songs include *When Irish Eyes Are Smiling*, Irish reels, and *Danny Boy* (unofficial national anthem for Northern Ireland and Eire).

NATIONAL AND INTERNATIONAL

(Homeland and Honeymoon).

Add national songs from the homeland of hosts and guests, or the honeymoon location. West Indian brides or those taking an exotic honeymoon might like the Caribbean song *Island In The Sun* (Harry Belafonte), or reggae. Australia's *Waltzing Mathilda* is popular. American music includes *If You're Going To San Francisco*, *New York New York*, *Chicago*, *America The Beautiful* and *Dixie*. Wordsheets accompany cassettes or records in music shops, or use library song directories.

Songs evoking European honeymoon locations include French, *I Love Paris In The Springtime*, or *After They've Seen Paree*. Italian music varies from Schubert's *Ave Maria* (Caruso), to *Que Sera Sera* (Whatever Will Be Will

Be), *Dimmi Quando Quando Quando* (Tell Me When). The Spanish favourite is *Que Viva Espana*.

DANCING

A drum roll is sounded before the first dance, traditionally the *Anniversary Waltz*, with the bride and groom starting the dancing.

SUGGESTED DANCES

Include party dances such as the Conga, the Twist, and the Charleston. For your exhibitionist guests play the Tango, and the Gezutski (a fast Russian dance, squatting, with your arms crossed and alternating each leg forward until exhausted!). Flamenco is jolly for a dance or two, especially if you provide castanets. Greek music, particularly *Zorba's Dance*, will encourage group dancing. So will the rousing Israeli *Hava Na Gila* danced to the Hora. Latin American Sambas and Rumbas are also lively. Communal dances such as the Hokey Cokey enable guests lacking dancing partners to join the fun. Children like *The Birdie Song*.

DANCE MUSIC VOLUME

Older people often prefer music quiet enough to enable them to exchange gossip. Check early in the evening that older people sitting talking are not shouting themselves hoarse. If so, ask the hotel manager whether he can switch off some of the speakers.

DISCO MUSIC

A separate disco can be held later in the day for the young people. At home you can provide music by hiring a live band, or a mobile discotheque. Discuss how loudly they will play, ensuring that the music will not deafen you and annoy neighbours. Ask for a list of suggestions and give them a list of your favourite songs. Supply them with discs they do not stock which you would like played.

RECORDED MUSIC

If there is insufficient space for a band you can use your own record player. Go through your cassettes and records and put suitable ones in order, or perhaps record a selection of your favourites, mixing lively tracks with mood music.

If your stereo system or cassette player is not loud enough to be heard above a roomful of guests attach larger speakers. Music can be played on a piano or electric organ, perhaps with a guitarist. Check that the piano is tuned and select suitable music scores.

LAST DANCE

If the band plans to finish dancing with a 'last waltz' the bride and groom should practise a waltz, especially if the bride has to whirl around in a long white dress and new shoes. End with relevant national songs or anthems such as the French *Marseillaise*. If you are playing the Israeli national anthem *Hatikva* or a Japanese song such as *Sayonara* (meaning good-bye), include a songsheet. *God Save The Queen* is played last at elegant formal dinners, or for a merry conclusion, *Auld Lang Syne*.

WEDDING GIFTS

MAKING WEDDING LISTS

For a quickly arranged wedding with few guests the bride's mother can send out a simple list merely stating 'a tea set' and so on. If you have time, compose a full list with columns indicating Brand/Style/Colour alongside each item. If you give several people the same list you risk getting duplicate gifts. But if you wait for each person to tick and return the list before sending to another, some guests won't get the list and may forget to buy a gift! You could divide your list into three, or ask guests to buy from a particular department store, even though you have not made a list there.

Older couples may already have one or two sets of everything. In that case presents relating to their personal interest might be the solution. For example, a couple who have a dining table and a dinner service but play bridge might welcome a card table.

CHOOSING A STORE'S GIFT LIST

Wedding lists can be placed at department stores or at specialized shops such as Chinacraft. Gifts can be delivered in advance, or all together to the new home after the wedding, or shipped directly abroad which can save VAT.

Harrods offers a 'Hold All Orders' option holding the money but usually sending goods all together up to 18 months after the wedding, allowing the bride to change her mind about any or all of them. Guests can order by phone. The purchase list is sent weekly so the bride can write thank you notes.

John Lewis, Oxford Street, and Peter Jones send a summary of gifts bought with donor's names at the end of the time period, which helps the bride to write thank you notes.

Items which must be installed before you move in can be bought with cheques from relatives who ask if you would prefer money.

Department Store name ....

Address ....

.... Tel. ....

Type of wedding list chosen ....

Deliver to ....

.... Date ....

WEDDING GIFT CHECKLIST

The   Store/Department/Brand/Colour/Received/Donor/Thanked/Exchanged.

☆ *INTERIOR*

- carpet .... ☐
- curtains .... ☐
- wallpaper .... ☐
- heaters .... ☐
- light fittings .... ☐
- mirrors .... ☐

vacuum cleaner .... ☐
wastebins .... ☐
secondary glazing .... ☐
curtain rails .... ☐

☆ *EXTERIOR*
doorknocker .... ☐
bell .... ☐
house number .... ☐
dustbin .... ☐
shutters .... ☐
locks or burglar alarms .... ☐
outside lights .... ☐

☆ *LIVING ROOMS*
settee and easy chairs .... ☐
dining table and chairs .... ☐
TV .... ☐
video .... ☐
pictures .... ☐
vases .... ☐
ornaments .... ☐
shelving or cabinets .... ☐
stacking coffee tables .... ☐
wine glasses .... ☐
sherry glasses .... ☐
coasters .... ☐
cakeslice and pastry forks .... ☐
carving set .... ☐
electric meat slicer .... ☐
coffee spoons .... ☐
grapefruit spoons .... ☐
serving spoons .... ☐
steak knives .... ☐
corn cob holders .... ☐
candlesticks .... ☐
cheeseboard .... ☐
toast rack .... ☐
cookery books .... ☐

magazine rack .... □
radio .... □
cassette player .... □
wine rack .... □
houseplants .... □
cache-pots .... □

☆ *BEDROOMS*
bed .... □
headboard .... □
mattress .... □
pillows .... □
bedding .... □
electric blanket .... □
duvet .... □
matching curtains .... □
bedside tables .... □
table lamps .... □
alarm clock .... □
teamaker .... □
convertible guest bed .... □
Cupboard fittings:
shelves .... □
clothes rail and tie rack .... □

☆ *BATHROOM*
shower unit .... □
blind .... □
towels .... □
bathroom cabinet .... □

Accessory set including:
toothbrush holder .... □
toilet paper holder .... □
linen basket .... □
bathroom scales .... □
hairdrier .... □
first aid kit .... □
bathmat .... □

shower rail .... □
shower curtain .... □
bidet .... □
taps .... □
extractor fan .... □

☆ *KITCHEN*

fridge .... □
deep freeze .... □
oven .... □
hob .... □
extractor fan .... □
dishwasher .... □
microwave .... □
electric kettle .... □
tin opener .... □
bottle opener .... □
toaster .... □
food mixer .... □
saucepans .... □
baking pans .... □
table and chairs .... □
tablecloth .... □
tablemats .... □
cruet .... □
cutlery .... □
crockery .... □
water glasses .... □
jugs .... □
clock .... □
coffeemaker .... □
tea service .... □
tray .... □
pinboard .... □
casserole dishes .... □
breadbin .... □
spice rack .... □
iron .... □

ironing board .... ☐
freezer bag .... ☐

☆ *GARDEN*

lawnmower .... ☐
wheelbarrow .... ☐
garden tools .... ☐
conifers .... ☐
fencing .... ☐
climbing plants .... ☐
fruit plants .... ☐
flower plants .... ☐
table .... ☐
chairs .... ☐
parasol .... ☐
sunloungers .... ☐
urns .... ☐
statues .... ☐
barbecue .... ☐
hammock .... ☐
hedge trimmer .... ☐
garden shed .... ☐
greenhouse .... ☐
watering can .... ☐
hose .... ☐
sprinkler .... ☐

☆ *BALCONY/PATIO*

folding director's chairs .... ☐
small table .... ☐
plants .... ☐
clothes drying stand .... ☐
windowbox .... ☐
pair of reclining chairs .... ☐
hanging chair .... ☐

☆ *GARAGE/UTILITY ROOM*

washing machine .... ☐
tumble drier .... ☐
deep freeze .... ☐

drying rack .... ☐
dustpan and brush .... ☐
broom .... ☐
shelving .... ☐
toolset .... ☐
paint and decorating items .... ☐
ladder .... ☐
workbench .... ☐

☆ *PERSONAL*
wedding clothes .... ☐
nightclothes .... ☐
night in honeymoon suite .... ☐

☆ *LEISURE AND PLEASURE*
backgammon set .... ☐
card table .... ☐
playing card set .... ☐
camera .... ☐
videocamera .... ☐
health club membership .... ☐
luggage .... ☐

☆ *STUDY*
desk .... ☐
chair .... ☐
shelving .... ☐
filing cabinet .... ☐
angle lamp .... ☐
phone .... ☐
typewriter .... ☐
computer .... ☐

☆ *HALL*
shelf .... ☐
hat rack .... ☐
doormat .... ☐
coat cupboard .... ☐
key rack .... ☐
mirror .... ☐
table .... ☐

telephone .... ☐
address book .... ☐
clothes brush .... ☐
shoe cleaning set .... ☐

DELIVERING GIFTS AT THE WEDDING

It is preferable for guests to send gifts and cheques in advance to British weddings. However, as a guest you will need to take money with you (clean notes), to French, Italian, Spanish, Greek and Japanese weddings. The French bride auctions her garter, or is paid for raising it inch by inch up her leg. The Greek bride has money pinned on her dress. In Italy and Spain at wedding receptions guests cut pieces off the groom's tie, paying money which is given to the bride. Guests also sign their names inside the bride's shoe and pay her for the privilege. For Japanese brides the usual gift is money, wrapped in pretty coloured envelopes.

GIFT DISPLAY

The bride should list gifts received and thanks sent. Organize the wedding gifts display at home, or in the hotel. Check insurance and security of gifts delivered to the reception hall or hotel. Arrange for the transport of gifts to the new home, perhaps by a security firm. Gifts should be moved promptly so that they are not unattended when the meal starts and do not need moving at the end of the evening.

THANK YOU GIFTS

Select thank you gifts for the best man, attendants, and bride's mother. Gifts for small bridesmaids could be dolls (Cindy, etc.) which wear many outfits including a wedding dress. Small reproductions of the Royal Family in wedding outfits are available from toy stores. So are plush dolls and bears wearing bridesmaids' dresses. These can be made to order with a reproduction of the bride's wedding dress or the bridesmaids' own dresses. Take a Polaroid photograph of wedding clothing, or save surplus material from the bride's dress hem, to help the toymaker.

Lockets, bracelets, or musical jewellery boxes are also popular. A teenage bridesmaid might like a mirrored make-up case with a light, ear-rings, a matching jewellery set of necklace and bracelet, a pendant, or a travel hairdrier. Pageboys could be given watches.

Gift for (name) ....

Purchased from (Store name) ....

Address ....

.... Tel. ....

Item chosen ....

Gift for (name) ....

Purchased from (Store name) ....

Address ....

.... Tel. ....

Item chosen ....

THE HONEYMOON

Choose a suitable honeymoon destination you will both enjoy, such as one based on shared interests like hiking or scuba diving. After the excitement of the wedding day you might like to spend a night in your new home. An airport hotel is convenient if you are travelling abroad early next day. Or if you have a long drive, for example from London to the Lake District, stay at a hotel near the reception.

UK WEDDING NIGHT IN RECEPTION HOTEL

Many hotels offer a free bedroom for the bride and groom if they have a sizeable catered reception held in the hotel. In addition or instead obtain a dressing or changing room in the hotel for daytime use. Luggage can be delivered to the hotel the day before if it is nearby.

WEDDING NIGHT AT ANOTHER UK HOTEL

Hotels with numerous reception rooms or several rooms with four-poster beds may have as many as five brides arriving on a Saturday evening. The check-in process can be speeded up if the best man goes ahead to deal with the receptionist and handles the luggage. If the bride has made the booking she should have noted in a handbag diary the date her booking was made, with whom and the quality of room promised. Better still carry the confirmation letter. Correspondence shows the name in which she made the booking. This helps sort out confusion when the bride has booked the bedroom in her maiden name, and the couple arrive expecting a room to be listed under their new married name.

Make sure the hotel room has a double bed. Even if you book a double bed there is not much you can do if when you arrive all double-bedded rooms are occupied. You are safest at a hotel where every room has double beds, such as a Holiday Inn. Book a hotel bedroom without a TV set if the groom is likely to spend most of the honeymoon night watching Match of the Day.

Budget honeymoon hotels in the UK, including inexpensive guest houses with four-poster beds, can be found through tourist boards. UK bridal suites can be found in the brochures of hotel groups or from reference books. Hotel wedding packages may include four-posters, jacuzzis, champagne, chocolates, flowers, a greetings card, and a porcelain gift. If no honeymoon package is available, have flowers, champagne, fruit and chocolates delivered to the room. Use Interflora, the hotel's shop and room service, or local shops.

SELECTING DESIRABLE DESTINATIONS ABROAD

European castles, French chateaux, Spanish paradores, and Portuguese pousadas are romantic. Heart-shaped baths are available at Niagara Falls, Canada, and Couples resorts in Pennsylvania, USA.

Travel agents can recommend tour operators who offer honeymoon options. Companies such as New

Beginnings organize Caribbean honeymoons and weddings. They tell you the cost and documentation required. In the Bahamas weddings can take place on beaches, or in the sea with the groom wearing a white tuxedo (dinner jacket) and shorts. The cost of the airport hotel, car parking, or transfer by train to the airport is included in some holiday packages.

Travel agent ....

Tourist board ....

Airline/shipping company ....

Airport/Ferry port ....

Hire car company ....

Bank ....

Travellers' Cheques ordered ....

Insurance ....

Vaccinations ....

Passport office ....

Hotel ....

Honeymoon suite/double bed requested No/Yes. Availability confirmed No/Yes. Honeymoon package gifts: Champagne No/Yes. Flowers No/Yes. Fruit No/Yes. Chocolates No/Yes. Others ....

.... No/Yes.

HAPPY EVER AFTER

MARRIAGE ANNOUNCEMENTS IN NEWSPAPERS

Announcements in *The Times*, *The Daily Telegraph* and *The Independent* follow the same format. To have the announcement of a Saturday wedding in the Monday edition of *The Times* you must send in the notice by the preceding Friday. Sample wordings:

MARRIAGES
Mr R. B. King
and Miss J. Hall
The marriage took place on Saturday March 26th, at St George's Church, Hanover Square, of Mr Romeo Bates King, and Miss Juliet Hall.
The Revd Edmund England officiated.
The bride, who was given in marriage by her father, was attended by Miss Anne King. Mr Ashley Jones was best man. A reception was held at The Savoy and the honeymoon is being spent abroad.

Mr R. Brown
and Mrs C. Smith
The marriage took place on Monday, January 1st, at Chelsea Register Office, of Mr Richard Brown and Mrs Cecily Smith.

(The title Mrs conveys the information that she is widowed or divorced.)

The Revd A. B. Smith
and Mrs V. A. Brown
The marriage took place at Camden Town Hall, followed by a Service of Blessing conducted by The Revd Thomas Windsor, at St Pancras Church, on December 1st, between Mr Albert Bland Smith and Mrs Verity Anna Brown. A family reception was held at 13 High Square, London WC1.

Shorter versions may appear. For example in *The Independent*:

Montagu/Capulet. On Jan 1st. Romeo to Juliet.

In *The Times*:

Mr B. Smith
and Mrs A. Brown
The marriage took place Monday, January 1st, at Chelsea Register Office of Mr B. Smith and Mrs A. Brown.

Local papers have chattier announcements with photographs. For example:

WEDDING BELLS
Montagu–Smith
A honeymoon in Italy followed the marriage of Romeo Montagu and Juliet Smith at St Michael's Roman Catholic Church, Harrow Weald.
The bridegroom is the son of Patrick and Maria Montagu of Kingston and the bride is the daughter of John and Ann Smith of Harrow.
The couple will live in Harrow.
Photo: Peter Watford Photography.

National newspaper name ....

Address ....

.... Tel. ....

Cost ....

Copy deadline date ....

Publication date ....

Local newspaper name ....

Address ....

.... Tel. ....

Copy deadline ....

Date published ....

Reprints of newspaper photos cost ....

PERSONAL MARRIAGE ANNOUNCEMENTS

Order printed business cards and business letterheads, home stationery letterheads, postcards, change of address cards and address stickers. The bank will require a note of the new name and address, also copies of the new signature.

THE NEW HOME

Arrange transport from the airport to your new home, perhaps a chauffeur-driven limousine. The couple might be welcomed at the airport or at the new home by their parents and chief bridesmaid. Food and flowers left over from the wedding can be placed in the new home. Door keys and security arrangements should have been arranged before departure.

Show the honeymoon film to the wedding hosts and selected guests at a family dinner. Pass around the wedding photo album. An effective audio-visual show can be made showing wedding slides accompanied by music you played at the reception (see pages 139–43), then honeymoon slides with evocative regional or national music.

Traditionally, the bride sends out new address cards plus an At Home card inviting guests to call round to see her and the new home on a particular date. As well as her husband, her mother, chief bridesmaid, or sister can help with catering and greeting newcomers while she is showing guests around.

ORGANIZING YOUR NAME CHANGE

Information on the bride's new name and address and specimen signatures may be required by banks, credit card companies, building societies, mortgage company, landlord, life assurance, car insurance, the Inland Revenue, Department of Social Security, and children's and stepchildren's schools. A new will should be made.

Bank ....

Credit cards ....

Landlord ....

Insurance ....

Tax office ....

DSS ....

School ....

Others including the doctor, dentist, hairdresser and local restaurants will also know the bride under her maiden name until informed. If bride and groom merge names, adopting a hyphenated surname such as

Smith-Jones, his business contacts must be told. The same applies if he Anglicizes his family name to make it sound better combined with her first name.

Get a paying-in book for cheques so wedding cheques can be paid into the new joint account. When cheques are made out to the bride's maiden name she writes on the back Pay ... (inserting her married name) and signs her maiden name.

FIRST ANNIVERSARY

A tier of the wedding cake can be kept for a baby's christening or the first wedding anniversary. Save the list of wedding guests in order to invite them to happy anniversary celebrations. Remembering anniversaries and birthdays is important if you want to stay happily married.

Anniversary date ....

Her parents' anniversary date ....

His parents' anniversary date ....

Bride's birthday ....

Groom's birthday ....

Interflora tel. .... Send fruit tel. ....

Send rose tel. .... Send tie tel. ....

Send cake tel. .... Send chocs tel. ....

Department store tel. ....

Telemessage tel. ....

PART 2

THE BRIDEGROOM

THE BRIDEGROOM'S POINT OF VIEW

This chapter deals with a few of the nitty-gritty aspects of planning a wedding. As bridegroom, you may not feel very involved in them – until someone asks you a question, and you realize you should be taking a keen interest in everything that is going on!

There may be times when you have the feeling that all your wedding is about is lists. You'd be right – it should be. For if something is not on a list, it could be forgotten, and there is nothing worse than finding that out on the day. Can your Aunt Annie manage the steps to the reception venue? Do you want any photographs taken in advance of the big day? When will the ring be ready? All details, maybe, but as the bridegroom, you are at the centre of proceedings, and you need to be involved.

INVITATIONS

This is one of the trickiest areas of any wedding. No matter how generous the numbers seem at first, by the time all the 'musts' have been written down, it often seems as if you will need a church and reception venue twice the size of the chosen ones!

Start by finding out the capacity of the place in which the ceremony is to be held. How many people will it comfortably seat? (Don't count the pew where you and the best man will sit.) The guest list can be divided into seven sections:

1 Bride's core family
2 Bridegroom's core family
3 Bride's other relations
4 Bridegroom's other relations
5 Bride and bridegroom's friends
6 Bride's parents' friends
7 Local 'musts'

The final two categories may be a surprise to the bridegroom, but if the bride's parents are bearing most of the cost of the wedding, it is probably on their 'patch', and they run the risk of offending a lot of local people if they cannot invite them. In a sense, they are hosting a party being held in your honour, to which you are allowed to invite some of your friends. Included in the local 'musts' if it is a church wedding is the minister conducting the service.

DIVORCED PARENTS

Some tact is required if either, or both, sets of parents are divorced or separated. In the bride's case, the invitations are extended in the name of the parent she lives with, or last lived with. It is up to the bridegroom whether both his divorced parents should be invited. In such cases it is common for them both to bury the hatchet for the day and attend, although the presence of any new partners can bring a certain amount of tension. You really have to trust them to consider your feelings and behave pleasantly on the day.

Another tricky point relates to whether you want young children and babies at the ceremony. They can be noisy and disruptive. On the other hand, weddings are a celebration of family life, and it seems a shame to exclude them. If you do want to avoid the risk of bored children or tired babies interrupting the ceremony, tactfully explain that you would welcome them at the reception but not at the service. Even at the reception, however, children can become restless and badly behaved, and may be occupying a seat at the same expense as an adult. If a lot of your friends and relations have young children, you could consider hiring several childminders and running a creche throughout the day.

Both bride and bridegroom should write down every member of their family who really must be invited. Consult both sets of parents about any relations who should be on the list. Continue through the rest of the categories, until you have the full list. Counting up, you are quite likely to find you have too many names. Now you have to be quite ruthless and put together an 'A' and 'B' list – the 'B's being a set of substitutes. They can be invited if people on the 'A' list decline the invitation, and/or can be asked to the reception, but not the wedding ceremony.

Even if your fiancée and her parents are organizing the wedding virtually single-handed, make sure you have your say now because if you miss out someone from your side of the family, it could cause a lot of resentment all round. The invitations are sent out by the bride's parents, and replies are addressed to them.

Invitations are usually sent out 6–8 weeks before the wedding. Sometimes they are issued much earlier, and in many instances the engaged couple help by addressing envelopes and sending out their own batch. It is sensible to include directions for finding the church or register office and the reception venue, in words and with a map. A list of local accommodation with addresses and telephone numbers might be appreciated by guests living far away. If close family are able to stay with the bride's relations, this should also be made clear.

If an 'A' and 'B' list is being used, ensure that if necessary people are chased up for a reply, so that if there are any refusals, someone from the second group may be invited. This is a complicated and time-consuming business, but there is no way of avoiding it.

Remind your friends and relations that they should reply promptly to say whether or not they can come. If names from your list are slow responding it could embarrass you in front of your future in-laws.

Once all the replies have been received, a table plan will be prepared if there is to be a sit-down meal. You may like to mix friends and relations together so that they get to know each other, or to seat guests with people they already know. If any guests do not get on, make this known so that they can be kept apart.

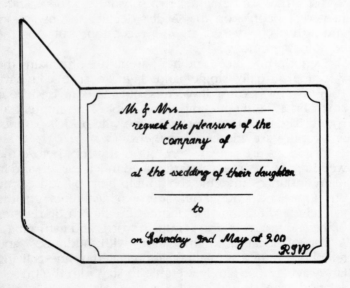

Mr & Mrs _____
request the pleasure of the
company of
_____
at the wedding of their daughter
_____
to
_____
on *Saturday 2nd May* at 2.00
RSVP

THE WEDDING LIST

This is one of the real fun aspects of weddings – the presents! People like to offer gifts to newly-weds. Although the traditional reason – to help a couple set up a home from nothing – applies less and less, the custom has remained. Because you and your fiancée probably have a fair number of possessions already, people need advice on what would be a suitable gift – something you have not got, and really want.

The answer is a wedding list. This is a comprehensive breakdown of gifts that you would be delighted to receive. It needs to be quite precise – people like to know where the items can be bought, and their code numbers so that they can be sure to buy the right thing. It makes sense to break the list into geographical sections, according to where most of the guests live:

1 Items available in the bride's parents area
2 Items available in the bridegroom's parents' area
3 Items available in the area(s) where the bride and bridegroom live

You will need to put more things on the list than you expect to receive, so that people have a wide choice. The best approach is to visit shops in each area together, picking out things you want, and ensuring that you select items in a broad price range. Many large stores offer a service whereby they keep a list of the items you have chosen, so that you can simply tell would-be present-buyers to ask to see what you still need.

'Shopping' for the wedding list is refreshing because you can choose things simply because you like them, not as to whether you can afford them yourselves. Don't get carried away! Think about what you may need not only for your home, but for example, there may be a sport you play together for which you would like new equipment.

Prepare the list at the same time as the guest list, so that it can be quickly despatched to those who request it. You and your bride can keep a record of who intends to buy what – or her mother may wish to do so. You may find you start to receive gifts as soon as the list is sent out, as people may prefer not to bring their presents on the day. Even if you see the giver the next day and thank them, always write a thank you letter and make a note of what they have given you.

Sometimes presents are displayed at the reception, so you may wish to keep all your gifts pristine for this. Note down who sent a cheque, so that their names can be written on a card (without mentioning the actual sums given) to be included in the display.

ARRANGING THE CHURCH SERVICE

Another important job requiring advance planning in which the bridegroom should be involved is arranging the church service. Sheets are usually printed with the order of service and words of the hymns, and the text must be given to the printer in good time to ensure they will be ready. You might have a favourite hymn (perhaps one from your schooldays or from some other time with fond memories). It will make the service more individual if you can include at least one of these.

Still on the musical theme, do you want music played while you are out of view signing the register or a hymn sung? You may have friends who can form a quartet and play, or you may want a special piece of organ music. Whatever you wish, make it clear early so that, say, the quartet can rehearse, or the organist can be sure he or she has a copy of the relevant music.

As for the rest of the service, most of it comes in standard form, but brides are often given a choice of whether they want to state that they will 'obey' their husbands (you might have differing views on this!)

PRESENTS

There are a number of people to whom the bride and bridegroom may like to give presents on the day of the wedding:

1 Bride's parents
2 Bridegroom's parents
3 Bridesmaids
4 Best man
5 Others who have made a special contribution – perhaps a friend made the bride's dress, or a relative arranged all the flowers in the church or decorated the cake, or the ushers.

These will be presented at some stage in the reception. Bouquets are a popular choice for the women recipients, but put your heads together to think of something for each person which they will really cherish as a souvenir of the occasion. Write a personal thank you on the accompanying card.

While discussing presents for parents, one very nice gesture is to write the week before the wedding, thanking them for all they are doing on your behalf and telling them how much you are both looking forward to the day. This adds to the store of goodwill all round.

ACCOMMODATION

If close friends or relations live a long way from the wedding venue, they may need help in locating accommodation. Firstly, find out if the bride's local family and friends can offer hospitality, and try to match like-minded or similarly aged people. Otherwise, and for other friends, supply a list of local accommodation and leave it up to them.

PLANNING THE HONEYMOON

The bridegroom traditionally arranges the honeymoon, sometimes keeping its location secret from his bride so that she enjoys a genuine surprise when she discovers where they are going. The honeymoon is likely to be your major holiday of the year – unless you had already booked one at some other time, in which case you may be restricted to having as little as a week or even a few days for your honeymoon. For this reason, you may like to discover from your fiancée if there is a special place she has always wanted to visit.

A wealth of travel packages is available, some catering specifically for honeymooners. You may choose to fly to somewhere sunny and relaxing, or to visit romantic cities such as Paris, Venice or Vienna. Perhaps you just want to book a few days in a luxurious hotel, or spend a week at a country club or on an activity break, learning to windsurf, or ride, for example.

The choice is wide, but bear in mind the following:

1 If you are travelling abroad, both of you need valid passports. If your bride wishes to change hers to her married name, she will need to fill in a form obtainable from the Post Office and send it in at least six weeks before the wedding. The form must be signed by the person who is to officiate at the ceremony. You may also need injections to immunize you against tropical diseases.

2 Even if you keep the destination a secret from your bride, she will appreciate knowing what climate to expect and how formal/informal the location will be, so that she can pack the right clothes.

3 You may be facing the expense of setting up a new home, which is very costly. Be sure you can afford the holiday you are planning – you could always splash out next year if you hold back this time.

4 Many hotels offer special terms for honeymooners and will appreciate being told in advance that you have just got married – this will invariably be to your advantage, for people like to make their own contribution to the happiness of such a special time!

5 Practical jokers, however, love disrupting honeymoons by cancelling bookings or 'hiding' tickets: it is therefore prudent to limit how many people know your destination.

6 You may prefer to stay locally on your first night, so that you can remain at the reception until late, or return for the evening party.

THE REHEARSAL AND WEDDING

Your wedding day should be one of the happiest and most memorable of your life. It will certainly be quite hard work.

One of the remarkable aspects of a wedding is that it is very likely to be the first and only time that a sizeable proportion of the bride and bridegroom's relatives and friends find themselves under one roof. They too should enjoy the occasion and will certainly have more opportunities than you to talk to old friends and meet new ones. In front of them, you will state your commitment to your bride, and with them you will celebrate your mutual love.

ON THE EVE OF THE WEDDING

The final preparations for the wedding start the day before.

THE REHEARSAL FOR A CHURCH WEDDING

It is customary, and certainly very sensible, to arrange for a rehearsal of the ceremony the day before the event, particularly if you are having a big wedding. You will need to arrange this with the minister or priest and the other parties – the bride's father, the best man and if possible the bridesmaids and at least one usher.

Although the atmosphere might be quite relaxed, do pay close attention to anything the minister or priest says about where you should stand and in what order events will happen. You can dress informally but make a mental note of, for example, where you would put your hat or gloves if you are carrying them, or where you might rest a prayer book.

The rehearsal might inspire you to learn your lines if you have not already done so. The minister or priest usually asks you to repeat his words when the time comes to give your vows. Some display the words on a card facing you, suspended from their service book. However, learning your lines will enable you to deliver them much more confidently.

Some couples actually ask the minister or priest not to prompt them as they wish to recite their vows on their own. This gives a very nice 'feel' to this important part of the service, communicating the couple's commitment to each other through their confidence. If you choose to do this, inform the minister or priest (who may have reservations) and keep a card with the words clearly printed on it with you at the altar just in case nerves get the better of you.

JOBS FOR THE WEDDING EVE

Check that all the items you are responsible for have been prepared and either delivered or collection arranged. These include:

☆ The order for buttonholes which often goes to the supplier of other flowers. Are there enough ordered for both fathers, the ushers, the best man, yourself and any other people who have requested them?

☆ If you have hired a morning suit, you need to pick it up and check it is complete. Try it on: are any alterations necessary? Check that your shoes are clean and your shirt ironed. Keep the entire outfit together in a wardrobe.

☆ Are all the taxis ordered?

If you intend to use your car for transport the next day, you will want to wash it, check oil and water levels, and fill up with petrol (nothing could be worse than running out on the way to the service!).

It is also worth getting hold of a curtain or similar ring just in case there is a disaster with the wedding ring the next day. The knowledge of that back-up in your pocket will do a lot to relax you!

In case you do not have time the next day, you will also need to pack your going-away clothes to change into after the reception, and your case for the honeymoon, together with all necessary documents including travellers' cheques, tickets and passport. It is also wise to give the best man any monies required for church fees which he is expected to pay tomorrow on your behalf. These should be in sealed envelopes with the name of the recipient clearly marked.

You will doubtless be called on to do various other jobs for the bride's mother, such as carrying guests' cases, and picking up and delivering the cake. It's going to be a busy day!

CHECKLIST: eve of wedding

☆ Check going-away attire
☆ Pack going-away clothes
☆ Pack honeymoon luggage
☆ Check wedding attire
☆ Buttonholes delivered?
☆ Wedding ring and substitute ring safe?
☆ Money for church fees obtained from bank?
☆ Taxis ordered?
☆ Car checked?
☆ Ushers briefed?

EVENING ENTERTAINMENT

Assuming you have wisely chosen to hold your stag party well ahead of the wedding, you will be free on the evening prior to the big day. If both sets of parents are in the area, it might be nice for you to have a meal together. This will help to strengthen the bond between the two families.

As it is supposedly bad luck for the bridegroom and bride to meet on the wedding day before the service, you will be staying in separate houses – perhaps at a hotel with your parents, and preferably under the same roof as the best man who should, of course, be included in any evening entertainment along with other special friends such as the chief bridesmaid. By all means celebrate, but remember that you don't want a hangover tomorrow.

THE MORNING

Being away from the hectic activity of the bride's parent's home, the bridegroom's wedding morning can be a fairly relaxed affair. You want to look and feel your best: sleep late if you can, and have a good breakfast. Shave carefully (cuts and plasters will haunt you in the wedding photographs for years otherwise!). It is a better idea to shave normally twice rather than try to do one extra thorough shave. Have a bath or shower, and make sure your hair has no stray 'antennae' sticking out.

If the wedding is in the afternoon, you have the morning to enjoy, but otherwise you will need to get dressed in your wedding apparel and check for broken shoelaces, rumpled ties, and so on. Don't forget the buttonhole. You will also need to give your best man any monies required for church fees, if you have not already done so.

CHECKLIST: things the bridegroom needs to check on the wedding morning

☆ Buttonhole
☆ Has the best man got the ring
☆ Substitute ring (just in case)
☆ Luggage
☆ Going-away clothes
☆ Spare change
☆ Taxi firm telephone number
☆ Crib sheet
☆ Speech
☆ Gifts
☆ Going-away car keys

As a little light relief, you could reflect on the superstitions surrounding the bridegroom on his wedding day. These are fewer than the bride has to endure, but include:

☆ You must not see your bride in her wedding dress before you meet in church

☆ Dropping the ring before putting it on the bride's finger is bad luck

☆ If the bride helps the bridegroom in putting on the ring, she will rule the marriage

☆ All money paid out on this day must be handed over in odd sums

☆ The bridegroom must not turn back for anything after leaving for the church

☆ Whoever goes to sleep first on the marriage night will be the first to die. Mind you, the first to kneel at the service will also die first according to superstition, so the answer is clearly to make sure you do not do both, and one cancels the other out!

☆ You must carry your wife over the threshold when you enter your new home

THE WEDDING SERVICE

This section assumes that the marriage service is taking place in a Church of England church. For other denominations, see pages 83–108. However, in whatever faith the service is being held, the bridegroom will want to be at the church on time.

WHEN IS ON TIME?

On time means early – half an hour before the service is due to start. Allow for heavy traffic and tricky parking (it is likely the best man will be driving the car to the reception, and he will want to be able to get there quickly.) This gives you a chance to check that the ushers are present and have been properly briefed, that there are sufficient service sheets (if you think they will run short, ask the ushers to give one to each couple, rather than each person).

Guests usually start to arrive from 25 minutes before the service. By then, or soon after, you should take your place in the front right pew, if possible walking down a side aisle. The bridegroom's role does not include greeting guests at the door. For some reason guests arriving at the service seem surprised if they see the bridegroom outside the church, and they will certainly start to worry if you are not inside it!

However, the best man may need to help the ushers out, and will want to meet the chief bridesmaid on her arrival (five minutes before the bride) to check all is well. He will also need to pay the fees due to the organist, choir, soloist, and bellringers – all in sealed envelopes which you should have handed to him previously.

This means the bridegroom can be left sitting at the front of the church, alone, nervous, for quite some time. Try not to fidget or turn round too much. Your family and friends will be seated in the pews behind you. Occasionally someone may lean over to say hello, and by all means have a quiet chat with them, but do not wander around the church exchanging greetings with people.

ARRIVAL OF THE BRIDE

On a pre-arranged signal (sometimes a flashing light, or maybe a wave from an usher) the organist will strike up the wedding march music to announce your bride's arrival. Everybody stands. Do not turn round at this moment, however tempted you are. Step forward to the chancel steps, facing the altar. Your best man will be a pace to your right and behind you. Now, with the procession well up the aisle, you can turn to give your bride a welcoming smile.

She will join you on your left, while her father stands behind and to the left of her. A bridesmaid will take her bouquet and if she is wearing one, lift back her veil. If there are no bridesmaids, the bride will hand her bouquet to her father, and you may lift back her veil for her. If this is the case, you must practise this several time the day before, to ensure you avoid catching her earrings or ruffling her hair. You should both turn and face the minister. At this point a hymn is usually sung, which gives everybody a chance to calm their nerves. Otherwise there may be a prayer and a reading from the Bible.

THE CEREMONY

The minister begins the ceremony, explaining the significance of marriage. He then asks if anyone present knows any reason why the couple cannot lawfully marry. Children and babies seem to sense the significance of the silence that follows, and often choose this point to yell or whimper. Actually if this happens it can break the tension, but do not let your concentration slip, for the vows come next.

First the minister asks you each in turn if you promise

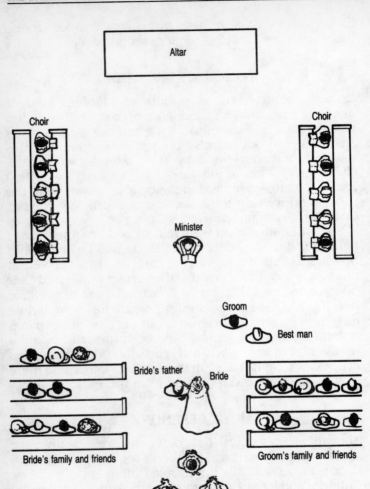

Positions as bride's procession approaches

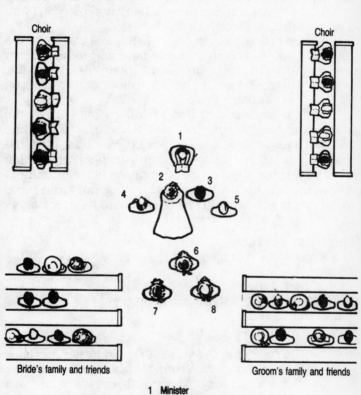

Altar

Choir

Choir

1

2   3

4

5

6

7   8

Bride's family and friends

Groom's family and friends

1   Minister
2   Bride
3   Groom
4   Bride's father
5   Best man
6   Chief bridesmaid
7 & 8   Bridesmaids

Positions for ceremony

to love, comfort, honour and forsake all others (in the modern version), and protect the other 'as long as you both shall live', to which the answer is 'I will'. The minister then asks: 'Who gives this woman to be married to this man?' This is a signal for the bride's father to step forward, take his daughter's right hand and place it, palm down, in that of the minister.

You then take the bride's right hand, and exchange the vows that you take each other 'to have and to hold, from this day forward; for better, for worse, for richer, for poorer, in sickness and in health, to love and to cherish, till death us do part.'

You then turn to take the wedding ring(s) from the best man. Alternatively, he places the ring(s) on the minister's prayer book to be blessed. You then push the wedding ring gently down the third finger of her left hand (the bride should not be wearing her engagement ring at this stage). If you are exchanging rings, the bride will then put your ring in place. Try not to let your fingers shake! You then say:

I give you this ring
as a sign of our marriage.
With my body I honour you,
all that I am I give to you,
and all that I have I share with you,
within the love of God,
Father, Son and Holy Spirit.

You may be repeating the words of the minister, perhaps reading from a card hung from his book, or be reciting the words from memory. Whatever it is, remember you are facing forwards, with the congregation behind you. Speak as loudly as you can without feeling ridiculous. That way everyone will hear your words, and will be impressed at your confidence and commitment.

The bride responds with a similar promise, and the minister pronounces you man and wife, often then making a short address to the congregation.

SIGNING THE REGISTER

At the end of the service, the wedding party – bride and bridegroom, both sets of parents, best man and chief bridesmaid (who usually acts as the witnesses) – join the minister in the vestry to sign the register. The bride signs first, using her maiden name, possibly for the last time. Photographs are often taken of the signing.

From now on, everything is much more relaxed, but the party should not linger too long in the vestry as any wedding due to take place shortly after would be delayed. You may need to wait for the ink on the marriage certificate to dry. The best man, or one of the mothers who is carrying a handbag, can take it away.

A signal should be given to the organist to commence the bridal march. You then lead the way from the vestry, with your new wife on your left arm. Behind you will be any small bridesmaids, the chief bridesmaid with the best man, the bride's mother with the bridegroom's father, the bridegroom's mother with the bride's father, and the bridesmaids, often escorted by the ushers. Walk as slowly as you can. Your guests will enjoy seeing you as man and wife for the first time, and you will be able to exchange smiles (but no words) with them as you progress down the aisle. Photographs are often taken at this time, so moving slowly helps with this, too.

LEAVING THE CHURCH

Your photographer may wish you to pose for photographs in the church porch or some other attractive location. Try to keep this session as short as possible since behind you there are often guests crowded around the door eager to come out to greet you. More photographs are taken when you leave the porch and stand in a position around which various other people can join you. Your best man can do much to organize the groups requested by the photographer. There tends to be

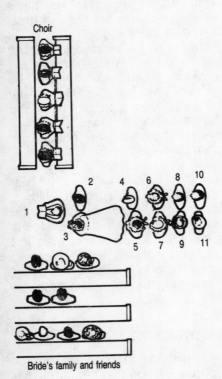

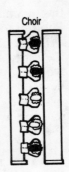

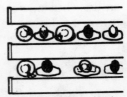

1	Minister	6 & 7	Bridesmaids
2	Bridegroom	8	Groom's father
3	Bride	9	Bride's mother
4	Best man	10	Bride's father
5	Chief bridesmaid	11	Groom's-mother

Order in procession to vestry

a lot of milling around by guests, while you seem to be stuck in one place as various people are brought up to stand next to you!

BEING PHOTOGRAPHED

There is a knack to being photographed. Get in a natural position and try to relax your body so that you feel comfortable. Change your position between photographs – you might put your arm round the best man's shoulders, or shake hands with your father-in-law. Resist any temptation to plunge your hands into your trouser pockets, and ask a bridesmaid or page boy to hold your hat and gloves. Try to look happy! When you smile, try to show your teeth, otherwise you may find you simply look terrified in the pictures!

If photographs are not convenient, or if you know there is a more attractive setting for them at the reception venue, you will leave the church area fairly soon. Be prepared for a shower of confetti as you approach the car (the best man should remind guests if the church has requested that no confetti be thrown).

LEAVING FOR THE RECEPTION

The wedding is over. You can enjoy a little time with your bride, confess how nervous you felt during the cere-mony, tell her how wonderful she looks, or just relax together. Behind you, an excited convoy is bringing your guests to the reception. You should have briefed the best man and ushers to ensure all guests have transport. For now, forget all that, and don't worry about a thing. You need a break before the next stint of hard work: the reception.

THE RECEPTION AND THE SPEECHES

Wedding receptions are very hard work for the happy couple – but very happy work, too. What could be better than celebrating your marriage with all your friends and relations? Your in-laws will have decided what kind of reception to hold: formal or informal, sit-down or buffet-style meal, whether to invite extra guests who could not be fitted in at the wedding ceremony, and so on.

THE RECEIVING LINE

You can be pretty sure your in-laws will have decided on a receiving line to greet the guests. This may seem over-formal, but it does ensure that you have some contact with every person who comes to your wedding, and they will value it. The usual order of the receiving line is: bride's mother and father; bridegroom's mother and father; bride and groom, although sometimes the happy couple stand in the middle.

Inevitably a queue will form as guests wait to greet their hosts and enter the reception. If possible, it is a good idea for them to be served with drinks while they wait. As people pass up the line you will hear them being greeted and/or introduced. Keep an ear out for this as it will help you to identify unfamiliar faces. The men will shake you by the hand, as will some of the women who do not know you, while the others may well offer their

1 & 2 Bridesmaids
3 Groom
4 Bride
5 Groom's father
6 Groom's mother
7 Bride's father
8 Bride's mother

Typical receiving line

cheek for a polite kiss. To avoid nose-jarring collisions, follow the rule that it is always the left cheek which is offered by both of you.

Standing exchanging greetings with perhaps upwards of a hundred people, some of whom you have never met, is tiring. Even if your hand is sore from shaking hands, and your mouth aches from smiling, keep going and stay cheerful – no one cares for a gloomy bridegroom.

There is also nothing worse than one who has drunk too much. You may have been offered a drink (which you will have to hold in your left hand to leave your right hand free for shaking hands); by all means sip it, but make sure you do not drink it too quickly. Firstly, you will be mingling with your guests and need to keep your wits about you – especially if you are under the unforgiving eye of a video camera! Secondly, you are later to make a speech which must be clear and coherent. Finally, you may be driving yourself and your bride away from the reception. For these excellent reasons, the bridegroom should abstain from more than a couple of glasses of wine at the reception. Keep your glass topped up with mineral water for the toasts.

Find something personal to say to as many guests as you can. If you remember what their wedding gift was (your bride may be able to prompt you on a few) then a specific 'thank you' for it will please them greatly. Perhaps you know a particular couple has travelled a long way, or you have heard their names many times but not met them until now. There is usually something personal you can say if you work at it! Listen out for clues from what they say to other people in the receiving line, too.

Try not to enter into long conversations, even with friends of many years – tell them you will seek them out later on. Queuing for the receiving line can be rather wearing for the guests, especially if they are waiting in the open air or in a draughty entrance hall.

As the line of guests peters out, wait for the bride's father's lead in breaking out of the line. If there are still some formal photographs to be taken, now is the time, while guests socialize over their drinks, or take their seats for the meal. In the latter case, you should aim to join them as quickly as possible, as conversation and patience can flag while people wait for the top table to be occupied.

If the meal is a more informal buffet style with no top table, they could start to eat – the best man or master of ceremonies should take the lead here, either by example or by making an announcement. The announcement may include the saying of Grace, which is optional but should certainly be said if a minister or priest is present. You should of course be there for this, but can then slip away for more photographs.

TOP TABLE

If there is a top table a number of seating suggestions are shown on page 190. The top table is occupied by the bride and bridegroom in the centre, both sets of parents on either side of them, best man and chief bridesmaid, possibly the other bridesmaids, depending on their age and the space available, and perhaps the chief usher. Obviously this will have been planned well in advance and there should be table cards to show people where to sit. Those sitting at the top table are invariably served first, or invited to go to the buffet first to be served if that is the style of the meal.

INFORMAL BUFFET

If the catering is buffet-style with no seating (and hence no top table) you will be free to mingle with your guests throughout the meal. Whether you go round the room separately or as a couple is a matter of personal choice. Many guests will enjoy seeing you together, but you will be able to get round to chat to more people if you split up. Perhaps the best solution is to split up initially, for you will inevitably meet up as you circulate. You can always send a message for your bride to join you if necessary!

One thing you must not do is settle down with your cronies in a corner: it is your duty to circulate as much as possible, and guests will think it very rude if you are not seen to be doing this. Equally, your friends are your ambassadors for the day, and it would be unforgivable if they were rude or unruly.

One problem for the bride and bridegroom at an informal buffet is that they are so busy circulating that

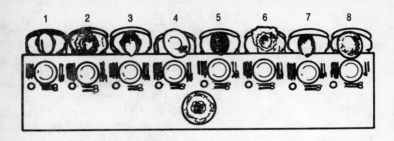

1 Best man
2 Chief bridesmaid
3 Groom's father
4 Bride's mother
5 Bridegroom
6 Bride
7 Bride's father
8 Groom's mother
9 Bride's family
10 Groom's family

Top table plan

they do not get a chance to eat! A solution is to have a plate with a selection of foods prepared and left in the room where you will change. That way you can be sure your stomach will not be rumbling as you make your exit from the reception.

THE SPEECHES

Now come the few minutes which three people have probably been dreading all day: the speeches. Comprehensive advice on planning and making a speech is given in Part 5. If you read this, and ask other people who have made speeches to give you some tips, you should be all right.

First to speak is the bride's father, or his representative, for he may invite an old family friend or relation to speak in his place. The speech will end with a toast to the bride and bridegroom, followed by a burst of applause.

Now it is your turn. Stay calm, give your speech as you have planned and rehearsed it, and speak as slowly as you can, as nerves give speakers a tendency to gabble. Your speech ends with a toast to the bridesmaids. If your bride wishes to say a few words as well, she should do so before this toast, which can then be proposed by both of you together.

The best man's speech is nominally on behalf of the bridesmaids. It is bound to include some jokes at your expense. Even if you find some of these hard to take, keep smiling and do not show your annoyance – if people feel the best man has gone too far, they will feel sympathetic towards you anyway.

The speeches over, you can breathe a deep sign of relief before cutting the cake.

CUTTING THE CAKE

The bride and bridegroom traditionally make the first cut of the cake together, after which the caterers whisk it away to slice it up frantically for serving to the guests. The ritual is always a focus of attention, and invariably photographed. The danger is that the icing will be so hard you will not be able to cut through it with your uncomfortable joint grip on the knife. A bit of planning avoids the problem: ask the caterers if the icing is hard, to make an incision through the icing while the speeches are being made. No-one will notice and you will be spared the embarrassment of a clumsy wrestling match with it in front of all the guests.

The bridegroom leads his bride to the cake so that they are both standing on one side of it. The point of the knife should be placed in the centre of the bottom tier, with the cutting edge towards the bride. The bridegroom then places his hand over his bride's, and together they push the handle gently down, drawing the blade slightly towards them. You are only making a token cut, and you may be asked to pause for photographs as you are slicing. Sometimes this ritual takes place before the speeches, giving the caterers more time to prepare portions for the guests to enjoy with their coffee. It is traditional to send pieces of cake to those who were unable to attend the wedding.

What happens next depends on what kind of reception is being held. If there is to be music and dancing, the bride and bridegroom lead the way to the dance area. They usually have one dance together, and are then joined by the rest of the top table, after which all the guests may dance if they wish. Some bridegrooms find this 'duet' more intimidating than making a speech. If you lack confidence about dancing in front of others, and do not want to invest in dance classes, you could at least practise with your bride in the weeks before the wedding. No-one is expecting a virtuoso display, but you will want to look and feel comfortable.

GOING AWAY

It is as well to plan the time of your departure. It helps the people who are running the event to have some idea of the timetable, and the going-away is important as it acts as a signal for other guests that they may now leave if they wish.

The bride and bridegroom retire to a room where their going-away clothes have been taken. The bride may

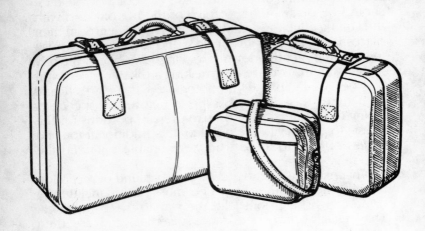

ask her chief bridesmaid to help her out of her wedding dress. Otherwise she will probably ask you, so it is best to help her before you start to change too. If you wore morning dress for the wedding, you will probably now change into a suit. If the wedding was less formal and you are already wearing a suit, you should still change into something more casual.

When you are both ready, make a final check that you have everything you need for the rest of the evening and, if you are going straight to your honeymoon destination, that you have all necessary documents and luggage, or that they have been packed in the car.

You are not expected to continue socializing once you have changed into your going-away outfits. Of course you may pause for a quick chat with anyone you missed while circulating, but you should really be heading for your transport now. Some couples have left their reception by hot air balloon, helicopter, speedboat, and even on bicycles, but chances are you will be leaving by car, either driving yourselves or in a taxi.

If your departure is by private car, it is very likely that the younger guests will have spent half an hour decorating it with streamers, confetti, balloons, and anything else that could be attached to the car. If there is shaving foam sprayed on the windscreen, use the wipers to remove it before setting off – otherwise you risk driving over a guest's foot and spoiling the day. Any other adjustments can be left until you have driven a few hundred yards down the road and can safely pull in and remove anything that restricts your vision or could be dangerous. For example, balloons tied to radio aerials can be pulled by the drag of the car and break the aerial.

Make your departure as much fun as possible for the guests – toot the horn, flash the lights, wind down the windows and wave. Although celebrations often continue for many hours, this is an important symbolic moment in the day and it is fun to make it memorable.

If you are to make a long car journey, it may be worth organizing a decoy car in which to make your exit from the wedding. You can then drive to where your own car is parked and continue your journey. Make sure the person who loaned their car is aware of the purpose of the ruse (and that they will have to clear up the mess!) and that there is some way of getting the keys back to them, unless they have a spare set with them.

Some couples hold a party in the evening after the reception. This gives them a chance to mix with their younger relations and friends without the inevitable restrictions imposed by a formal reception. Now you can let your hair down and really enjoy yourself with no responsibilities to worry about, except that if you both drink, you should take a taxi to where you are to spend the night.

THE HONEYMOON AND AFTER

The honeymoon marks the start of your married life together. The significance of this was perhaps much greater in years gone by. Today, for many couples it provides an opportunity to enjoy a special holiday, perhaps to a far-flung destination, or maybe just of a longer duration than usual.

After all the excitement of the build-up to the wedding and the big day itself, it is not uncommon for newly weds to feel a slight sense of let-down after the ceremony. So much planning and energy went into it, and now it is over. It can also feel very odd to have left behind all your friends and relations having a great time together. Don't be afraid to voice such thoughts – marriage is all about sharing, and you can help each other get over these feelings. Relaxing together will help, too, and will provide the best foundation for your new relationship.

MAKING A WILL

It is commonly assumed that when one of you dies, your estate passes directly to your spouse. This is not always the case. There are limits prescribed on how much can be automatically transferred in the absence of a will, and the legal aspects of death are made far more complicated if there is no will. There are plenty of books giving advice on how to make a will, or you could ask a local solicitor to explain what you have to do.

INSURANCE

If you already have a life assurance policy, you will probably wish to make your wife its beneficiary. If you do not have one, now is a good time to consider taking one out as it would help to provide for her if you died.

If you have moved into a new home, make sure you take out a policy to cover its contents – including all the wedding gifts. Even if you are now sharing a house or flat one of you owned, or were already living together, you will need to add any expensive items you were given to the contents policy.

STARTING A FAMILY

Even if you are not planning to have children at all, or not for many years, once you are married people tend to assume it is on the cards. Either or both of your sets of parents may be very keen for this to happen, especially if they are not already grandparents.

It is best to be prepared for questions and comments, and the first step towards this is to agree with each other on whether, and when, you would like to have children. Modern contraception methods allow us a choice in this matter which was more difficult for previous generations to make. You may have talked this through during your engagement, but even if you did, your or your wife's thoughts might have changed. Allow a lot of time for your discussions – one exchange of views will not be sufficient to map out the pattern of the early years of marriage.

MAKING MARRIAGE WORK

There is a lot of rubbish written and said about how to

make marriage work. Phrases like 'Love is never having to say you're sorry' give a misleading idea that a loving bond is all you need to see you through life's challenges. It isn't. You have to work at marriage in the same way as you work at a job: make allowances, communicate your feelings, and think about your partner's need as well as your own. About a third of today's marriages end in divorce, which is rarely amicable. If you show consideration to each other, and try to understand and work with each other, you might be able to avoid being part of that unhappy statistic.

If you do, you will have many wedding anniversaries to celebrate. Your wife will appreciate your remembering them without being prompted. If necessary, write the date into your diary at the start of each year! The anniversaries are listed below – you might have some trouble finding an appropriate gift for all of them!

Anniversary	*Wedding*	*Anniversary*	*Wedding*
First	Cotton	Fifteenth	Crystal
Second	Paper	Twentieth	China
Third	Leather	Twenty-fifth	Silver
Fourth	Books	Thirtieth	Pearl
Fifth	Wood	Thirty-fifth	Coral
Sixth	Sugar	Fortieth	Ruby
Seventh	Wool	Forty-fifth	Sapphire
Eighth	Bronze	Fiftieth	Golden
Ninth	Pottery	Fifty-fifth	Emerald
Tenth	Tin	Sixtieth	Diamond
Twelfth	Silk and linen	Seventy-fifth	Second diamond

PART 3

THE BEST MAN

WHEN YOU ARE CHOSEN

You may be chosen as best man, anticipating the delightful prospect of dressing up at a grand wedding and making a speech. To be chosen as best man is an honour. You are a close relative or friend of the groom, and he is relying on you for assistance on one of the happiest and most important occasions in his life.

ACCEPTING THE ROLE OF BEST MAN

Are you going to accept? Why not? Should you, must you, can you? First check the wedding dates. Assuming that you are not obliged to take a pre-arranged holiday abroad, go into hospital, or take an exam on the groom's intended wedding date, you should be able to express your desire to accept.

You may wish to consider the location of the wedding – if the bride lives far away for example, what expense and time the travelling will involve. Going to India can involve more than 24 hours flying, and you can hardly arrive just a few hours in advance, because of the risk of flight delays.

It is not usual for the groom to pay for the travel and accommodation expenses of the best man and ushers. If he paid the travel of ten people to India he would have to spend a considerable sum. But as a close relative or friend you may be able to stay with your family, or share travel expenses and hotel costs with another of the ushers or guests.

TACTFUL REFUSAL

To refuse is rather delicate. Sometimes a blunt expression of the problem and your regret is the best solution, by phone for speed. If you are going to be abroad, follow it up by a friendly letter along the lines of: 'It's just the week you are getting married. What bad luck! I'm really sorry I can't be there. But I hope you have a truly splendid day. I shall certainly be thinking of you and we all send our best wishes.'

A brother returning from abroad especially for the wedding would not have time to act as organizer in the months leading up to it. He can be given or ask for other roles instead, such as giving a speech, acting as toastmaster, or being head usher.

In a second marriage the question arises of how much to involve the children from the first marriage. A widow re-marrying might wish to give a prominent role to a grown-up or teenage son. If the groom agreed, her son could be best man. Not every boy would feel at ease doing this. He, too, might prefer to be an usher.

If the groom wants you to be the best man when you can see that your older brother really expects to be chosen, as would be correct, you may be able to keep family peace by expressing a preference for being head usher. Pretend that you prefer less responsibility. The alternative is to suggest that your rival be appointed chief usher.

Find out from the groom what he thinks your responsibilities will be. These depend on the circumstances of the wedding, the wedding size – which may increase as the period of the engagement lengthens – and the bridegroom's age, especially if he is a lot younger or older than you are.

WEDDING CLOTHES

It is up to the groom to tell you how formal the wedding will be. Clearly it would be absurd if you wore informal clothes when the rest of the bridal party was in formal clothing. If it is going to be a black tie or morning suit affair you do not have to buy a new outfit, but you will be responsible for its hire, together with providing a shirt, and your own shoes. The groom may advise you where to obtain them, or you could take on the task of comparing the different hire companies.

However, the groom may provide the ushers with matching ties and handkerchiefs and buttonholes to give the wedding group a unified look and enable them to be identified.

SPEECHES

As best man you are not always obliged to make a speech. It would be possible to have no speeches at the wedding. The groom may not require the best man's speech if there are no bridesmaids. Or he may simply have another older friend of the family, perhaps a colleague of the bride's father, proposing the toast to the couple, a reply from the groom, and then a reply from the bride's father.

BEST MAN'S WEDDING GIFT

Being invited to be best man gives you a closer relationship with the bridal couple, and the best man normally gives a larger wedding gift than he would have done had he been an ordinary guest.

As a close friend or relative, you will naturally want to give the happy couple a wedding present. It is usual for any guest to give a present after being invited to a wedding, whether you are able to attend or not, although the tendency is to give a larger present if you are attending. The best man, like close relatives, gives a larger present than more distant relatives and friends, although of course this depends upon his circumstances and budget.

BEST MAN'S WIFE OR GIRLFRIEND

Does being a best man give you more or less right to bring along your wife or girlfriend? Naturally your wife will be invited, though she will not be with you throughout the wedding.

While the fiancée or long-standing girlfriend would normally be invited, if you are changing girlfriends every other week, or likely to change girlfriends before the date of the wedding ceremony, the bride's mother will not necessarily want to send out invitations to a succession of your acquaintances. Nor will you necessarily want an ex-girlfriend to appear at the wedding as well as your new girlfriend when the time of the wedding comes around.

It is not right for a total stranger or very recent acquaintance to arrive at the wedding, just because you met her the week before and you hope she will become a long-term friend. Of course the size of the wedding affects this. You could not expect a new girlfriend to be invited at the last moment to a dinner where seating plans have already been made. But it is quite possible to ask if a girlfriend may come along to a stand-up buffet, providing the invitation comes from the bride's family (or host).

INVITATIONS

The printed invitations will probably be sent out about six weeks before the date of the wedding. The best man and ushers, as part of the wedding party, already know they will be present. Others must wait for their formal invitations. If your long-standing girlfriend lives at a distance, the groom's mother may ask you for your girlfriend's address in order to send her the invitation. If the bride's mother or wedding dinner host is more cautious she or he may decide to send an invitation to you 'and guest'.

If the invitation goes to the best man and his wife, or the best man and his fiancée or girlfriend, he is responsible for a wedding gift from both of them. If a separate invitation is sent to the girlfriend, she may wish to send a separate gift, or contribute a proportion of the cost in order to enable you to buy a larger joint gift.

USHERS' GIRLFRIENDS

The single ushers – particularly if there are as many as six ushers, are less likely than the best man to be invited to bring along girlfriends who are unknown to the hosts.

The host may have printed only the number of invitations required for the guests, and not for the wedding party themselves. If you do not receive one but you know there are spares you can reasonably ask for one 'as a souvenir'.

THE GROOM'S OLDER BROTHER

If you are married, you have had the experience of a wedding before. Therefore you are in a good position to help and advise, though you cannot expect your brother to do exactly as you did at your wedding.

CHILDREN

If the best man's wife or usher's wife is invited to the wedding it does not necessarily follow that their children will be invited to the reception. The children of the groom's or bride's brothers are probably known well to the bride and groom. If they are part of the ceremony as bridesmaids or pageboys they will usually be invited to the reception, unless this is long past their usual bedtime in which case you must book a babysitter. (Remember that granny, other relatives, colleagues and neighbours may be busy at the wedding.)

When the bride has no bridesmaids and there is a seated dinner the wedding reception host may have good reasons for not including children. There is likely to be a limit to the number of seats, and to the cost of each dinner ordered from the caterers. Small children do not sit still easily during long dinners and speeches. If the bride's mother invites one set of children she may create ill-feeling if she does not invite the children of other brothers and cousins, which could add another thirty to the catering. Older teenagers are sometimes invited to come along if there is a dance after the seated dinner.

GROOM'S BEST FRIEND/WORKMATE, COLLEAGUE, OR BUSINESS PARTNER

If you do not already know the bride, the sooner you get to meet her and her family the better. When organizing the wedding, advising the groom, and writing your speech, you will want to appreciate the bride's family's lifestyle and fit in with her, as well as the groom's family's lifestyle and his aspirations. If your groom is of a different religion or nationality, check the location of the wedding, then what your responsibilities will be.

You are presumably chosen because the groom knows you well and likes you a great deal and has no brothers or close relatives. The bride's family will be regarding you as the groom's right hand man, representing his friends and the sort of person he is or would like to be, and your good conduct will reflect on him.

If you work with the groom, don't talk shop at the wedding in front of the family and the guests.

BEST GIRL

If you are not happy with the unconventional idea of being best girl, you might hint that you would be happier being maid or matron of honour, or chief bridesmaid. This might involve you in an equal amount of dressing up and fun, but with responsibility for helping the bride write invitations and thank you letters, dressing her, and organizing her clothes, rather than helping the groom with his clothes and the honeymoon – which is sometimes supposed to be a secret from the bride.

Assuming that you accept, you will want to meet both sides of the family and make sure that they are happy with your role so that the ceremony goes as expected and having a best girl instead of a best man is not a big surprise to everyone.

At a formal wedding you will probably wear a smart day dress, perhaps with a corsage of fresh flowers pinned to your lapel bodice to distinguish you from the other guests. At a second marriage where the bride is wearing a suit, you could be similarly attired.

Even if the bride is not wearing white, the bride's mother and groom's mother are normally a generation older and can be distinguished from the younger bride. However, if you are of similar age to the bride and groom, or look young, you will want to ensure that the bride wears more distinctive clothes or flowers than you do. You should also avoid wearing an entire dress or large areas of colour which will clash with the rest of the wedding party. If the others are wearing pink and purple, that may rule out a bright orange or red dress and accessories.

Your clothes will be different from those of any bridesmaids, though if there are ushers you might have a corsage paid for by the groom, and a sash or shoes to echo the groom's family or team colour. If you are in the armed forces, you could also be co-ordinated with the groom and ushers by wearing a dress uniform of your military regiment.

Bridesmaids are required to wear dresses which are identical or co-ordinating with each other, often in a paler colour such as pink, or yellow and green, echoing the bride's dress and accessories. As best girl you also pay for your own outfit, but are not required to co-ordinate with the bride, matron of honour, or bridesmaids.

ORGANIZING THE STAG PARTY

A stag party is not obligatory but it is often staged by members of clubs and groups, particularly by all-male organizations such as football teams when one of their number is getting married. The best man is the organizer, but who is the host and who pays? The best man is the host and issues the invitations and therefore he pays, but usually with the help of those attending if it is a large gathering.

At a pub the best man would buy the first round of drinks. Probably others would then offer to pay for subsequent rounds, or at least for the groom's refills. At a restaurant dinner the best man organizes it, warning the guests in advance roughly what it will cost, having first verified this with the restaurant manager. At the end of the evening the bill is then split between the guests, with the exception of the groom who does not pay.

The guests will normally be mostly the groom's young friends – those he would go out with on a Saturday night, weekend nights, or see regularly for sports, rather than his elderly relatives. The guests can be the groom's choice or a surprise. It would be hard to stop well-wishers drifting along if you set off in a crowd from the office or held the event at your local pub. Numbers can range from the groom and best man having a drink together, to a small group such as the groom, best man and two ushers having dinner together, to a full scale party with 20 or more guests.

THE DATE OF THE STAG PARTY

A party which includes the groom and relatives or friends flying in from abroad specially for the wedding has to be held as near the wedding date as possible, but not the night before. The groom, best man and guests may have last minute arrangements to make for the wedding next day, and they want to be wide awake to enjoy the day, rather than dozing and hung over.

LOCATIONS

Possible locations are pubs, clubs, wine bars, restaurants, or private homes. If the stag party will be attended mainly by people from the workplace or office, the ideal location is a pub or other location near by. Many pubs have a separate room which can be hired or sometimes used at no cost.

The cheapest drinks party is one organized at somebody's home, with drinks bought in bulk, glasses borrowed from an off-licence, or paper cups used. If the home is that of the bridegroom or a best man who lives nearby, anyone who gets tipsy can stay there until they sober up enough to walk or drive home safely. You could start at the local and end up at home.

FOOD FIRST

The first thing to provide at a party is food, otherwise guests will sneak off early to get something to eat. Sufficient food must be provided, something for later arrivals, and provision for those on a diet. Peanuts, prawns, pork sausages, sherry, beer, whisky, and spirits will leave most of your Jewish, Muslim and Hindu friends or workmates with little to eat and drink except peanuts and water. Orthodox Jews eat kosher meat and no shellfish. Muslims eat Halal meat. Hindus are vegetarian. Jews, Muslims and Hindus don't like to get drunk, so even if they are non-orthodox and imbibe, some of them will prefer low alcohol drinks rather than spirits. So try to include some cheese, vegetables, fruit, and wine. You must also have some juices, soft drinks, and non-alcoholic beers for the drivers.

DRINKS AND JINKS

Drinking on an empty stomach would make half of your guests sleepy and the other half noisy and belligerent. You probably know the way your group behaves under the influence of drink. You must make sure that the guests have fun but matters do not get out of hand. It is the best man's job to ensure that no one gets too drunk, particularly the groom.

SOBERING UP

Now it is generally known that drinking an excessive amount is dangerous and could have fatal consequences, even if the groom does not mix alcohol with drugs, or try to walk or drive home. There have been cases of grooms being delivered home unconscious and having to be hospitalized after drunken stag nights, which have never been popular with their brides. So you need to keep all the party reasonably sober, particularly the groom, or at least get them sobered up before they leave the premises.

Give the guests food before they start drinking, plus a liberal supply of non-alcoholic drinks. Mix a punch containing decreasing amounts of alcohol as you replenish it. Offer more food and coffee before they leave. Arrange entertainment to keep them busy and otherwise amused. If all else fails you will have to water down their subsequent drinks, 'lose' their car keys, and drive them home yourself or call a taxi.

ENTERTAINMENT

Rather than making the groom a source of unintended merriment, some form of entertainment can be organized. This can follow the interests of the groom himself or the group as a whole.

BE A SPORT

If the groom is a keen sports player, arrange for him to have a professional coaching lesson to improve his play. Leisure centres hire sports facilities with a coach in attendance. You could snorkel in a swimming pool, have a deep sea diving lesson with a club, and take pictures with an underwater camera.

An afternoon could be spent watching or trying stock car racing, or spend an evening at the cinema. Or even spend a whole day on an organized Survival Game or some activity the groom's wife-to-be might not enjoy.

PHOTOGRAPH IT, FILM IT

Don't forget to take a photo of the groom in action. Both Polaroid and 35 mm cameras would be useful. Polaroid will provide instant pictures to pass around and discuss.

A conventional camera will take good quality photographs to be enlarged as souvenirs. The latest automatic 35 mm cameras made by Pentax have a zoom for close-ups. If the groom looks impressive perhaps a good photo can be blown up to poster size. The Polaroid photos of the stag party can also make an interesting beginning or end to wedding day photo albums.

Better still, record the groom's play on video: you can either hire a video camera for the day or get a company to take the video film for you. You might be able to arrange a deal with the company that plans to video-record the wedding day itself.

VIP TREATMENT

You could take the groom for a test drive in the car of his dreams or, if money is no object, hire a chauffeur-driven Rolls Royce for the evening. Then use a ticket agency to obtain tickets for an historical play or opera, Ascot, the races, or an equally popular match or show. This could be followed by drinks in a traditional gentleman's city business club. Alternatively an upmarket agency such as Crème de la Crème will get your group tickets for a concert, or theatre, with pre-show or interval drinks in the private rooms which are used by royalty and VIPs.

WINES AND VIEWS

You could arrange an evening on a wine company's premises or at a nearby hotel, calling in a wine company representative for a wine-tasting session. Those present could then give the groom a case of the wine he likes the most. Afterwards, if it is not a secret, you could show a video of the honeymoon destination, which the groom can then keep as a souvenir, so he will be able to get maximum enjoyment from trips around the honeymoon country.

GOURMET BANQUETS

Or you could arrange a dinner at a restaurant featuring the cuisine of the honeymoon country, dining on specialities not normally on the menu. These dishes must be ordered for your group several days in advance. Again this enables the groom to be better prepared to enjoy his honeymoon. The menu can be kept by the groom as a souvenir, signed by all the guests. You might like to order a vintage wine, champagne, or port, or two or three different wines from the country, and ask the wine waiter to describe them.

LIVE ENTERTAINERS

If you want live entertainment, the most personalized songs will come from a revue put on by the groom's own friends, a sort of amateur 'This is Your Life', with a few key guests arriving one by one, from the old school, previous workplace, or home town. All you need is a big banner, unfurled when the groom arrives, half a dozen photos borrowed from his mother and stuck in one of those magnetic page albums, a microphone, and a Polaroid camera. If you can get a few accessories, such school caps, football team or college scarves, and the words of the old school song, so much the better.

You could also try phoning one or more of the groom's distant friends, or an old school headmaster, or the teacher of the subject at which the groom was most successful. Ask if the friend or teacher remembers John, or whoever, and record the reply on a telephone answering machine. Make sure it is on the start of a new tape so you can locate it easily.

Your guests may include some talented amateur actors or singers who can make up amusing songs, strum guitars, mime to music, sing or dance.

PROFESSIONALS

If you would rather spend money than time, live entertainers can be hired. Identify the groom's musical tastes, whether they are orchestral, opera, or jazz, or rock, reggae or pop. A live performance can be teamed with the gift of musical records or cassettes, or a stereo or CD player.

Make sure your act is good and reliable. At one party the palm-reader failed to arrive because she was taken ill at the last moment. Whether she had seen this coming was never known, but the host had not!

You will also want to be sure that your entertainers can find their way across town to the venue through rush hour and arrive at the right time. Both the agent and you need to have their phone numbers at the location they are leaving from. You also need a note of the agency's phone number. Phone on the morning of the day to confirm. Then if they have forgotten, double-booked, blown up the transformer, got lost on the motorway, or fallen ill – you will be surprised at the comical excuses – you will have time to arrange something else. It is always a good idea to have a back-up of disco music, video tape or other entertainment just in case they fail to turn up on time. Avoid engaging unknown dubious entertainers. What sounds like a funny strip act might degenerate into an unsuitable audience involvement rugger scrum in which the guests lost half their clothes. Anyone who wakes up next day unable to remember what happened will imagine the worst happened to everybody else, though not to himself.

To ensure that you are booking a professional and acceptable act, try to engage a group which has been recommended and go to see them perform elsewhere first. If you want a particular singer or comedian, make sure that your arrangement with the company specifies this.

You cannot prevent the lead singer falling ill, but you can make it clear that you expect the group to consist of those you have met and not others using the same name. There was one particularly bad experience with wedding photographers which you could learn from. The family booked a wedding photographer whose work they liked and with whom they had rapport. In fact they chose between two companies on the basis of this man's personality. However, the extrovert man who made the presentation to them and showed them his work was merely the rep on this occasion. More bookings for other weddings reached him for the wedding day and he sent someone else to take the wedding photos.

DINNER SHOWS

A less original but safer approach is to visit a gourmet ethnic restaurant or supper club which has public performances on stage. A well-known restaurant could be chosen, or one with a particularly attractive menu which is worth framing, or a restaurant which specializes in dinner shows such as flamenco dancing, Indian dancing, or Middle Eastern belly dancing. If you want something different, there are restaurants specializing in magic or medieval banquets.

STAG PARTY SPEECHES

When you hold a stag party in a private room at a restaurant, this is a good place to have some after dinner speeches and to present a gift to the groom.

The general tone of the best man's speech is a humorous one. Relate how the groom spent his time as a single man. Recall his achievement and cleverness, and unaccountable rare moments of stupidity. What are the qualities of the perfect married man? Does he possess them? The bride to be seems very charming. Has she made a wise choice? Look forward to the enormous improvements which could be made in him. And express fears about the occasional disappointments that will occur, when his bride attempts to change things! Finally extend the good wishes of yourself and all those present, and give him the gift which you trust will assist his new life, and contribute to the happiness of him and his new wife.

If you have had an evening out on the town, the whole group can see the groom home safely and make the presentation either at his home, or at the best man's home *en route*.

Assuming that the groom is making a speech in reply, take along a tape recorder. You can then put together a tape of the stag party speeches, adding the wedding day speeches later.

MAN TO MAN CHATS

The married best man, usher, or father may take this opportunity to advise the groom on marriage conduct and bedroom behaviour. Advice from different sources – proverbs, for instance – tends to conflict.

HEN PARTIES

While all this is going on it is only fair that the bride-to-be should be gathering with her girlfriends for a similar hen party organized by the Maid of Honour or Matron of Honour. If you are collecting photos from the boys' bachelor party, combine them with photos from the girls' hen party in the wedding book.

Girls should perhaps beware of trying to turn the tables on the boys by calling in a male stripper. One best man informed the groom who, when he heard of his plan, turned up in disguise and did a strip show, finally revealing all – including his identity, to the horror of the bride!

JOINT BACHELOR PARTIES

If there is a best girl, rather than having her organize a bachelor boys' party, hold a combined party for the singles. In a private house you can have the girls in one room and the boys in another. Or at a restaurant have a boys' table and a girls' table.

This is a last chance for everyone to contribute 'My mother's ten rules for a happy marriage,' and 'My father's ten rules for a happy marriage.' The rules which no longer apply – such as grandparents' advice to your mother and father when they married, will raise a few laughs. You could even have two opposing speakers, as in a debate.

If the party is held at home start with practical demonstrations such as 'How to make hospital corners on beds; cakes, biscuits, and meals made in ten minutes'.

When meeting in a restaurant swap lists and present a book of tips such as: 'What to do if the car won't start'; 'How to be sure you never lose your doorkey.' Later you might discuss how to avoid arguments; and how to keep him/her happy. Details of American bachelor parties are given on page 251.

PRE-WEDDING PLANS

For some best men there is a lull until the days immediately before the wedding. However, a large wedding with many attendants requires forward planning. Even the calmest wedding creates a flurry of activity and excitement in the last few days.

DUTIES DURING THE ENGAGEMENT

First the best man and ushers will be invited to a family dinner or the engagement party to meet the family.

MEETING THE BRIDE

If you cannot think of anything else to say you can admire the ring, and tell the bride how you know the groom, and what a good choice they have both made. Since you are aiding the groom in organizing his side of the wedding, it is worthwhile finding out his bride's taste in music, clothes, colours, food, furnishing (you will be buying them a wedding present) and anything else which might be relevant.

MEETING THE BRIDE'S AND GROOM'S PARENTS

Naturally you will express pleasure at the forthcoming marriage and say how pleased you are to be part of the wedding party. The bride's parents who pay for the wedding will be making decisions as to the number of guests and ushers.

MEETING THE USHERS

The best man has overall charge and he directs the chief usher. A meeting is usually held at which he briefs the ushers. They have three chief areas of concern: clothes, church seating plans, and transport.

WEDDING CLOTHES

The best man will be supervising fittings for either formal and informal wedding clothes, co-ordinating outfits and accessories, in a style which establishes them all as members of the wedding group, but distinguishes them from the groom. A truly energetic best man will investigate all the clothes hire firms and locate one which has a convenient location, a wide choice, and reasonable prices. The best man may even negotiate for the groom to get complimentary clothes hire if he is bringing them the business of, for example, the hire of six ushers' outfits. Major hire companies have leaflets showing which accessories go with which formal outfits.

Black, white and grey men's suits and accessories will go with most colours the bridesmaids might choose. A heavy black will look better against strong colours in the girls's dresses, while pale grey offsets the paler pastels, so make a note that you must discuss the girls' colour schemes after the bride has decided.

PRELIMINARY SEATING PLANS

Detailed seating plans of the church cannot be made until the numbers of guests and their relationships to the bride and groom are known. However, the best man can make a rough plan. The ushers should be given the basic rule to remember, to seat the bride's family on the left and the groom's on the right, which echoes the bride's and groom's position as they progress down the aisle.

TRANSPORT

The best man must check hire car costs and advise the groom. The car which brings the bride to the church, transfers the bride and groom to the reception, and then takes them to the hotel or airport can be one car hired for the day, driven by the best man. (Why not? It saves money. And although it takes time and trouble, the best man might enjoy the pleasure of driving a Rolls Royce.) Rolls Royce produce a booklet on the correct behaviour of a chauffeur driving a Rolls, which includes the wearing of driving gloves and opening car doors.

Alternatively a chauffeur-driven car can be ordered for each segment of the journey. If a car is hired for a minimum of one hour but the distance between the bride's home and the church is very short, the best man could arrange for the chauffeur to take the bridal couple for a spin in the Rolls Royce on the way.

Alternatives to the Rolls Royce are a Daimler, a stretch limousine, a tandem bicycle, or a helicopter for departure from the hotel where the wedding reception is held to the airport. If the bridal couple are marrying abroad there are many locations where horse-drawn carriages or Surreys are popular.

Hire company addresses can be found in the yellow pages of local phone books, or in advertisements in bridal magazines, or motoring magazines. Obviously you must remember to inform the hire company that the car is required for a wedding, so that the appropriate white ribbon can be placed on the bonnet.

The wedding party cars can be Rolls Royces, some years and models being more expensive than others. If you cannot get this year's model, you might go to the other extreme and choose a vintage car. Horses and carriages can be hired.

It is a good idea to suggest to the bride's mother that when guests telephone her she should check how they intend to reach the church and reception. Drivers can be sent maps indicating routes and parking. Those without transport can be put in touch with others coming from their area. Elderly relatives can be collected by others, or a note can be made to ensure that one of the ushers transports them from the church to the reception.

If guests speak foreign languages find out who can translate, and arrange for their mode of transport from the church to reception to be organized in advance. You don't want to be standing outside the church on the day trying to find out whether a silent, smiling Japanese lady has transport to the reception, and whether she has indeed been invited to the reception – a delicate question, even without the language difficulties.

GIFTS

The gifts to the bride and groom will depend on the finances of the best man and ushers, whether the couple already have separate homes, and whether they badly need any major items such as bedding or curtains. Maybe they already have two sets of crockery, and do not need more, but cannot afford to re-carpet their new home, in which case a large rug might be welcome.

PAPERWORK

An older groom may wish to take charge of most of the practical details. But a younger one might rely on the assistance of an older brother to organize the paperwork. A groom who is arriving from abroad, or has heavy commitments to work or study, may also rely heavily on the best man. To prepare for the wedding there are applications for marriage licences, arrangements to meet the minister, and enquiries about the costs of the church service.

HONEYMOON ADVICE

A budget must be made for the honeymoon, investigating possible honeymoon locations and comparing package tour prices. The groom will have to make reservations for the honeymoon transport and hotel, booking a honeymoon bedroom suite, and ordering extras such as champagne on arrival. The best man may have to chase up tickets which are not delivered, collect them and keep them safe, and confirm the flight.

The best man may be able to advise on the suitability of transport, hotels and bedrooms. Cruise ships and trains rarely have double beds, and package tours frequently give twin bed rooms. The best man might suggest that the groom tells the hotel he is on honeymoon and requires a double bed, or books a honeymoon suite with a double or four-poster bed.

There are numerous guides to UK locations. Local tourist boards can suggest hotels which have honeymoon suites, including the budget options such as bed and breakfast places with four-posters.

If the groom cannot afford any of this, the groom and ushers could club together and pay for the bride and groom to spend a night at a hotel with a honeymoon suite, or buy a couple of curtain rails and a curtain and, aided by the chief bridesmaid, rig up an improvised four-poster at home.

If the honeymoon is to be abroad, allow at least six weeks to order passports, visas, and vaccinations – which may have to be administered in two batches at widely spaced intervals.

INSURANCE

The best man should allocate a safe place, such as a body belt, or an inner pocket which buttons down or closes in the suit he is hiring, for keeping the bride's ring and the groom's suitcase keys. Car keys and doorkeys should also be kept safely. A key-ring can be attached by a black ribbon to an inside pocket so the keys can be extracted quickly, and never put down and lost. A set of duplicate keys can be given to the head usher, if the best man holds the main set. The best man could keep duplicate keys if the groom has the originals. Insurance can be taken out to cover possible loss of the ring, luggage and honeymoon holiday expenses, and the wedding itself.

It is also worthwhile checking on insurance policies to see whether items in the best man's care are covered by his household insurance, whether the policy for the bride's and groom's new home will cover presents delivered there before they move in, and whether clothing and wedding presents on display at the wedding reception are protected by insurance.

Receipts for deposits, dry cleaning receipts, and claim tickets for hired clothing and hire cars must be kept.

SPEECH

The best man should prepare his own speech, if necessary advise the groom on speechmaking, and keep a duplicate copy of the groom's speech. Make careful note of the spelling of family names, nicknames, titles of the family, friends and ministers or other VIPs whom you or the groom should mention in your speeches.

Your library and bookshop will have many books on speechmaking. Sample speeches are given in Part 5.

ENTERTAINING THE GROOM BEFORE THE WEDDING

The stag party is never held the night before the wedding in case the groom ends up with a hangover. But the best man may need to keep the groom happily and harmlessly occupied while the bride-to-be is busy with wedding preparations. If the groom is saving up for all those wedding expenses, he might need to stay at home with the best man sharing a drink from the off licence, rather than spending money on expensive rounds of drinks in bars and pubs. The night before the wedding you might like to hear the groom rehearse his speech.

NEAR THE DAY

Helping to calm the groom's pre-wedding nerves is one of the tasks, best achieved by unflappability, good organization and careful attention to detail. Giving advice will be your pleasurable task if you are older and more experienced or already married.

In addition to hiring and returning his own morning dress the best man will collect the groom's. He should keep two telephone and address lists, one in his pocket and one taped by the telephone at home, giving the contact numbers for all major participants, relatives, ushers and other attendants, church, minister, caterer, hire car company, jeweller, and travel agent.

FINALIZING SEATING PLANS IN THE CHURCH

Visit the church when no wedding or service is taking place so that you can draw up a pew plan. Then make a seat plan, filling in the names or status of guests, e.g. bride's mother. Pew cards can be made for reserved seats. You need to be clear about the seating of divorced parents (see page 230).

WEDDING REHEARSAL

A dry run or dress rehearsal can be held for the attendants, checking that you know when to produce the ring, where you will be standing, and when you will be speaking. Obtain copies of the church service for the groom, the bride, and yourself and other attendants.

You may want to do a dry run for the groom in your living room. He should have his clothes laid and ready and try them on in advance in front of you. That way you can check he isn't missing a collar-stud, wearing odd socks or a pair which don't match the shoes, or shoes which need new heels. The groom may go to church with the bride and watch another wedding the week before their own ceremony to see how it is done.

It is also handy to gather with the groom and ushers and look at some family photographs so that on the day you will instantly and enthusiastically recognize the bride's grandmother, stepfather, her real father, the other important people who need to be greeted and seated.

THE WEDDING DAY

Careful planning should make for a smooth-running and happy day. This is the day when the bride and groom are like king and queen with nothing to do except relax, smile and be joyful.

GETTING READY

Probably everybody will wake up early. But you should set two alarms to get yourself up, perhaps a clock plus a telephone alarm call. Then phone the groom. After that call at his home and help him dress. Take spare studs. Check that he has his marriage licence handy. Phone the ushers to ensure that they arrive at the church one hour in advance of the ceremony.

PARKING

Earlier this century when few people owned cars the ushers were responsible for organizing hire car transport for all the guests. Nowadays it is only the wedding party itself which arrives at the church in grand hire cars. Most guests drive themselves to the wedding and need help with directions and parking. Some of the guests may need help finding transport to the church, and to the reception, and cars may be hired to meet particular trains.

When there is a car park near the church but no attendant, one of the ushers must remove any chain barrier and then direct into the car park the wedding guests arriving by car. Spaces should be reserved for some or all of the wedding party cars, unless they can be left in the road immediately outside the church without obstructing traffic. In city locations shoppers and passers-by looking for parking places can be courteously re-directed to other nearby public car parks.

A NO PARKING sign may be obtained from the church or one can be made to prevent shoppers from parking too near the church door where the bride's car will be drawing up.

THE CHURCH DECORATIONS

The ushers should arrive at the church about one hour in advance in case any of the guests arrive early. If the best man has given the pew cards to the chief ushers these can be placed on the pews to reserve seats for important people. When the ushers arrive the flowers will probably already be arranged around the altar or wedding canopy, or the florist might be making the finishing touches. If by any chance the expected flowers are not ready or seem insufficient, the chief usher should phone the bride's mother or florist.

USHERS' DUTIES

If the weather is wet or snowy, the ushers must take large umbrellas with them to the church and one or more ushers should open car doors, hold umbrellas overhead and escort guests into the church so they do not get wet. Similarly when guests leave they must escort them back to the cars.

Those ushers who know most of the guests should greet them and direct other ushers to lead the guests to their seats. The immediate family are identified by their buttonholes or corsages.

The family will be given the seats nearest the front with a good view of the ceremony. The bride's mother and the groom's mother will normally have been given corsages earlier in the day so they can arrive wearing them, especially the bride's mother who arrives at the last moment. The ushers may be distributing the flowers to them or other guests. Sometimes a flower is given from a huge basket of flowers to everyone arriving. But the wedding group always wear different flowers so they can be identified.

The groom and best man may wait seated in the front right hand pew (Christians in USA) or stand, (Christians in UK and Jewish). Those taking part in the ceremony require seats reserved in the front row – including the best man himself who will sit down after handing over the ring.

Other guests may be colleagues, neighbours, or friends. Those guests who are not known by the ushers are asked, 'Friends of the bride or groom?' The bride's friends sit on the left. The groom's sit on the right. Ushers should hand out order of service sheets, and prayer books to guests as they arrive.

In theory those arriving first should go to the far end of the pew so that others can get in without pushing past. In practice the early arrivals may take the aisle seats with the best view on a first come first served basis, tenaciously guarding their places by stepping out into the aisle to let the latecomers take the inside seats. If there seems to be any disagreement pending, the ushers can quickly move the latecomer to a second aisle seat further back.

Ladies with strapless dresses or other clothing unsuitable for church can be tactfully advised to keep their coats on during the service. Where the place of worship requires men to wear hats or ladies to cover their hair with lace headcoverings these can be distributed. If men and women are sitting separately, as in a synagogue, newly arrived persons who are unaware of this fact should have it explained to them.

SEATING PRECEDENCE

Generally the closest family are given the seats nearest the front. Those partaking in the ceremony are given seats in the front row so that they can quickly and easily leave the seats and return to them.

If the bride's mother has remarried but her first husband, the bride's father, takes part in the ceremony he sits next to the bride's mother. The bride's stepfather, her mother's second husband, sits behind. Do not seat him alongside his rival, nor on the other side of the bride's mother as if the two men are competing for her attention. Even if the stepfather is paying for the wedding, the bride's own father may be the person who is closest to her and chosen to take part in the ceremony.

If the bride's mother and stepfather are hosts and taking part in the ceremony, the bride's father and his second wife will be given seats in the row behind. Apart from saving them the embarrassment of sitting next to each other, this saves the guests confusion. The wording of the wedding invitation itself should have indicated to both ushers and guests who the hosts are.

Seats near the front need to be saved so that small children who take part in the procession as bridesmaids and pages are not obliged to remain standing throughout the service. A seat must be allocated to a nanny or childminder if the child's mother is partaking in the service.

Families with babies or small children can be seated near a door at the back so they can make a quick exit if necessary. A few spaces near the back should be saved so that late arrivals can slip in unobtrusively. Similarly spaces should be saved for those with sticks or wheelchairs who do not wish to negotiate long distances. However, be sure that spaces with obscured views of the ceremony are not allotted when other places affording a better view are left free. Try to ensure that tall people with large hats are not seated in front of children or small people, but further back.

USHERS' BEHAVIOUR AND DEPORTMENT

The ushers should all be wearing carnations of the same colour, different from the colour of the one worn by the groom. The bride can be presumed to know who's who. But this system is a great help to short-sighted great-uncles trying to sort out which of the twin boys or similar brothers is getting married, and the bride's mother's friends from the shop or office – who know neither bride nor groom. It makes sure the photographer doesn't keep photographing the head usher instead of the groom. If the ushers' carnations match the colour of the brides-maid's dresses or flowers, e.g. pink, and the groom's carnation matches that of the bride's dress or flowers, e.g. white, it is clear to onlookers who is partnering whom.

The ushers should not engage in long conversations with each other or friends, ignoring and delaying arriving guests. If a fond aunt tries to block the doorway and engage in extended conversation say something like, 'Aunty, let me find you a seat . . . I must go back now but I look forward to talking to you later.' If the aunt has arrived well in advance she can be introduced to the person sitting next to her which will deflect her from distracting the busy usher.

The ushers should be calm, dignified and poised, not dash around looking agitated. They should also stand upright and not lounge against door pillars or recline on the sides of pews. Since they are conspicuous and likely to appear on camera during the day, they should remember not to jingle coins in their pockets, and avoid stroking their hair, and moustaches, lips and beards. When they are not occupied they can stand with their hands folded together, looking outward from the doorway to meet the eyes of approaching guests.

When several guests arrive together the chief usher might escort somebody important such as an elderly grandmother. If there is a group, the usher takes the oldest or most important person to lead the way. He offers his right arm to a single lady or to support anybody needing assistance.

At any time during the day when the best man, bride's mother or photographer seem unduly busy, an usher who is not occupied might offer to help, asking, 'Is there anything I can do for you?'

BEST MAN'S ARRIVAL AT CHURCH

The best man accompanies the groom to the church. In the olden days he would have been with the groom, theoretically to be ready to defend the groom. Nowadays this custom is followed so the groom knows the best man will 'get me to the church on time'. They may enter together from an east right-hand door and stand waiting for the bride. The best man stands to the right of the groom and slightly behind him. The organist plays quiet music.

The bride's mother arrives last before the bride, with the smallest bridesmaids and pageboys, who are often her grandchildren. The only exception to this is when the HM the Queen attends, in which case she is the last to arrive before the bride.

An usher waits by the church door for the arrival of the bride and informs the church choir so that the organist can strike up with 'Here comes the bride' or another appropriate tune which will arouse the attention of the guests in the church, and cause them to rise to their feet, stop talking, and look towards the bride.

Preceded by the minister and choir, the bride enters on the arm of her father or whoever is giving her away. It could be a stepfather or uncle if her father is deceased, sick, abroad or unable to attend. After she has entered the church an usher shuts the church doors and ensures that nobody enters and walks down the aisle in the middle of the ceremony. It is useful to be equipped with a spare handkerchief in case the bride or bride's mother bursts into tears.

SAFEGUARDING THE RING

The best man has charge of the ring given by the groom to the bride. Many couples have his and her wedding rings and the best man may be entrusted with both. If he is right-handed for maximum convenience he must keep the ring (or rings) in his right-hand pocket, or inside left pocket, and take out the gold or platinum band when required. Jewellers usually supply a ring box with a new ring. If this is too bulky for the best man's inside pocket, small zippered or buttoned purses are made for jewellery. A valuable heirloom ring or secondhand ring usually has a protective box. A ring which is not new may need cleaning before the ceremony. A jeweller will advise on how to clean it without damaging it or leaving marks.

The best man should not take the ring out of the box and carry it loose in his pocket. It can drop through a hole in his pocket into the jacket lining, or gather fluff inside the pocket. It is possible for the best man to transfer the ring into his hands just before the ceremony starts and wear the ring on his little finger so as to be able to produce it immediately.

The ring is placed upon the Bible held by the minister. The ring will be placed on the bride's fourth finger of her left hand by the groom. The best man may have taken it upon himself to remind the groom that in some European countries rings are worn on the other hand. Catholics follow a more elaborate ritual for placing the ring on the bride's hand. In Jewish ceremonies the ring may be placed on the bride's middle finger.

If by chance the ring rolls off under the pews during the ceremony, you do not want the bride and groom and ushers crawling around on hands and knees hunting for it, while the minister and guests wait anxiously. The best man should produce another ring. The ceremony then continues. When the proceedings are over the best man or chief usher should retrieve the ring after the guests have moved and it is easier to find.

After the minister has blessed the ring and passed it to the groom, the best man may sit down.

AFTER THE CEREMONY

THE REGISTER

The register is signed by the minister or registrar together with the bride and groom and two witnesses, who can be the maid of honour and best man, or two of the parents. If the minister has covered the register showing the bride's signature, which is in her maiden name, do not try to remove the cover. He may be discreetly concealing some personal detail not known to others outside the family such as the fact that she is adopted, or was the daughter of her mother's previous marriage.

SETTLEMENT OF CLERGY FEES

Payments are made to the clergyman, choir, and bell-ringers. The groom sometimes gives their money to the best man the night before to minimize the amount of last minute activity on the day. The most discreet method is to place the money (notes or cheques) in envelopes. Each envelope should have the name of the recipient neatly written on the outside. This enables the best man to recall the names and say, 'Thank you Mr Brown,' and ensures you do not mix up the envelopes and give the wrong amounts. The envelopes should be sealed. The minister of the church is entitled to payment, even if another minister has taken part or all of the service.

The best man leaves the vestry to summon the bridal car and when he returns the bridal group gather for the Recession.

THE RECESSION

It is bad form to try to enter the church interrupting the ceremony and an usher can ask latecomers to wait outside or until a suitable moment before entering. The usher should not lock the doors or obstruct anyone from entering, however, since this might be construed as forcing the bride to marry under duress, or preventing anyone with an objection to the marriage raising it. This is unlikely, but it is an important technical and legal point. Sometimes a latecomer or someone who has slipped out to the cloakroom manages to sneak into the back of a large church unobtrusively.

Generally the guests all wait to see the bride returning down the aisle on the arm of her new husband, but an official photographer may wish to leave ahead of them and fix up his tripod by the church steps.

The bride and groom walk back down the aisle. If it is a double wedding they are followed by the second bride and groom. The best man and the maid of honour or chief bridesmaid follow, together. Other ushers are paired with bridesmaids. Finally the parents of bride and groom bring up the rear.

THE GUARD OF HONOUR

A guard of honour may consist of soldiers or other groups in uniform, sailors, RAF, police, nurses, Boy Scouts or Girl Guides. They are seated at the back so that they can leave fast to form a human archway with raised arms holding banners, flags, batons or swords through which the bride and groom emerge. You will want to arrange matters so that the photographers are ready to capture this moment promptly, and guests are briefly delayed in the church entrance hall or directed to other exits so they do not flood out of the church into the back of the group being photographed.

CHURCH PHOTOGRAPHS

The best man and head usher probably both wish to be in the photographs taken on the church steps. If necessary they can both be in one photograph, then take turns at being in the photographs while the other attends to the guests. After the photographs are taken in front of the church, the bride's parents and those who will be on the receiving line leave first so they can get to the reception hall ready to receive the first guests.

AT THE RECEPTION

The house or hall where the reception is held should be made as easy to find as possible. Check that there is a sign with the hall or hotel name at the turning off the main road and the entrance to the driveway. If possible indicate that the wedding reception is held there by adding some wedding symbol such as carnations and balloons with slogans such as congratulations.

Have the cloakrooms and toilets checked earlier in the day. Management should fix missing locks, replace missing light bulbs, stock up with spare toilet rolls, add flowers, spray the Ladies with perfumed air freshener and generally make the place welcoming. The bride will be unable to get into a small cubicle if she is wearing a dress with a long train. Even if she is not staying the night at the hotel, they may make available a bedroom with *en suite* bathroom where you can leave the honeymoon luggage, secure wedding presents delivered on the day, and where the bride and groom can change into their going away clothes.

The groom's, best man's and ushers' top hats and gloves may be left in a cloakroom or left in the bedroom used as a changing room. The best man can take charge of the groom's hat so that the groom can go straight to the receiving line.

RECEIVING LINE

Compile a guest list to give to the toastmaster. Toast-masters usually have loud voices but if he requires a microphone, check it is in place and ask him to try it out and inform the management if it is not properly connected and adjusted. If there is no toastmaster, go through the names, checking how to pronounce them all. Announce the guests as they approach the receiving line.

Ushers should direct guests to drinks and chairs, make introductions and talk to anyone who is on their own. If you are having a wedding breakfast early in the day the drinks before the meal may be dispensed with.

CAKE-CUTTING

The timing of the cake-cutting will depend on the size and duration of the meal. When the cake will be a dessert, or will follow dessert with coffee after a light meal, the best man or master of ceremonies announces the cake cutting which is then followed by speeches.

However, if the meal is large and a long evening of dancing follows the coffee and speeches, the best man will call the bridal group back to the tables and summon the photographer for the cake cutting ceremony. The toastmaster might make the announcement after the best man has gathered everyone together or the best man may use the microphone belonging to the band if there is dancing. The cake is then passed around to accompany tea and coffee served later, with light sandwiches or Danish pastries for those who arrived after dinner, are still hungry, or do not like wedding cake.

The ushers should see that a drink is taken to the band. Wedding cake will be saved for those unable to attend the wedding and the caterer will put it in a box at the end of the evening. It may be too heavy for the bride's mother to carry, in which case the best man or chief usher can carry it to the car for her.

The parents of small children not invited to the wedding may gather up leftover petits fours. However, rather than leaving the guests to wrap up oddments surreptitiously, the ushers and attendants could be encouraged to offer the petits fours to guests who are likely to want to take them home, presented in silvery wrapping paper or teeny baskets. The European custom (especially in Italy) is for voile bags of sugared almonds in pink, white and silver to be given to the guests.

SPEECHES

Speeches begin after the guests have finished eating. Waiters should be instructed to fill wineglasses ready for the toasts. Announcements are made by the toastmaster or best man, 'Ladies and Gentlemen, you may now smoke,' and 'Pray silence for (name of speaker) who will propose a toast to (name)'.

After checking the microphone, the toastmaster or best man introduces the first speaker, and in due course the other speakers. Speeches should be delivered calmly with a confident, happy manner. Ushers can admit latecomers between the speeches, greeting these guests with enthusiasm and finding them something to eat and drink.

TELEMESSAGES

Telemessages may have arrived from relatives and friends overseas, those who are old or living far away, and those who are obliged to work on the wedding day. There may also be telemessages from groups of friends belonging to social organizations, school, college, or work colleagues.

If the best man is the groom's father, or the older brother who is head of the family, and wants to orchestrate every detail of the wedding to make it a wonderful occasion uniting the family from far corners of the globe, he might have reminded distant brothers and cousins to send cables, and suggested quotations which he is not using in his own speech.

The master of ceremonies, if there is one, must be handed the telemessages by the best man, who can sort them into order of importance, starting with the nearest or oldest relative, ending with those from friends or if possible an amusing telemessage.

If there is no master of ceremonies the best man reads the telemessages. Large numbers of telemessages would take time to read. Those from nearest relatives can be read in full. Others can be summarized, 'John Smith sends his best wishes.' Afterwards the telemessages should be kept safely by the best man and returned to the bride's mother, or sent to the couple's new home. The best man can keep them in a large white envelope labelled Wedding Telemessages to (bride's and groom's names) so that they do not get crumpled. The bride may wish to stick them into a wedding book with a copy of the wedding invitations, photographs, cutting from the local newspaper, and wedding menu.

Sending telemessages is traditional. But if a relative has thought to send a cassette with a message instead it might be worthwhile playing that – remember to bring along a cassette recorder.

If many relatives cannot attend, perhaps because the bride and groom's families live in different countries, the best man could have arranged to have a brief video made of a group of relatives or friends on an army base in Gibraltar, faraway Hong Kong, Singapore or Australia, saying how glad they are to be able to speak, that they send their good wishes, and that they are thinking of the bride and groom and opening a bottle of champagne.

The video should be rewound so it is at the start of the tape. The VCR and TV must be set up in advance, with a dry run to ensure all the plugs and switches are on. If the VCR is taken to a hotel or hall, the best man should make sure that it has been gathered up at the end of the evening, complete with all leads, and the tape, which should be clearly labelled with the subject and the bride's address, to guard against loss.

DANCING

Should the best man dance with the bride? Yes, but only after she has danced with the groom and her father. The best man should dance with the chief bridesmaid if she is single and unattached, although if she is engaged to be married he would not monopolize her. He does not have to dance with all the bridesmaids. That is the ushers' job, though it would be a nice gesture to dance once with each of them, especially if he sees one of them sitting alone.

The ushers need not confine their attention to the bridesmaids, but might offer to dance with any of the lady guests, especially those who are tapping their feet, strumming the table, clapping, or swinging their heads in time to the music, without having yet been invited to dance.

Elderly guests stuck near a loud band can be moved, or the band can be asked to play more quietly, or to play a slow number. Ladies who are sitting with their backs to the band, clearly not interested in the music, might welcome a few minutes conversation instead. Girls or women who are dancing together might be pleased to be introduced to a couple of male dance partners. At the end of the dance or dances the usher or best man should thank the lady and escort her back to her seat.

Any young lady who is stuck with her family on a far table can be invited to join the young people when some of them get up to dance and vacate seats. Similarly teenage children who arrive after the dinner because they were not invited to the full meal can be asked to join the other youngsters. Whether or not the best man dances with all the single lady guests depends on the size of the gathering. It is an option. He should certainly see that no lady is left sitting alone after all the others on her table have got up to dance.

PHOTOGRAPHS

The best man might organize some photographs to be taken out of doors before the meal while there is still good light outside. He will have to retrieve the top hats and gloves if they have previously been taken away. He should summon the bridesmaids and get the ushers to pose with them for photographs. Also he should find grandparents, step-parents, siblings, children, and other VIPs for photographs.

DEPARTURE FOR HONEYMOON

The best man should know the groom's flight and destination but keep the information secret.

He should watch the clock or set a timer on his watch to ensure that the bride and groom do not miss their flight. He should remind the bride and groom when to change clothes, have the going-away outfits ready, and collect the wedding clothes in a protective container with the hire documents.

The best man who has been keeping the documents now hands over the honeymoon travel tickets and passports and he reminds the groom to check that no vital documents have been left in the pockets of the wedding suit or left at home. The best man then ensures that the going-away car arrives, with Just Married adornments. Phone for a hotel porter or despatch ushers to carry the honeymoon luggage to the car. Call the family to wave goodbye to the honeymoon couple and clear a path through the crowd so the couple can reach the car. Give the groom the car keys, or drive the couple to the airport. Return the groom's car to the couple's new home and return to the scene of the reception.

Alternatively he could drive the couple to their honeymoon hotel. Sign in for them. Check that champagne is waiting for them on ice in their bedroom. Check that luggage is in the room or send up the bellboy immediately with the luggage.

If the couple are staying the night at the same hotel as the one where the reception is held, he can arrange to have leftover food and drink kept for the couple, as a midnight feast or breakfast in bed.

CLEARING UP

Return to the reception hall and collect telemessages, wedding presents and any found items. Report any lost items to caterers, cleaning staff, and hotel management.

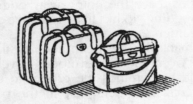

INFORMAL WEDDINGS

A best man is still usually required at an informal wedding, though if there are no bridesmaids, and/or not more than fifty guests, it is not necessary to have ushers.

The informal wedding is less demanding in terms of finance and etiquette. However, it offers more opportunity for ingenuity in finding ways to make the occasion personal and special. The do-it-yourself wedding is great fun.

PREPARING THE CAR

The best man should clean the car. He may have to take his own car or the groom's to a carwash. Fill the car up with petrol. Clean out the car interior. Clean the car boot and if it is dirty line it with old cleaned carpet. Place a large golfing umbrella in the boot just in case it rains. Borrow a big umbrella if you do not have one, or buy one from an umbrella specialist, or the lost and found departments of the London Underground. A large black umbrella can be decorated with white or silver decorations. A large white one could be decorated with flowers to match the bride's outfit and used as a parasol if it is sunny. Or simply tie a couple of white balloons to the handle.

CLOTHES

Clean your shoes, and have your suit cleaned – or hire one or even treat yourself to a new one. Buy a new shirt. Select a tie and socks.

PHOTOGRAPHS

Bring a camera and some spare film. See if a local camera shop stocks cheaper film in bulk.

AT THE CHURCH

Drive the groom to the church. Accompany the maid of honour, if there is one, in the Recession. Drive the couple back home or to the reception. If they are going away, drive them to the airport and plan to collect them on their return.

THE RECEPTION

At the reception gather the guests for the cake-cutting and group photos. Remind the groom to thank his in-laws personally. Have some spare alcoholic drink available. Keep spare coins for phone boxes and cash for emergency purchases.

Buy the first round of drinks at the bar. Organize a surreptitious whip-round for more drink, take-away food, or a gift for the couple.

When they leave for the honeymoon, remind the bride

and groom to phone home to absent relatives such as divorced parents. Fetch coats for the guests. Check that everyone has a lift home. Or persuade them to club together for a minicab. Walk people who live nearby home.

Finally clean the Just Married sign off the car belonging to yourself or the groom.

DUTIES FOR DIFFERENT CEREMONIES AND CUSTOMS

When you are attending a wedding in another country or one hosted by the bride's parents who are from another country, you should be prepared for the customs of their weddings. If you are involved in planning a wedding in the UK at which the bride's family from abroad will be attending, you need to make sure that the incoming best man or ushers know how our customs differ. It would be a nice gesture to incorporate some of the rituals which will be familiar to them.

ROMAN CATHOLIC WEDDINGS

The best man, as in other marriage ceremonies, accompanies the groom and safeguards the ring or rings before handing these over to the priest at the correct time in the ceremony. Most commonly the best man and groom arrive at the church about 20 minutes before the bride and wait at the front right-hand side of the church for the bride. An alternative Entrance Rite is for the best man, groom and bridesmaids to await the bride at the church door, where they are greeted by the priest. A procession to the altar then ensues, led by the priest and other officials, followed by the bride and groom, the best man, bridesmaids, and the parents of bride and groom.

ORTHODOX ETHNIC WEDDINGS

The ushers may have to explain to non-Jewish guests that men entering the synagogue are expected to wear head-coverings, but non-Jews are not obliged to wear a prayer-shawl. It would be a thoughtful gesture to ensure that non-Jewish visitors have somebody Jewish next to them who can explain what will happen. At the most orthodox synagogues men and women sit separately. In ultra-orthodox communities women wear a head covering too. You do not kneel in a synagogue, but simply stand and sit when the others do.

Headcovering for guests is provided by the host. In the synagogue men wear headcovering and prayer shawls. Paper skullcaps called couples or kipot (Hebrew plural) may be provided on a table by the door for any guests who have forgotten theirs, or for non-Jewish friends. If you are not wearing a top hat as a member of the bridal party, you will probably want to wear your own more elaborate embroidered velvet couple. Get it out in advance and check that it is in good condition and does not need sewing, cleaning or ironing. If you want a new one they can be bought from Jewish shops specializing in religious gifts. You may need a hair grip to keep the hat on your hair.

During the ceremony, and when attending the syna-gogue the week beforehand, the groom may have to recite in Hebrew, and the best man might help him practise this in advance.

The orthodox seating tradition is for the bride's family to sit on the right but reform communities reverse this. There are four systems of procession. (Details in books obtainable from the Jewish Museum and Bookshop, London, which also runs a video about Jewish customs.) Under the canopy the best man stands on the left, beind or beside the groom.

Remind the groom that he has to place the ring on the bride's index or pointing finger – which is chosen so that she can show the ring to the witnesses. The ring must belong to the groom. So if the second ring is used because the real ring is too small or gets lost (see Troubleshooting guide) any extra inexpensive ring belonging to the groom would be acceptable – providing the bride accepts it. This would be better than a ring borrowed from his mother which she might decide to reclaim after giving it to him. The groom might want to carry a spare signet ring, or entrust it to the best man.

The Hebrew marriage document is signed after the ceremony at reform synagogues. The best man will hand over the fees including any travel expenses to the rabbi and cantor (singer) after the ceremony in a sealed envelope.

At the wedding reception the best man does not stand in the receiving line. At the reception you may have to satisfy the more orthodox elderly guests as to whether their kosher food has been provided if the rest of the guests are not getting kosher food.

EUROPEAN VARIATIONS

The wedding car will not necessarily be decorated in the British manner in other countries of Europe. It could have a pink or white bow tied to the car radio aerial, and more bows tied to door handles and anything to which a bow can be attached.

FRENCH

The best man is called the *garçon d'honneur*. During the wedding reception the bride may expose the garter on her leg. The men in the audience shout out offers of money if she will raise the garter higher up the leg and lift her skirt to expose more leg. While perhaps the very richest families would not do this, for the average couple it is a popular way of obtaining money to make a better start in life and pay for the honeymoon and spending money. The immediate family and closest friends, such as the best man, will shout more often and louder, and offer larger denominations of money when the garter is very high up the thigh and the auction is more intense.

GREEK ORTHODOX

Note the position the best man stands in church – slightly behind the groom because the best man has to change over the head-dress worn by the bride and groom which is swapped symbolically. The best man is invited to choose the bridal couple's child's name and will give presents to the child.

AMERICAN

In America a wedding rehearsal is held the day before the wedding and a rehearsal dinner is held the night before the wedding. The Bachelor Dinner is held two nights before the wedding, so that it takes place when everyone is in town. The day after the wedding a breakfast is held for the departing guests by the groom's family – no speeches here.

The groom wears one colour, perhaps a white tuxedo to match the bride's white dress, while the best man wears another colour such as grey. Or the groom can wear light grey, the best man and ushers (also known as groomsmen) dark grey. The tuxedo is a dinner jacket – a 'regular' suit jacket or tails. Matching the jacket are white, black or grey trousers – sometimes grey with a stripe.

White shirts are standard wear, but coloured shirts were previously worn, with pink being popular. Swathes of black are appearing on sophisticated evening gowns for girls, so black jackets for their escorts' suits may make a comeback. Keep watching the advertisements in bridal magazines for the latest fashion. The ushers wear ties of the colour matching the bridesmaids' gowns – usually bow ties, possibly cummerbunds in the same colour, or sashes.

At a less formal wedding men wear a suit in black, white, tan or light grey. The white shirt may have many pleats down the front. An Ascot neckerchief, or cravat, might be worn.

For a fancy wedding the groom wears a top hat and carries a cane, and sometimes the best man and all the ushers do so too, and the bridesmaids wear hats.

THE WEDDING CEREMONY

At a large wedding there may be a professional paid wedding organizer. The best man wears a gardenia; each usher has a carnation in his buttonhole. This is called a 'boutonnière'. In a church the head usher takes the best man's and groom's boutonnière to the vestry. The best man pays 'the officiant' either before or after the ceremony.

THE BEST MAN'S WEDDING RECEPTION SPEECH

At the wedding reception the best man gives the first toast to the bride or groom as soon as the champagne is poured. A longer speech is optional and often has a fairly impromptu air, although he may have made notes and privately gone over what he wanted to say beforehand. A summary or expansion of what he and others said at the bachelor party will be news to the rest of the audience. The speech features the bride and groom. He might talk about how he met the groom, how the groom has changed, what they have done together and why they are good friends.

Then he will mention the bride, explaining that when he first saw her he was so impressed that he wondered 'what does such a lovely girl see in you, my brother?', which is supposed to make the bride look better by comparison. Finally he might wish 'my brother and his lovely wife luck, love and happiness,' or 'peace and harmony,' or 'everlasting love and happiness'.

HOMOSEXUAL MARRIAGES

Homosexual marriages are conducted in communities such as San Francisco, usually by ministers who are themselves homosexual. Is there a best man or 'third man', a fourth man, or a groom's maid? Since the homosexual marriage is a recent innovation there is no tradition which you are obliged to follow. Certainly ushers can follow the practice of directing families and friends of each partner to the appropriate side of the church to join those they already know.

ISRAELI

A British boy marrying in Israel would have a best man although Israelis have no best men or ushers. The bridal car, carriage, or tractor, is decorated with flowers.

Weddings are often held outdoors with a canopy held aloft over the bridal couple. Check whether the canopy will be fixed in the ground on poles or held up. If it is to be hand-held, your four canopy holders should be lads of similar strength and height, and should practise co-ordinating.

Check the appropriate clothing. Men in the immediate

family wear suits and ties. On an Israeli kibbutz in the hot summer the guests might arrive wearing shorts. Extra food is prepared because food is inexpensive and catering is not elaborate, so uninvited friends of guests are welcome.

MIDDLE EASTERN AND ARABIC

In Tunisia you may be in a wedding reception hall with men only, while the bride sits in state on a throne with the women in another hall.

As always make yourself agreeable by finding out whether there is anything you can do to help and expressing an interest in the family, but find out about local etiquette. In some countries you should enquire after the health of a man's family. Do not pay direct compliments to or about his wife, as this will offend him or at least make him distinctly nervous. That is like saying to an Englishman, 'I've noticed that your wife is extremely attractive, and has lots of sex appeal. She's very interesting. In fact, I rather fancy your wife.'

A way round this, if you do not know the bride well, is to ask the bride's fiancé or father, 'Tell me about yourself and the bride and her/your family', or 'Tell me more about your daughter/your new wife and where she has been/will be living.' When you learn of her talents and achievements you can say to the bride's father, 'You must be very proud of her and her good work,' or 'She is a credit to you'; to the groom's parents, 'She will be a credit to your family'; or to the groom, 'I am very pleased for you,' or 'She will be a credit to you'.

In some communities you should not ask too closely about the future plans and hopes because this might bring bad luck (the evil eye), and because only God can decide the future. Remarks by your host and yourself may be prefaced by 'God willing ... we/you/they will ...'. When you have established the rules, you can brief other ushers or guests from your home as to correct behaviour. If they act inappropriately it may be better to explain their actions to your hosts, rather than making the guests unduly embarrassed after the event.

In some Middle Eastern and European countries you are expected to pin money onto the dress of the bride as a wedding present. Have a supply of paper money ready – crisp, clean new notes.

HINDU

Remove shoes when entering a temple – a general practice in very hot countries. On entering a Hindu temple every person rings a bell to inform the God of their arrival. The Hindu groom traditionally tied a ribbon around the bride's neck and ties a knot in it – hence our saying tying the marriage knot. Parsees tie the groom's hand with a seven-stranded cord, seven being a sacred number.

AFTER THE PARTY

After the party it seems as though everything is over, but for the wedding couple their life together is just beginning; and if you are the groom's best man you have proven yourself to be his most stalwart ally, and a reliable and trustworthy new friend for the bride. Your lifelong relationship with them as a married couple is just starting.

Back at the hotel where the reception is held you may be called to collect lost and found items. Technically the guests should depart after the bride and groom have left, and the hotel or hall may wish to lock up. But guests do not necessarily want to go back to their homes or work, leaving family and friends they have not seen for years. You must politely persuade happy guests to leave. If you wish, ask some of them back to your home (providing this does not rival a similar invitation to call at the bride's mother's home).

TRANSPORT

See that anyone inebriated is sent home safely in a taxi or under the care of a more sober driver. See the elderly or single safely to their homes by arranging lifts for them if they live at a distance, or take them back yourself if they live near your home.

CLOTHES

The morning after the party you will return your own and the groom's hired clothes to the hire company. Or you can take your clothes and his to the cleaners, later collecting them and returning the groom's clothes to his new home.

GIFTS

If you have been safeguarding presents which were delivered on the day to the reception hotel, or displayed there, you will take these to the groom's home immediately, or keep them at yours since it is safer in an inhabited house, and deliver them to the groom's home on the day he is due back.

The groom may ask the best man to order flowers, pot plants, a garden bush, or a fruit tree to be sent to the bride's mother with a thank you note from the groom the day after the wedding. This can be done through Interflora, and would be a nice gesture in winter or spring. However, there may be numerous flowers left over from the wedding, or the bride's mother might have an abundance of flowers in her own garden if it is summer time.

An alternative would be to send a large box of chocolates, a bowl of exotic fruit, a personalized gift, theatre, opera or ballet tickets, or a book or gift featuring the lady's favourite hobby or pastime. The best man might be able to suggest this to the groom, as well as making the necessary arrangements, and to find out what would please the bride's mother.

Personalized gifts are advertised in bridal magazines and Christmas catalogues, charity catalogues, mail order catalogues, and by mail order companies advertising in the popular tabloid newspapers as well as the heavy Sunday papers and their magazines, and general women's magazines. Libraries keep reference books listing major companies, department stores which deliver worldwide, brand names and products, plus specialist magazines advertising mail order goods. A handsome picture frame for the wedding photographs would certainly be useful.

NEWSPAPERS

You will need black and white photographs if you wish to send them to local newspapers. Newspapers can convert colour prints to black and white but this costs them time and money. If the local paper did not send a photographer you might like to despatch to the newspaper a wedding photograph and a typed note of who married whom, when, where, in what clothes, and where the honeymoon will be. Look at a previous issue of the paper to see how much detail they give. If you can mention the bride or groom's school or workplace, or where they will be working, that might increase your chances of getting them mentioned in the paper. If the bride or groom or either of their parents works in a local restaurant or large office or factory, that will be of interest to many of the newspaper's readers. Any minor disaster or narrowly averted calamity, (the car broke down on the way to church and the milkman gave the bride a lift!) should make the news page of the local paper, or one of the more popular nationals.

This information should reach the newspaper as fast as possible, while it is still news. You may wish to phone the newspaper to check their deadline and take the typed copy and photograph round to the newspaper in person.

Check when the vital edition of the paper will be

appearing and buy at least one copy, preferably several. You might want to send clippings to relatives abroad, bridesmaids, ushers, and others, or have an extra copy to pin on the notice board where the bride and groom work.

THANK YOU NOTE

Finally you will thank the groom and bride in person and/or in writing for bestowing on you the honour of being their best man, or usher, for a delightful day, and for their thoughtful gift to you which you will treasure.

AFTER THE HONEYMOON

WHEN THE BRIDAL COUPLE RETURN

Naturally if you are the groom's best friend, immediately after the honeymoon either you will telephone him to ask how he enjoyed the destination and holiday, or he will phone you.

UNFINISHED NEW HOME

If the builders and decorators have not kept to schedule the bridal couple might return from honeymoon to find their home not complete. The builder's excuse might be sickness, lack of staff, or the non-arrival of some vital part such as the cooker. The best man, if the bride and groom's parents are not nearby, could check that all is well while they are away, chase up the builders or supplier, and fix things up for the day of their return. He can turn on the heating, deliver flowers, fruit, milk, or food, and leave a note welcoming them back. He could also offer to invite them around for a snack or sandwich, or encourage the maid of honour to do so. Another possibility is to form the ushers into a painting party before or immediately after the couple's return to get at least one room ready.

NO PHOTOGRAPHS

Photographs can fail to arrive for a variety of reasons, such as the non-appearance of the photographer, the camera jamming, the flash failing, the batteries running out. Guests forget cameras, and run out of film. The pictures may be taken out of focus, with heads cut off, or the camera wasn't loaded.

Wedding photographs can be re-taken at a photographer's studio, the bride's home or the hotel or other location, after the honeymoon. This is quite a common practice in America where the time-consuming posing of photographs by professional photographers would unduly delay the wedding reception.

Have a professional photographer in addition to your amateur photographers, but make sure you are not committed in advance to buying several expensive photographs. The photographer may charge such high prices that only a small number of framed photographs are ordered. Wedding guests may wish to pay the photographer for duplicates. But instead or in addition amateur snaps can be duplicated and given to the guests at less or no cost.

It is best to inform the local newspapers in advance so they can send their own photographer. Newspapers will sell photos to the public on request. Don't rely on the newspaper photographer's attendance. Any major event in the vicinity will deflect the photographer to news coverage. If the reception is in one district and the bride and groom live in adjoining areas, you may be able to inform more than one newspaper.

Duplicate copies of the local newspaper can be bought on the day of publication or later – usually for a slightly higher fee. With a bit of ingenuity the newspaper's front page masthead and the account of the wedding can be pasted together and photocopied to make a wedding poster, and reduced in size for sending airmail to relatives abroad.

The bride who is disappointed because she has no wedding day photograph will cheer up considerably if a posed wedding portrait is transferred to a souvenir wedding plate. Bridal magazines carry advertisements for such services. So do certain photographic suppliers, who duplicate photos and transfer them onto tablemats, greeting cards, and Christmas cards, particularly around Christmas time.

POST HONEYMOON FILM SHOW

Normally the bride and groom will be keen to entertain in their new home and will first hold a get-together to show their honeymoon slides, photos or videos. Naturally you will take round your photographs of the wedding and settle up any financial or practical arrangements, such as return of the deposit for the groom's hire clothes, or the receipt for the cleaning of the clothes for which he will reimburse you. You will be returning the tele-messages and any other leftover items from the wedding. You may be required to load a projector or video screen for the slide film show.

WEDDING ANNIVERSARIES

You will want to send the bridal couple a card on their first wedding anniversary, when they may be holding a party to eat a tier of the cake they have saved. It is a good idea to contact the groom in advance and subtly remind him of the forthcoming date, and perhaps enquire what he will be getting his wife. If he has no idea you might tell him what the traditional anniversary symbol is. If the bride and groom hold a party each year, these are the appropriate presents.

WEDDING ANNIVERSARY GIFTS

	Traditional/Modern
1st	Paper/clocks
2nd	Cotton/china
3rd	Leather/crystal/glass
4th	Books/electrical appliances
5th	Wood/silverware
6th	Sugar, chocolates/wood The 'Wooden Wedding'
7th	Wool, copper/desk sets
8th	Bronze, pottery/linens, laces
9th	Pottery, willow/leather
10th	Tin, aluminium/diamond jewellery The 'Tin Wedding'
11th	Steel/fashion jewellery
12th	Silk, linen/pearls, coloured gemstones
13th	Lace/textiles and furs
14th	Ivory/gold jewellery
15th	Crystal/watches The 'Crystal Wedding'
20th	China/platinum The 'China Wedding'
25th	Silver The 'Silver Wedding'
30th	Pearl/diamond
35th	Coral/jade
40th	Ruby The 'Ruby Wedding'
45th	Sapphire
50th	Gold The 'Golden Wedding'
55th	Emerald
60th	Diamond The 'Diamond Wedding'
75th	Second Diamond

ONCE MORE?

The best man may have muddled through doing the minimum the first time around, or surprised and pleased both his family and friends by his efficiency. Either way, it is always easier to be best man the second time. If there is anything you would do better on a future occasion, make a note of it – or send a note to the publisher of this book so that we can incorporate your suggestions in future editions. Make a file labelled Weddings, if you have not done so already, and keep a copy of your speech, names of dress hire companies, music groups, the master of ceremonies, caterers and other suppliers. While it is fresh in your mind, note whether you would avoid choosing them again, ask them to do things differently, or highly recommend them rather than any rivals who might be considered.

If you have shown yourself to be an efficient best man and an amusing speaker, perhaps you will be asked to be best man again. If the chief bridesmaid has caught your eye, or the bride's sister, or the happiness of the bridal couple has convinced you that it is time to settle down, perhaps you will get engaged and choose the groom to be your best man!

TROUBLESHOOTING GUIDE

PREVENTING AND DEALING WITH MISHAPS

Most mishaps at weddings are minor ones. Momentary embarrassments have included the missing ring, a missing organist, and microphones which don't work, difficulties which can soon be solved. There have also been reports of weddings where the minister refused to marry the bride, or the wedding party guests were arrested for fighting! More serious difficulties at weddings of my family and friends have included missing wedding luggage (which appeared from the hotel luggage room at the end of the honeymoon), and wedding presents stolen from the boot of the car in the reception hotel car park.

The best way to prevent or put right these problems is to anticipate them and have contingency plans. Those who organize events regularly, whether caterers, or hotel managers, automatically arrange for a back-up plan to cover eventualities they have previously experienced, to guard against financial loss and guarantee goodwill. If you can learn from the mistakes of others you can avoid encountering major difficulties yourself, and you will have the confidence to face small hassles calmly and deal with them quickly.

THE WEDDING CEREMONY

LATE BRIDE

Brides are often a little late. Exceptional lateness can be caused because the bride's car will not start, because town-centre traffic or a road accident is blocking the main road, or the hire car company has taken the bride to the wrong church.

A quick phone call to the bride's home around the time you expect her to leave, and/or after she should have left, will give you a clue as to what has happened. If she is arriving in an ordinary hire car, it should have a car phone so phone the head office and ask them to radio to the car to find out where the car and bride are.

You can fill in time by getting the organist to play more music, and send the ushers around talking to the guests and explaining what is happening before they get agitated.

CEREMONY ETIQUETTE

The minister and church authorities may object to the throwing of confetti (creating litter) the making of a video in church, or the recording of the choir, who may ask for additional fees. Check these points in advance. It may be possible to throw rice (an Indian custom) or flower petals rather than confetti, or to take the video of the couple entering church and the procession after the end of the ceremony itself.

REPLACING A LOST RING

Check that the ring is the right size for the bride. If she has put on weight the ring may be too tight. Her fingers may swell in summer time. See that the ring is insured. Store it in a safe place. Move it into a secure pocket immediately before the ceremony. Some jewellers will provide a spare ring of nominal value just in case. In theory if the ring is forgotten or lost inside the coat during the ceremony – or rolls off down the aisle, time can be saved by passing the bride another ring.

However, the ring is supposed to be a token of the groom's offer to support the bride financially, and a Jewish marriage may be invalid if the ring does not belong to the groom or his family, or the bride is misled as to the value of the ring. The best solution is for a spare ring to be worn by the groom's mother, which can be swapped over later.

AN INVALID CEREMONY

If the wording is incorrect, or the best man ends up married to the bride, the ceremony can be repeated immediately. If it is discovered at a later date that the ceremony was invalid, if the minister was bogus, for example, it can be repeated at the time of discovery.

SPILT WINE

The worst problem is red wine – on a white dress. You might ignore this and leave the problem to the maid of honour – unless it's your glass of wine which got spilt over the bride's dress. Perhaps champagne or sparkling white wine is chosen for weddings for good reason.

The Jewish groom and bride however sip a cup of red wine during the wedding ceremony. This is supposed to add joy to the occasion, not to be a test of steady hands and good housekeeping.

If the groom or bride spill wine, first she should wash the stained area immediately. If the bride has a dress made to order she can carry a handkerchief of the same material, and in the event of a mishap this can be pinned or sewn over the stain to look like a pocket.

If the accident happens late in the day the bride can change into her going-away outfit early. A professional photographer will have taken photographs all day, starting with the bride in her dress at home with her parents before she leaves for the wedding ceremony, so there should be some photographs of her in the immaculate dress.

NO ORGANIST

It would be useful to have the home phone number of the organist and any stand-in who can take over if the organist falls sick. If your guests include musicians there may be one who plays the church organ and can take over.

CHANGE OF MINISTER

Sickness in the family – anything from bridesmaids with chickenpox, to the death of a parishioner requiring the minister's attendance at a funeral, can mean that the date chosen for the wedding is no longer possible for the preferred minister. It is a good idea for the best man, groom and bride to meet other ministers to the same congregation so that they feel at ease if there is a last minute change.

TODDLER HORRORS

Babies and toddlers can cry through the ceremony, crawl the wrong way up the aisle, laugh or wet themselves, fight over the ring, injure themselves on rose thorns, eat the icing off the wedding cake, or merely turn up when uninvited. But the bride loves the little darlings, doesn't she? So the bride's sister, the little darlings' mother, will tell you.

During the wedding ceremony ushers should seat guests with babies and young children in aisle seats for a quick exit and as near the back as possible. Alternatively a children's corner can be created with a nanny or childminder while the parents are engrossed in the ceremony. (You'll need to check with the officiating minister if this is possible.) Ushers and other uncles and close friends should have child-distracting toys or games ready. At the first whimper the child can be removed. If the parent asks why you can explain that you thought the little darling was crying because he wanted to go to the toilet.

At a hotel wedding reception the tinies can enjoy a separate room with special treats for them. Ushers at the exit door of the kiddie room and the entrance door to the main hall can fetch parents to the kiddie room if the children want their parents.

If the wedding reception is held at home the children can be placed in a separate room with children's size tables and chairs, suitable foods, and entertainment. The bride should visit them at some point so they can see her, and be photographed with her, preferably before they are covered with sticky cake.

NO CAR

If the groom's hire car fails to turn up in time, or his own car refuses to start or runs out of petrol, the best man must be prepared to provide transport quickly by paying for a taxi or using his own car, which of course is in perfect running order and filled up with petrol. If the best man's car is not nearby he calls upon his mother, father, the groom's father or brother, his own or the groom's boss or employee, landlord, a passing police car, or whatever his initiative suggests.

PARKING TICKET

Everybody loves a lover and most people love weddings. You can get away with anything if you're in the process of getting married. One bridal attendant received a parking ticket while the wedding ceremony was in progress, but when he explained the circumstances to the police they tore up his parking ticket!

THE WEDDING RECEPTION

SHORTAGE OF DRINK

If you run out of drink, go home and raid your drinks cupboard, or get front doorkeys and go to the bride's father's house for extra drink. Drive to the nearest off-licence and get more drink and glasses. At a sit-down dinner, caterers usually allow a certain number of bottles per table. Some hotels providing catering will not permit you to take in your own drinks. Others are flexible. If just a small number of elderly guests want port or after-dinner liqueurs which were not in the original budget, you may need to obtain some.

LEFTOVER DRINK

The groom or bride's father or whoever is paying for the wedding should have discussed what will happen to opened or unopened bottles of drink. Are these provided on sale or return basis, perks for the caterer's staff, or paid for whether used or not by the host and therefore his property to take away? If the latter is the case the leftover bubbly can be collected and given to the newly weds in their honeymoon suite, sent to their new home or delivered to the father-in-law who has paid for the wedding.

Similar questions can be raised concerning the flowers. Can the cost of church flowers be divided between the two or more wedding groups using the same church? Can the cost of table decorations be divided between two wedding parties using the same hotel restaurant on the same day? If not, are the flowers merely hired, or are they the property of whoever pays for the wedding?

If flowers belong to a groom who is paying for his second marriage, he may wish to have leftover flower displays sent up to his honeymoon suite, given to his mother, mother-in-law and bridesmaids, distributed among the guests, or saved for planting in his garden or placed on the windowsill of his new home. If the groom is flying off, the best man might assist the bride's mother, with the help of the ushers, in distributing the flowers.

SHORTAGE OF STAFF

At one wedding the caterers unfortunately placed the food buffet style although a sit-down dinner had been ordered. The caterer said there were not sufficient staff to serve all the food at the tables, and staff had been paid to serve a buffet, but not wait at table. As many guests had travelled distances, and elderly relatives were expecting a sit-down dinner, this was not acceptable. The bridal group considered asking the hotel management to supply extra staff. They could also have had the ushers deliver platters to every table, but this would have meant they had to leave the top table and female guests alone at the young people's table.

The solution reached was that the ushers placed *hors d'oeuvres* platters on the dinner tables. The bride's father tipped the serving staff extra to wait at table providing the main course and dessert. The financial dispute with the caterer was sorted out later.

MISSING OR MARRED CLOTHES

Cuff-links can be replaced with others, and big buttons replaced by smaller buttons – the chances are most people will not notice. If major items go missing the possible remedies are to go home and look again, buy, borrow, or improvise. Large hotels sometimes keep spare ties and bow ties for restaurant guests.

If the reception is being held at a grand hotel where the honeymoon couple will be staying for the first night of their honeymoon, your guests probably include VIPs already well known to the staff. But it is always worthwhile getting to know the head receptionist, hotel duty manager, restaurant manager or head chef. Then if a problem occurs later you will feel at ease phoning your contact on the hotel's internal phone or going round to see them.

You will be surprised at the staff's helpfulness and ingenuity in solving problems. A missing buttonhole can be replaced by one from the hotel garden, or a flower arrangement replaced by a girl who has much more skill with a piece of wire and tin foil than you would have. A professional chef can rescue the sinking wedding cake in a trice. A trainee waiter will be delighted to demonstrate napkin folding and make hats for small children.

LOST RINGS – AGAIN!

The best man is not the only one who might lose a ring, but he can be trusted to help if a ring is lost. The best man might suggest engraving the rings with the owner's name, and he may be able to track down missing rings – about which the public seems singularly sympathetic.

Engraving his and hers wedding rings with the names of the bride and groom and dates of the marriage is not a one hundred per cent guarantee that a determined thief will be discouraged from keeping or disposing of rings.

But it does help a public-spirited finder to trace the grateful loser.

The groom's receipt for the ring, the valuation for insurance, and a photograph of the ring on the bride's hand, will be useful in advertising a reward, issuing notice of the loss to the police, claiming insurance for a loss, or obtaining an identical replacement.

A guest lost a ring which she had left in the hotel bedroom and hesitated to ask the chamber maid in case she thought she was being accused of stealing it. She told the best man who had no hesitation in asking the hotel if anyone knew where it was. The hotel staff showed her they had merely placed it for safekeeping in the top drawer of the bedside table. Top marks go to the hotel whose member of staff found a man's wedding ring left behind on the hotel bedroom washbasin, and rushed to return it to him at the local airport.

A LOST SPEECH

You should keep duplicate copies of your speech and the groom's in a place where the duplicates can be found in a hurry. A long speech is best retrieved. If the speech is short you will have to extemporize. The rehearsal of the speech the night before will alert you to the location, or absence of the vital notes, and the rehearsal will enable you to remember the gist of both speeches.

DRUNK, SICK OR SILENT GROOM

The drunk groom or guest can be sobered up with water, food, and coffee. Prevention is better than cure. If a drunk groom gets to the microphone you will have to get him away as fast as possible. Pretend the groom was joking. If necessary switch off the microphone or the amplifier and get the band to strike up. Improvise something such as, 'I don't know if you all caught that, the groom actually said, in Esperanto, that he wanted everyone to start dancing.'

The sick groom or guest can be removed to the cloakroom or taken to a bedroom to lie down. You can say he just went out for some fresh air and will be back shortly. If he looks seriously ill of course phone your home doctor, the ambulance service, or get the hotel to call a doctor. If you have a large number of guests you can appeal for a doctor or nurse. This may alarm the other guests. As soon as possible put their minds at rest by informing them that nobody is about to drop dead in their midst. Tell them if the guest will rejoin them shortly, has gone home, or been taken to hospital. If he regularly has such turns and recovers from them they will be glad to know that too.

If the groom is totally silent when he should give a speech you will have to say something funny to cover up. For example, 'He promised he would not give a long speech, and he didn't. Would you like to hear it again? It was better the second time, wasn't it?' or, 'He's shy and hates making speeches so as I am the best man I am going to thank (name) and propose the toast,' or 'He's the strong silent type, but he just muttered to me that if he's employing me as best man, I should do the work of speechmaking!'

STOPPING ARGUMENTS AND PREVENTING FIGHTS

Saying 'Come outside' has many advantages. By the time you get outside the argument may not seem so serious. Insults repeated in front of a lamp-post are not so annoying as those said in front of your family and friends. The dangers of wrecking the hotel property, the decorations, or picking up wine and food and throwing are reduced. The cause of the dispute may have been left behind. Other guests are not drawn into a fight which can become a free for all. You can offer some threat, bribe, or apology you might not make in front of others.

MISSING PERSONS

Keep a check on the whereabouts of the bridal group, and notice if any of the chairs at the wedding dinner remain unoccupied in case a guest has got lost. If the bride's mother's house has an answering machine, check back for incoming messages from anybody who has got lost – they may say that have given up and gone back to their hotel, in which case you can contact them.

Outgoing messages should not reveal that the family is away but say that you are very busy and if the caller wants to check wedding arrangements call the number of the hotel where the reception is held. That will give anybody who is calling to say they are lost a number from which they can obtain directions to the hall.

ENTERTAINERS

Entertainers should be selected by going to hear them play, and instructing them as to the volume of sound and variety of music required. You need to make it clear how long they are required to play, to find out what will happen regarding substitution if any of the band fall ill. They might break down on the motorway or lose their way. Their equipment could develop faults. If you have a back-up system, such as cassette-playing equipment, friends who have guitars nearby, or if the hotel where the reception is held can supply music tapes and players at short notice, you are well prepared.

MISSING OR STOLEN WEDDING PRESENTS

You will need to list all the presents and their values in order to inform the police and the insurance company. Stolen cheques can be cancelled. Notify the senders and banks immediately. The bride and groom will cheer up if replacement gifts can be ordered from the stores.

FINDING LOST TRAVEL TICKETS

If both the groom and best man think the other has the travel tickets you must reconstruct where you last saw them, the location, and the clothes you were wearing, and where you have been since. Tickets for scheduled flights can be replaced more easily than those for package tours. Given lack of time you will have to try to queue-jump and see supervisors rather than wait in long lines only to be referred elsewhere. Any other documents you may have – such as hotel numbers, phone numbers of travel agents and so on, will be useful.

THE HONEYMOON

Honeymooners like to escape from the cares of home and work and keep their destination a secret from family and colleagues who might phone up and disturb them. Brothers who might play practical jokes are not given hotel phone numbers and addresses. However, if the groom trusts the best man he would give him a number to be contacted in emergencies – such as the illness of a parent at home. Nowadays most ferries, trains, and planes have telephones.

The time when it is hardest to contact a couple is when they are motoring, with hotel destinations picked on a daily basis. One way to contact them as they travel is to put out an appeal over a radio station. If the couple do not hear it on the car radio, they may be identified by hotel staff or hotel guests when they stop.

Another way of contacting the honeymoon couple who are travelling across several countries through Europe or elsewhere is to contact an embassy abroad. They will notify the border-crossing officials who will ask the couple to contact the embassy for information.

HONEYMOON BEDS

Hotels with several ballrooms can hold up to five weddings the same day on a busy Saturday in springtime or summer. The wedding couples may be given a free bedroom in which to change clothes, or a free bedroom in which to stay the night before flying off the next day. The honeymoon couple are sometimes told that they will receive the honeymoon suite with the four-poster bed and/or Jacuzzi or the best available room. If there is only one honeymoon suite with a four-poster bed it can only be given to one of the honeymoon couples, or it may be given to a paying guest, not to any of the honeymoon couples.

PASSPORTS

The usual system is for a bride to apply several weeks in advance for a new passport in her married name to be issued dated for the day of the wedding. The bride can travel with a passport which is still in her maiden name. Many married women continue to use their maiden names.

When the bride, groom, best man or usher urgently needs a new passport because of losing the passport in a burglary or needing to travel unexpectedly because of sudden illness in the family abroad, you will need to provide documentary evidence such as a police report, doctor's letter on headed notepaper, or telegram.

Sometimes passports are left behind when travelling on the honeymoon and again package tour operators may help the honeymoon couple to re-route – to see Niagara Falls from the American rather than the Canadian side for example, or the Canadian side if a US visa has not been obtained. Crossing borders is much easier if you have good evidence of your identity. Passport photos are useful for obtaining identity cards. Advise the groom to take with him identity cards which contain his photograph and signature, a professional membership card, or a driver's licence to show his age and address.

INSTANT CHECKLIST OF BEST MAN'S DUTIES

Although not all of these duties may apply to the wedding you are attending, it is useful to check that these eventualities have all been considered.

BEFORE THE WEDDING

☆ Meet bride, and parents of bride and groom
☆ Appoint ushers or discuss their appointment with groom
☆ Attend engagement party
☆ Organize or attend stag party
☆ Organize or discuss seating at church, register office and reception with bride's mother
☆ Check through necessary documents with groom: reading of banns, marriage licence, marriage certificate
☆ Check through necessary clerical payments with groom: minister, choir, bell ringers, organist
☆ Arrange transport to church for self and groom, and check transport arrangements for bride, and to reception
☆ Arrange hire of clothes for self and groom
☆ Organize buttonholes for self and groom, and ushers
☆ Discuss music, bells, flowers with groom, bride and bride's mother

WEDDING MORNING

☆ Collect hired clothes for self and groom if not before

☆ Dress, and check groom's outfit
☆ Collect buttonholes
☆ Liaise with bride's mother over any last minute chores
☆ Take wedding ring and any honeymoon documents from groom for safekeeping
☆ Entertain groom until ceremony

AT THE CEREMONY

☆ Conduct the groom to the church or register office in good time and take up position
☆ Produce ring when required
☆ Sign register
☆ Join procession out of church
☆ Take part in photographs and help find needed relatives or bridesmaids
☆ Help with transport from the ceremony to the reception

AT THE RECEPTION

☆ Supervise ushers and parking arrangements
☆ Receive and introduce guests
☆ Make speech on behalf of the bridesmaids
☆ Hand over honeymoon tickets, car keys etc. to groom before departure
☆ Organize decoration of car
☆ Supervise loading of luggage

AFTERWARDS

☆ Assist bride's mother in clearing up after the reception
☆ Return hired clothes of self and groom
☆ Take wedding presents to the couple's new home
☆ Check arrangements for couple returning from honeymoon and arrange to meet them or a welcoming gift

PART 4

THE
BRIDESMAIDS

WHEN YOU ARE CHOSEN

You can expect to receive a phone call or a letter with details of the time and place, who will be paying for the bridesmaids' dresses, where you can stay, and so on.

ACCEPTING GRACEFULLY

The tone of your letter depends on how well you know the bride. If she's your best friend she will probably have told you in person or phoned unless you live so far away that she has had to contact you by letter. In that case you just write expressing how happy you feel and follow up by phone as soon as you can.

REFUSING

If expected to pay for your own clothes and unable to meet this cost, you can decline graciously, especially if this would be the third wedding that year and the novelty of being a bridesmaid has worn off.

HANDICAPS AND ILLNESS

There is no reason why wheelchair-bound people should not be able to be bridesmaids. Sisters and friends with permanent disabilities can be included in the ceremony as bridesmaids or other attendants. A mentally handicapped adult who is not eligible as legal witness can still be a bridesmaid.

(See handicapped weddings, blind, deaf and wheelchair users, pages 325–9.)

REFUSAL LETTER AFTER ILLNESS/ ACCIDENT/OPERATION

Dear (bride's first name)
Thank you so much for inviting me to be your bridesmaid. It has made me (and whoever) very very happy to hear your good news. Unfortunately I am still weak after the foot operation and cannot be sure how soon I shall be able to travel and resume normal activities. Rather than disappoint everyone later I shall decline from the outset and plan to attend as your guest. My thoughts are with you. It must be such fun. I'll phone you soon to check that all is going well for the big day. All my/our love

Other reasons for refusing are exams, pregnancy, death in the family or contagious sickness or long illness, and inability to travel with children or leave children behind.

CANCELLED WEDDING

Listen sympathetically until a week has passed and the tiff or cancellation seems permanent. Then unflappably locate lists of gift donors and offer to help write brief notes accompanying returned gifts. Produce the newspaper phone number so the bride can announce the cancellation. The bride-not-to-be returns the engagement ring, engagement presents, shower gifts, wedding presents and is expected to refund the bridesmaids for any deposit on dresses.

Keep in touch to cheer up your friend. 'These things happen. Anyone can make a mistake. It's probably all for the best. There's someone for everyone.'

You cannot expect to be chosen as bridesmaid at the next wedding. The bride might have a smaller wedding and need to choose the groom's sister. She could hold the wedding far away where her new man cannot encounter people discussing her cancelled engagement. If you are chosen again repeating previous plans seems easier, but she may want to start afresh.

CLOTHES

BRIDESMAIDS' DRESS STYLES

Styles must co-ordinate with the bride's dress but also suit the ages of the bridesmaids. Long ago children were dressed like miniature adults, but nowadays the tendency is to have different styles for different ages. For example a fifteen-year-old prefers and looks more appropriate in a reasonably sophisticated dress, not too much like a little girl's frock.

MATRON OF HONOUR'S CLOTHES

The matron of honour's clothes are different from those worn by younger unmarried girls, and may have to look suitable for going to a registrar's office. A matron of honour staying at the bride's house the night before needs a neat outfit for travelling there, with clothes packed in a smart overnight bag or suitcase.

A matron of honour's dress can be bought from the mother-of-the-bride section in bridal wear shops. Needless to say, a lively slim young woman in her twenties doesn't want to dress like a staid stout woman of fifty. An older matron of honour must be distinguishable from the bride's mother if they are similar ages.

The matron of honour may wear something removable to provide the bride with 'something borrowed', such as blue garter or blue brooch. The borrowed item symbolizes friendship, and remains a popular tradition at many weddings.

YOUNGER BRIDESMAIDS

It is well worthwhile choosing an outfit for younger bridesmaids which is suitable for wear afterwards.

FLOWER GIRL

The flower girl can match or dress differently from other bridesmaids as is appropriate, although she often wears white. She carries a small posy or a basket of paper rose petals, basket and flower colours co-ordinating. Flower girls and pages, if paired, could dress in white silk or satin.

PAGEBOY

Pageboy outfits are found in men's outfitters and bridal wear shops. Traditional pageboy outfits have tight pantaloon trousers fastened below the calf with buttons or ribbons. A red velvet suit with a red velvet tie can be hired.

Small boys often wear white, blue or grey miniature lounge suits, sometimes three piece, *i.e.* with a waistcoat. A junior kilt outfit with black velvet jacket looks good if the family is Scottish and the groom also wears a kilt. The jabot, the frill on the shirtfront, and the sporran, the fur-covered pouch hung in front of the kilt, are hired with the outfit. Accessories may be included or could cost extra.

To match a bridesmaid in white and blue a pageboy could wear a blue and white sailor suit. Little Lord

Fauntleroy and Kate Greenaway suits with high waist trousers fit romantic period fashions. Tiny boys are sometimes paired in co-ordinating colours with junior bridesmaids in orange, brown or peach colour satin trousers and peach colour shirts with frills. Baby pink for toddlers, which is rather girlish, can be edged with blue piping.

You can see the different styles such as the Eton suit by writing to hire companies for their leaflets or looking in illustrated dictionaries and encyclopaedias. If you are having bridesmaids' dresses made, velvet pageboy outfits can be designed with lace collars to co-ordinate with the bridesmaids' and bride's dresses.

RING-BEARER

The ring-bearer always dresses in white, goes the tradition, but others say he can be dressed in blue. In summer the ringbearer can be all white, wearing white suit, white shirt, white tie, white socks and white shoes. The ring could be pinned onto a white cushion.

BABY BRIDESMAID

The child's Christening gown can be worn or any frilly white party dress to co-ordinate with the bride if there are no other bridesmaids, or a coloured dress matching other bridesmaids.

COLOURS

The aim is always to co-ordinate with bride's outfit. Any colour goes except all-white which can be confused with the bride and detracts from her uniqueness.

Don't be identical to the bride's colour or clash with it.

A cream-coloured bride's dress might co-ordinate better with a peach colour dress and flowers. Dresses could be in rainbow colours, or graduated shades of the same colour. Two blonde bridesmaids could wear pale blue, two brunettes darker blue or silver grey in the same style.

Bridesmaids in the 1990s wear peach, lilac, lemon, blue, or turquoise dresses. Pink, blue and gold are said to be lucky, and red and green unlucky. Green is considered unlucky in Ireland because it is the fairies' colour and the fairies might steal the wearer away. Superstition should not affect your rational judgement. Deeper colours, the modern fashion, look striking on dark-skinned brides and bridesmaids at sunny outdoor weddings surrounded by brightly coloured plants. Red and white is popular at Christmas time. Red and pure white looks harsh like 'blood and bandages', they say in army-base towns. Ivory white softens the contrast with red and other colours.

Check the church carpet colours and whether red carpet will be laid down, clashing with orange, pink or purple dresses. If so, you could ask the florist to supply white carpet.

BLACK DRESSES

Avoid complete black as it looks like mourning and is less jolly. A few people wish to reverse the trend and wear black at weddings to look sophisticated, and white at funerals to express confidence that the departed was a pure innocent soul who is now in heaven. Until the trend reverses completely this is likely to cause confusion. It also offends conservative grandparents who don't wish to be reminded of funerals and who like the bride in traditional white and bridesmaids in cheerful colours.

Patterned bridesmaids dresses are comparatively rare, though vertical pink and white striped cotton or pink and lavender mottled sheen satin dresses have been chosen. The joins of patterned fabric look neater when separated by piping in a plain colour such as pink along seams.

STYLE

Avoid inadvertently offending others or deliberately disregarding convention. Outfits which appear amusingly different in the shop can look very odd in church and halls full of elderly relatives. You might regret your decision too late on the day.

NECKLINES

Revealingly low necklines are unsuitable in church. If you want a strapless dress for dancing later, wear a bolero or jacket of matching material in church to cover your shoulders, upper arms, and suggestive cleavage. A removable collar can be added to a dress, and another option is to wear a shawl.

Enquire whether the minister objects to sleeveless, strapless dresses, for he might feel you were showing disrespect, making a mockery of him and his church.

In hot countries such as Australia, especially in summer, church authorities may be more easygoing. Unusual wedding outfits were accepted on one occasion by a minister in robes conducting a marriage in Sydney. The bride, wearing a tight white strapless dress, was followed by three bridesmaids in tight black strapless dresses. All the dresses had love heart plunge necklines. This wedding was filmed and replayed on Australian television. The effect was stunning because the bride was exceptionally glamorous.

Brides can marry in less conventional clothing such as flowing white trouser suits in UK register offices.

MAKING THE RIGHT IMPRESSION

Some brides go as far as hiring an image consultant to spend a day or two shopping with the bride and bridesmaids and advising them. On their shopping day the bride and bridesmaids and the consultant visit many stores and come home with notes to discuss what they like most. When the bride or chief bridesmaid particularly like a dress the shop will put it aside for a day or two while you dream about how you look in it.

The bridesmaids' dresses must not clash with the girls' uniform look. The bridesmaids' lipstick will be the same colour as the bride's but can be a darker or lighter shade to tone with their skin colouring. For example, a black bride having a register office wedding chose a white dress with navy trim and a matching hat with navy trim and navy shoes. To brighten the outfit the colour consultant suggested pink lipstick and flowers. The bridesmaids wore pink lipstick in different shades and navy dresses.

Discuss how the style of each dress suits each bridesmaid. The height of the girls affects the style but the length of different parts of her body determines which features should be disguised or enhanced. For example a short girl with long legs might be advised to wear a short jacket to the waist to emphasize her long legs, or not to wear a contrasting colour belt but a self-colour belt of the same material as the dress in order not to cut the body in half but accentuate the upward line. Small girls should avoid large patterns. A print with huge flowers will look odd if there's only room for one complete flower on your bosom. Also consider accessories. A small hat will not dwarf a smaller girl.

Generally a dark-skinned girl wears strong colours, dark colours or bright colours because these suit her skin tone but personality affects this too. A shy girl might prefer quieter colours. White comes in many shades. Ivory is a slightly yellow tinge. There are also grey whites, blue whites, pink whites, and green whites. Accessories can tone in, such as the navy accessories with a blue white.

When asked your opinion do not insult the bride by making her feel she has shortcomings. Avoid saying, 'that would look lovely on someone taller', implying she is too short. Don't upset the shop assistant by saying that a dress is terribly old-fashioned or the price is ridiculously expensive. You may be upsetting a customer who was considering buying it or another girl could emerge from the fitting room wearing it. If asked your opinion simply say to the bride, 'It's not you,' or 'It doesn't suit you'.

SEASONAL CLOTHES

A strapless gown supplied with a matching jacket is useful covering outdoors in cooler weather, or indoors in air conditioning and evening. Otherwise you may need a wrap. Clothing must be adaptable to the time of day. In hot countries it can be hot at noon and chilly at five o'clock after the sun sinks. Fans are handy in scorching weather in summer in Mediterranean countries, the Caribbean, much of the USA, Hong Kong, Japan or China. In the UK romantic fans fit period costumes.

Fabrics are heavier in winter. Bridesmaids could wear velvet dresses with fur trim and overjackets, warm muffs and fur-trimmed hats. For a register office attendants can wear coat-dresses.

THEMES

The reception surroundings and decor can inspire themes, such as Victorian, Edwardian, Art Deco or Roaring Twenties. Locations such as a lake, river or seaside suggest boating and sailor blue. Country gardens inspire green accessories and greenery in a hall or marquee with pillars decorated like trees to resemble a forest.

ALTERATIONS AND FITTING

An appointment is made for fitting dresses which have been made to order. A return visit is made about a week later to check that alterations are correct. When several bridesmaids have dresses of the same length it is well worth making an appointment to ensure that hem lengths are the same.

The alterations department may agree to adapt your dress afterwards so you can wear it again. In wartime dresses were made as blouses and skirts so that one half could be easily adapted for other occasions. The bridesmaid's dress could be altered by shortening the skirt and removing ribbons. Otherwise you could advertise the dresses for sale in local newspapers stating the sizes and colours, or take pictures and place advertisements in local shop windows.

Bridal shops supply dress covers in varying lengths. Clear covers are better for identifying bridesmaids' gowns. A white cover conceals the bride's secret dress. A bridal and ballgown clothing cover, flared to accommodate full skirts, can be bought through dry cleaning shops. It will protect long dresses in wardrobes and is useful for transporting clothes to the bride's house for dressing there on the wedding day or when travelling abroad.

MADE TO MEASURE MAIL ORDER

A London-based bridesmaid went to a wedding in the USA where all the bridesmaids had the same design dress made to measure in advance. She posted a list of her measurements for the dress to the USA. When she arrived in the USA and put the dress on it fitted perfectly. She had bought her own shoes in England which she had dyed to match the swatch of material she was sent.

DYEING ACCESSORIES

Obtain a fabric sample from the dress if you are dyeing shoes to match and send the sample to out-of-town bridesmaids. Plain or moiré silk shoes can be dyed to match dresses or sashes. Satin shoes should retain the sheen to match the dress or sash after dyeing, and cheaper shoes may turn out matt. Ask the dyers in advance if the shoes will retain their texture.

Shoes and clutch bags can be professionally dyed to match several outfits for the big trip to a wedding abroad. Use tea in a stainless steel bowl to dye all the bridesmaids' tights to match and turn shoes, stockings, gloves and lace from white to beige cream colour. Practise on old cloth first.

SHOES

The same shoes should be worn by all the bridesmaids for a uniform appearance. Court shoes and satin pumps are popular for wearing with bridal gowns and bridesmaids' dresses. Clip-on bows individualise the design. Ballet slippers with suede soles can be made up with your own fabric for child or adult bridesmaids (needing half a yard or more fabric per pair).

For weddings and formal occasions such as the rehearsal dinner, do not wear open toes nor backless or strapback shoes because they look too casual. Smart silver and gold strap sandals exposing feet look wrong with clothes that cover women up to the neck and down to the ankle. Edwardian bootees go with Edwardian dresses and bonnets from days when a lady did not expose her ankle, and top hats match Edwardian ladies' long-skirted riding habits.

Choose shoes that are easy to walk and dance in. Ankle straps help to anchor shoes, and you can also roughen the soles with sandpaper so that you do not slip. Wear in new shoes around the house in advance and ease tight leather shoes using a liquid product which stretches shoes while you wear them.

HEEL HEIGHT

A chief bridesmaid who is no taller than the next bridesmaid can wear higher heels to show who has precedence and neatly grade heights in the procession and photographs. One-inch heels with wider bases are better for walking than the spindly two-inch heels, or wobbling on glamorous but impractical three-inch heels.

CHILDREN'S SHOES

Black patent shoes can be worn by the pageboy. Little girls often wear white shoes and white party socks which can be bought from smart dress shops or bridal outfitters, socks made of finest cotton with trimming of lace and little white bows.

HOSIERY

White, ivory or flesh colour stockings and tights can be obtained, patterned with wedding bells, heart and ribbons, horseshoes, glitter hearts, usually on the back of the ankle. A line of pearls can be worn down the back or the outside of the leg. Avoid stockings with black seams.

UNDERCLOTHES

Lingerie will include pretty petticoats designed to be seen when you are dancing. A basque is worn under a strapless dress. Bra straps should be fastened to loops under dress shoulders. Underwear should not show through see-through materials and do not wear black underwear below pale colour dresses. Don't forget the garter!

Frilly underpants may be chosen for girls aged up to six and tomboys likely to do handstands.

ACCESSORIES

Sashes and other accessories might co-ordinate with the colours of the groomsmen's ties and cummerbunds and flower colours. Either give a dress material swatch to the groomsmen when they go to the hirers to get the right shade of blue or pink ties, or have cravats and accessories made up to match the dresses.

GLOVES

At formal weddings with short-sleeved dresses long gloves are worn, with long-sleeved dresses short gloves. An orthodox bride in a short-sleeved dress wears long gloves. From the 1920s until the 1950s a bridesmaid might have worn long gloves with buttons down the centre of the inner forearm. She wore the gloves when shaking hands but removed them from fingers for eating. They were not removed entirely but unbuttoned and the hand covering section was folded inside the forearm section. To match a dress with a net bodice wear net gloves.

JEWELLERY

Bridesmaids wear the minimum of jewellery to achieve a co-ordinated look. Accessories should not destroy the image or period the bride has created. Avoid incongruous colours or styles, no modern jewellery with old world clothes. Don't rival the bride, nor distinguish yourself from the group. Co-ordinate with the bride's jewellery whether gold, silver or two-colour jewellery combining gold and silver. Don't wear three pairs of ear-rings, heavy gold chains around ankles, or jingling bangles which are a distraction during the ceremony and speeches. The bride may be giving you jewellery. (See also Jewish weddings.)

To cover bitten nails you can buy false nails, which should not be obtrusively long. Nine carat gold nails (available at shops or through jewellery and mail order catalogues) are suitable only if the bride wears them.

WATCHES

Don't forget to turn off a watch alarm so it doesn't sound during the ceremony. With evening clothes wear a suitable dress watch *e.g.* goldplated with diamonds or diamante stones set in the watchface. Smart black-face watches with small glinting stones can be found at reasonable cost.

Watches co-ordinating with bridesmaids' dresses are available in solid colours, for example an all pink watch with pink face, pink edge and pink watchstrap can look wonderful. Watches can be bought with five interchangeably coloured bezels to match the bridesmaid's dress and party clothes.

SPECTACLES

Ultra-modern frames are incongruous with period wedding gowns, so the bespectacled bridesmaid may prefer to remove her glasses for the procession. If glasses are needed for reading to sign your name, or driving, keep them in a padded glasses case in a wristbag.

Red glasses look wrong with pink dresses. For ultimate glamour the bride and her sisters can buy glasses in several colours matching dresses for entertaining.

PARASOLS

Pretty parasols, purely decorative in most English summers, are supplied in matching fabrics by bridal wear or accessory shops. When marrying abroad in hot countries parasols are practical for shielding you from sunburn, stickiness and exhaustion, helping you look cool and calm. The Caribbean is subject to sudden showers so a waterproof parasol is handy. Wet monsoon seasons strike South Pacific areas such as Hong Kong, Singapore and Australia.

HEAD-DRESS

Hats with matching handbags can be hired. Hats made to order using dress material or contrasting fabric can be kept or sold back to hat hire shops after one use.

Flower wreaths can be worn in the hair using reasonably priced fresh flowers in spring. Matching flower head-dress and posies can be made of silk flowers, a circlet of flowers for the smaller girls. Shapes include combs with attached flowers and mock pearls, arcs, diadems, glittering tiaras (popular with Indians), circular caps with hanging ribbons, ribbon roses and veils, and huge saucer shape hats.

FLOWERS

Flower colours contrast or co-ordinate with the dresses or overall colour theme *e.g.* red, white and blue; white, yellow and green; or shades of pink to purple in graduating colours.

The bride carries the most dramatic bouquet, the bridesmaids carrying similar but smaller or less elaborate flower arrangements. Bouquets should suit heights and builds of bridesmaids; cascades for tall girls, small flowers in the hair of dainty girls, and affordable flowers on wrists for economy. Pomanders attached to the wrists are convenient when holding the bride's train. It might be a good idea to attach the lightweight flowers a small bridesmaid carries to her wrists with bands of ribbon. Small children need styles which are almost indestructible!

The maid or matron of honour has different flowers from the bridesmaids. If you are slightly pregnant, confide in the bride and perhaps you will be able to hide the bump behind a big bouquet.

The groom pays for the flowers and his mother may accompany you to the flower shop. You have to agree on whether to have fresh or false flowers of silk or other fabric. The main considerations are the cost and avail-ability of fresh flowers (although fresh lilies can be flown in), whether you plan on preserving the bouquet, and whether attendants have allergies.

Different bouquets are provided for honour attend-ants, corsages with street clothes, bouquets with short dresses. Long-stemmed sheaves are carried on the outside arm with flowerheads pointing outwards. Baskets and bouquets are carried in front. Heather is used with Scottish dress. Small girls can carry hoops entwined with ribbons and flowers.

ALLERGY

You don't want to sneeze throughout the ceremony. Hay fever and asthmatic attacks are inconvenient and embar-rassing. The church or register office may be already decorated with flowers so you might have to endure them briefly. Sometimes at the church or synagogue the bride for a following wedding has paid for flowers to be installed, so you might get a nasty surprise! Small flower displays at the reception probably won't affect you providing you are not sitting next to them.

Avoid spending hours carrying a bouquet of fresh flowers. Dried flower bouquets are not necessarily the solution – one bouquet had to be left with a relative for six months until it stopped causing irritation. Fortunately fake flowers can be indistinguishable from real ones, and these are often the answer to this problem.

RING-BEARER CUSHIONS

Ring-bearer cushions are sold in the UK, USA and Australia. The cushion often has a lace frill around the edge, a strap underneath for the hands to hold it when not in use, and two ribbons which can be used to tie on the ring with a bow. The ring cushion can be heart-shape, circular, oval, oblong or square. A heart-shaped motif can be outlined in mock pearls in the centre. The chief bridesmaid may have to carry the cushion and give it to the child at the last moment, or supervise the child holding it. The ring might be tied on in advance, but practise making a neat bow. Alternatively the ring can be tied on in the church entry hall before proceeding. To practical people symbolic rings seem pointless, but are sometimes carried by toddlers to give them a role.

CHECKLIST: clothes

Bridal wear shops:

Name ....

Address .... phone ....

   opening hours .... late night opening ....

   nearest train/parking .... our assistant ....

   dress styles preferred .... cost ....

Shoe shops ....

Groom's clan kilt ....   Toastmaster's clan kilt ....

Scottish thistle and heather buttonholes. Scottish heather in bride's bouquet. Welsh daffodils.

Bridal dress stocklist ....   delivery to shop date ....
fitting date ....   delivery to home date ....

Bride's dress fabric, bride's dress colour; bride's dress style;

Her shoes, head-dress, gloves, tights; bouquet, parasol, jewellery.

Something old ....   Something new ....

Something borrowed ....   Something blue ....

Chief bridesmaid's dress fabric, colour, style, ribbon colour, head-dress, gloves, shoes, tights, jewellery, flowers. Parasol/other accessories ....

Flower girl's dress colour, shoes, tights, flower basket.

Pageboy's outfit, shoes, and accessories (e.g. ring cushion).

Co-ordinating colours: groom and groomsmen's suits, their accessories ....

Mother of bride ....   Mother of groom ....

Matron of honour; female witness;

Church carpet ....   Reception carpet ....

Car colours ....

For travelling and hanging bridesmaid dress covers.

(Bridal dresses should not be stored indefinitely in polythene or they may go yellow.)

Clothes supplier's names and address and phone ....

Delivery date and time ....

Guard of Honour's uniforms and flowers, school scarves, hockey sticks, tennis raquets, golf clubs, fencing swords, swords?

Is bride's father paying for clothes? ....

Insurance (your household policy, bride's wedding insurance policy)

OTHER PRE-WEDDING PLANS

If the bride is a laugh-a-minute, accident-prone type whom you might have to help out of scrapes, get her organized. If you share a bedroom, rearrange it so she has everything to hand in a top drawer with a folder containing vital papers. Give her an address book with reference headings such as Caterers, Florist, Hairdresser and so on to help her keep on top of the job.

You may later be involved in planning transport, speeches, listing gifts the bride receives, plans for supervising children, and giving honeymoon advice. Don't take the bride's wedding decisions for her, but be available to escort her. You might offer, 'Monday is my day off. I can drive you, if you like.'

STATIONERY

Order floral or decorative stationery suitable for writing thank-you cards. You may be asked to help with writing invitations and placecards, too, unless the bride employs professional calligraphers and printed cards. Look at lace-trimmed wedding cards at stationers and printers, and help the bride plan the order of service and music. Cassettes of wedding music are available from music stores.

COMPUTERIZED INVITATIONS AND CARDS

There are computer programmes which design individualized greeting cards in black on white paper or in colour if you have a colour printer. Such programmes can be used on compatible personal computers.

Computer graphics programmes can also create designs such as outsize hearts. Fold them to make heart-shaped cards, or stick cut-out hearts inside a card on horizontally cut folds to make pop-up designs. Outsize cards can be made using a colour photocopying machine which expands the picture size. It is fun experimenting to make a card to present to the bride at a hen party, invitations to surprise parties, a personalized thank you card, or an anniversary card. Small numbers of cards are fun to make and embellish with silver sprinkles, bits of net and lacy ribbon. Personalize invitations with silver writing and borders, spray-on glitter, silver stars, miniature plastic bags of confetti, stick on confetti, or a foil-wrapped chocolate (not in hot weather). Visit Christmas and party shops for ideas. Attach tokens such as silver shoes from cake decorating shops.

For a hundred or more invitations you need grander and less time-consuming cards. Specialized business promotion companies make individual theme designs with pop-up centres, cake, bride and groom, church.

PLACECARDS

Experiment with fibre tip pens or, better, a fountain pen and inexpensive white paper. For placecards use wide oblongs of glossy card. To make a projecting heart draw the heart in colour centrally. Rule a horizontal line half way up outside the heart. Cut the outline of the top half of the heart above the line. Fold the card in half horizontally along the pencil line without folding the heart. Write neatly inside the heart the name of the person who sits there. The wedding date and name of bride and groom can be added in the corner.

SHOPPING

THE GROOM'S GIFT

For the man who always considers himself last when buying presents, buy what he needs. The bride can find out what he would like. If the groom is a student, you could buy smart clothes for his new office job, a matching shirt and tie, personal organizer, or expanding briefcase.

For the man who has everything, you could always follow his sporting interests. There are many accessories or gifts specially for golfers, footballers, fishermen, and so on. Another idea that would be appreciated is a watch. Co-ordinated 'his and hers' watches are available or you could have a design created especially for him. For the practical type, or one who should be more practical, how about an electric drill?

PAGEBOY'S AND JUNIOR BRIDESMAID'S GIFTS

In the UK the groom traditionally buys presents for the ushers and best man. The bride might be asked for advice or be delegated the shopping by a busy groom, especially if she is buying for the pageboys. The smallest children might like a watch decorated with a cartoon character or the lastest hero craze.

The traditional gold or silver bracelet loses its novelty for a small girl who has already been a bridesmaid. However, a charm bracelet allows her to add charms each time. Visit children's shops or use their mail order catalogues.

GIFTS FOR CHILD BRIDESMAIDS

Jewellers sell name necklaces, matching necklace, bracelet and ring sets in silver, and charm bracelets with teddy bear motifs or rocking horses.

GIFTS TO ADULT BRIDESMAIDS

The bride chooses a gift, ideally engraved with the wedding cake or the initials of the recipient. Identical gifts should be given to prevent jealousy unless ages make it impractical. The maid of honour and the best man get larger gifts. Traditional choices are items of value in gold or silver, a heart-shape locket, pendant with charm representing a thimble, scissors (for hairdressers), cat, dog, ballerina, opening boot, saxophone, drum and guitar, darts, ice skate, and football, brooch, compact with light, illuminated make-up mirror, musical jewel box, embroidered jewellery case, engraved picture frame, luggage or clock. Inexpensive silver sets of matching necklace and ear-rings are available. Pick a perfume she likes but cannot afford, a silk scarf, failing all else a gift certificate from her favourite shop.

The older matron of honour who has a home might appreciate a tray, silver candlesticks, a silver religious item or picnic set.

GIFTS TO THE BRIDE AT ENGAGEMENT AND SHOWER PARTIES

The bride might like a ring-minder for the kitchen or bedroom. Silver or gold charm bracelets are suitable. Add charms representing church, opening bible, bride and groom, stork, and I love you.

GIFTS TO BRIDE AND GROOM FROM BRIDESMAIDS

Various shops supply cushions with jokey messages including, 'I'm not perfect but I'm perfect for you', 'If you ever leave me I'm going with you', 'Marriages are made in heaven. So is thunder and lightning', and 'Behind every successful marriage there's a surprised mother-in-law'. For the second marriage perhaps, 'Eat drink and remarry,' or 'Older men make better lovers'. These sayings can also be inscribed in pill/pin boxes.

Brides not employing a photographer, who normally sells an album as part of the package, might like a wedding album. Silver-plated and heart-shape photograph frames are also available.

Large toy and games departments in major stores sell backgammon, playing card sets and green baize tablecloths marked with cards. For the couple who have everything, consider unusual furniture such as a cardtable, rocking chair or hammock. Perhaps best of all, ask what they want.

GIFTS TO BRIDE'S AND GROOM'S PARENTS

Find old family wedding photos. If you find a suitable one you could have it copied, retouched and framed for the bride's mother or mother-in-law as well as, or instead of, the usual bouquet at the wedding reception. A bridesmaid who is the groom's sister can organize this for the bride as a gift to the groom's family.

GIFT WRAPPING

Don't forget to remove the price before wrapping the gift! To enable the recipient to change the gift leave the price on a book jacket, or enclose the bill in a sealed envelope passed to the recipient's mother. French shops automatically wrap gifts at no extra cost. Some shops gift-wrap for a small charge.

CHECKLIST: shopping

Bridal doll sources: ....

toy supplier tel: ....

Menswear shops for groom's gifts: ....

Ladies' wear shops for trousseau: ....

Jewellers: ....

Health club address: ....

Department store with wedding list: Name, address, phone ....

Shopping List:

Keepbook; Ostrich plume pen for signing register; Wedding reception guests autograph album; other ....

Obtain lucky symbols: silver colour horseshoe or real horseshoe, or cardboard lucky black cat; buy silver sixpence or threepence from coin shop or have five pence handy for bride's shoe; four-leaf clover; organize lucky chimney sweep.

ARRANGING ACCOMMODATION

The bride tries to give accommodation in her house to the chief bridesmaid and the immediate family or friends who cannot afford hotels. For those who want the hotel comforts, and don't wish to impose on the bride's family, she can find out the availability of hotel accommodation and make a booking on her guests' behalf. The chief bridesmaid may offer accommodation to other bridesmaids, or meet and greet them, seeing them to their hotel.

BEAUTY TREATMENTS

Share exercising and dieting together, or perhaps visits to a health club, aerobics classes, swimming, sunbed treatments or a suntanning holiday. The bride could visit a health and beauty club for the day, perhaps as an engagement gift from the chief bridesmaid. Spend a day together dieting every weekend.

No time or will power? Spend a weekend or day at a health farm. It might be fun (and useful too) to attend a lecture by a colour consultant. They select a member of the audience, hold colours to her face and choose the range of colours which suit her best. For a fee, the colour consultant selects your colours and gives you a swatch to match when buying clothes, so bride and bridesmaids can reorganize their entire wardrobe.

Beauticians can do a pre-wedding make-up consultation colour analysis, tint eyelashes and brows, shape brows, and on the day make up the bride and three bridesmaids.

For spots and sores zinc ointment available from chemists is a skin soother. Natural products and caffeine-free herbal teas are sold by health shops. Various preparations claim to help acne, calm nerves and provide vitamins needed when taking the contraceptive pill. Ask your doctor's and pharmacist's advice.

DENTAL TREATMENT

Missing, broken, crooked, stained or discoloured teeth can ruin that perfect wedding smile. Visit the dental hygienist for advice and treatment.

STOP SMOKING

Join the bride in attempting to give up smoking. Avoid being photographed holding a cigarette at the wedding, and don't blow smoke over newly-washed hair or clothes which need dry cleaning.

HAIRSTYLE

Hair should not be too flowing in church completely covering the dress so that you look as if you are naked underneath like Lady Godiva. Long tresses can be held back neatly with flowers. Try the chosen hairstyle the week before, taking the hair adornment to the hairdresser. Some hairdressers will do your hair and manicures at home. Don't surprise the bride by turning from brunette to blonde. Apart from anything else, it can alter the colours which suit you.

BEAUTY SLEEP

Allow time to recover from jet-lag after a long plane journey. Apart from feeling exhausted you look haggard until sufficient sleep restores your schoolgirl complexion and white eyes. Have an early night before the wedding day. If you share a room with the bride and she is too excited to sleep, walk her up and down until she is tired.

CHECKLIST: health and beauty

Have all the bridesmaids' hair done by the same hairdresser.
Doctor's name, address and phone: ....
Dentist's name, address and phone: ....
Family Planning address, tel: ....
Bride's appointment date and time ....
    Does bride want a companion? ....
Health Club address and tel: ....
Class dates, times, costs ....
Hairdresser's name, address and phone ....
    appointment date and time .... Assistant ....

CHECKLIST: packing

Dress(es) .... Hat .... Shoes .... Hosiery ....
Underclothes .... Outdoor clothes .... Swimwear ......
Cosmetics bag .... Toiletries/medicaments bag ....
Dictionary .... Passport .... Address list ....
Gifts .... Tickets ....
Speeches and music .... Camera ....
Instruction book ....
Film ..... Batteries .... Mail order developing envelope ....
Other ....

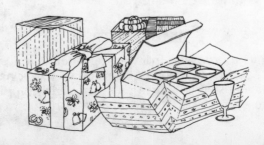

PARTY PLANNING

An event as important as a marriage need not be celebrated with merely one party alone – a reception – there are many other opportunities to celebrate the event, and you can help to organize them.

ENGAGEMENT PARTY AND WEDDING VENUES

The bride usually chooses her wedding reception venue (and sometimes the engagement party) from local hotels, village and church halls. You can also entertain in a private room at a restaurant, hotel or at home. In case she asks for advice here are more ideas. Check local guidhalls, medical centres or halls connected with the families' work. The engagement party is often arranged at short notice. Wedding reception venues, like churches, get booked up over a year in advance for summer, so rapid fact-finding and decision-making are essential.

If the bride asks for help in choosing a venue, you could investigate unusual museums, the zoo, or whether there are private function rooms at public buildings. In general, unusual venues are more appropriate for engagement parties, and grand hotels and castles are better for more formal wedding receptions. Wherever you live in the world, once you start looking for venues you will be surprised at the wide choice available.

ENGAGEMENT PARTY CLOTHES

For a formal engagement party such as a dance at a grand hotel ballroom you can buy or hire evening gowns. With an evening dress in black and blue or black and red you might wear matching long black gloves and black shoes. For an afternoon party you might wear a sophisticated Italian pink dress with matching pink hat, gloves, shoes and handbag, all one colour. If you want a secondary contrasting colour, accessories should co-ordinate. It is simplest to match black accessories for winter evenings, white for summer, silver or gold if you have silver and gold evening shoes. Satin shoes can be dyed one colour or mottled to match a dress.

THE HEN PARTY

The hen party is the bride's last fling, a girls' night out with no-one expecting her home to cook dinner or account for her whereabouts. The bridesmaids often organize the hen party at a date close to the wedding, usually a lunch or evening event. But at a weekend they could start in a single sex sauna or leisure centre, whirlpool bath, return home for simple entertainment such as listening to cassettes and admiring wedding gifts, or go out to a club or dinner.

Plan in advance any announcements, speeches, thanks you don't want to forget, and photographs you may wish to take. Organize transport sharing cars so the bride-to-be does not have to drive.

ENTERTAINING IN HOTEL SUITES

At all-suite hotels each main bedroom also has a sitting room usually containing a fridge-bar and sink, and sometimes a microwave. This helps economize on meals and drinks, providing you don't consume too much hotel-price alcohol. Use the room to entertain, hold a hen party, or reciprocate invitations from the bride's family.

LIVE ENTERTAINMENT

You might attend a medieval banquet at a stately home. Ask banquet entertainment organizers if there are souvenir records or cassettes of the evening which the girls can buy for the bride-to-be. Tell the organizers in advance that she is in the audience so she can be called out as a 'volunteer' for games. They might seat her in a place of honour with a good view near the front, convenient for a singer to come forward from the stage to sing to her, or for her to be called on stage. If your guests need special diets or are teetotallers, warn the caterers.

GIFTS

Find out the bride's interests and choose something appropriate. For example, for someone who takes vitamin pills, a pill box, for someone who is always late, an alarm watch, for someone who wears lots of jewellery a jewel case. Visitors' books with a quotation on the left page and lines for names and addresses are another idea – or why not give the bride-to-be a book about a Royal Wedding?

PARTYING AT HOME

If the party is to be held at a house, it might be fun to organize a pink party and a pink cake containing a symbol such as a ring, thimble or lucky charm – an omen that whoever finds it will be the next bride.

Play party games adapted to the wedding theme, *e.g.* wedding crosswords; wedding Scrabble; wedding bingo (Bride's bingo is sold in America); unscrambling words (names of wedding group as well as marriage-related items); pin the carnation on the groom; pin the bouquet on the bride; where will she wear the ring?

MUSIC FOR A HEN PARTY

Records and songbooks will give you the words of songs such as *Jolly Good Company*, *The More We Are Together*. Or you can have a guessing game, playing the first bar of the tune, and the guests have to guess the name, who, what, or where. Use songs with the bridesmaids', bride's, ushers' and groom's names, for example, *Oh no John, no John, no John, no!*, or *When Johnny Comes Marching Home Again*, or play around with placename songs such as *Sweet Lass of Richmond Hill*.

You can string songs together to tell a story with a compere or narrator, beginning with the fact that the engaged couple are rushing into marriage, or have known each other so long that you wondered whether they would ever make up their minds. You could have a chorus singing the verse from a well-known song such as the music hall number *Daisy, Daisy*, using the tune everybody knows but adapting the words, 'Will she, won't she, give me your answer do!'

TRANSPORT

Groom and ushers or boyfriends should be briefed to arrive at the end to admire gifts and give girls lifts home. Alternatively call taxis, or pay a cab to make a round trip delivering all the girls, ending at the home of the chief bridesmaid so that she is last to alight and pays the fare.

CHECKLIST: parties

Who is tidying, clearing up, rearranging furniture? ....
Washing up? ....
Returning attendants' clothes? ....

Returning cake and leftover food and drink? ....

Returning wedding gift display? ....

Entertaining late-night revellers? ....

Organizing transport? ....

Providing beds? ....

Who is up early next day to let in workmen collecting the marquee? ....

Who makes breakfast/brunch the morning after, and lunch or dinner? ....

THE WEDDING

All those hours of planning come to fruition on the big day – but your priority must be to stay alert and help the bride look and feel her best.

THE WEDDING REHEARSAL

A rehearsal is helpful and usually takes place the day before the wedding. A rehearsal usually takes place in church to familiarize attendants with where to enter, order in the procession and recession, distance apart and speed of walking, and where to stand during the ceremony. You need to practise mounting steps and carrying the train, perhaps with a stand-in wearing a white paper imitation train. Watching another wedding from pews the previous week is helpful, but does not give you the same confidence as actually standing in position.

The wedding rehearsal could be held the night before the ceremony. A dress rehearsal is useful so attendants can practise walking in long dresses. Wear shoes and correct pinching using shoe stretch liquid if necessary. Try on the head-dress to be sure it won't slip off. You may need pins to hold it.

Check underclothes. Prevent bra straps slipping off shoulders or peeping above the neckline of the dress, dark underclothes showing through light dresses, tight underwear making lines across the back of the skirt, loose hems catching high heels and small size tights splitting as you put them on or getting snagged by jewellery.

A rehearsal dinner or bridesmaids' and ushers' dinner can be held for out-of-town members of the wedding party to meet each other and be entertained. Remember that guests might also like time for shopping and sightseeing. If the bride's family are busy, book guests tickets for an open top bus tour and meet for a late tea, dinner or buffet supper. Discuss the receiving line positions.

PREPARATIONS

If you are attending a morning ceremony followed by a wedding breakfast you must be up early. Run a bath for the bride and if required drive her to the hairdresser. The chief bridesmaid should dress herself and help dress younger bridesmaids and the bride. This may entail hairstyling and manicure, or retouching a chipped or broken nail if the manicure has been done the day before. When the fresh flower circlet is delivered sew it to the bride's veil. Clean the bride's engagement ring with an old toothbrush. Remove price tags from the base of new shoes so they don't show when she is kneeling in church. Supply concealer cream for last minute spots. Calm the bride's mother if necessary.

Be ready in time for the photographer who will photograph the bride alone, also with the maid of honour, then the bridesmaids. Beware: the video camera may find you all dressing in your underslips pulling on dresses and zipping them up! You may wish to remove wires normally used to straighten teeth.

If the reception is held at home before leaving for

church check the marquee to see that the placecards are ready.

BEING PHOTOGRAPHED

As a bridesmaid you are right at the centre of things – and that means getting used to the unblinking eye of the camera! In group photographs the bride's sister stands nearer the bride and groom than distant relatives. Tiny pages and bridesmaids stand or sit in front so they can be seen. On steps outside the church and inside the reception hall or hotel, the bride stands at the top of the steps and the bridesmaid drapes the bride's train down the steps.

Fetch a champagne glass so the bride can be photographed as if raising the glass for a toast. Arrange the bride's dress. The train is usually draped in front of her so it can be seen in the photograph, and you should spread her skirt on the staircase in fan shape. If required, you could help and call guests as they are to be photographed. The bride is photographed with child attendants, then all attendants.

Bridesmaids who have not removed their glasses for the procession might do so for photographs. It is usual to photograph bridesmaids individually, chief bridesmaid and best man, bridesmaids with ushers, child bridesmaids with their parents, bridesmaids with their boyfriends, and the matron of honour with her husband. A traditional group photograph of bridesmaids shows them revealing garters.

TAKING PHOTOGRAPHS

You have so much to do that you may be best advised to lend your camera to a friend to take photographs – that way you can be in the pictures too! However you may be able to step to one side and take some snaps yourself. Carry extra film in case your camera jams or someone forgets film and needs more. Take photographs of the hotel name, the wording on the cake and the car with numberplate. These shots make opening credits in an album and help identify film if it is lost by processors. Don't forget to carry spare batteries.

POSES TO CHOOSE

To create height for a bride and groom with taller attendants have the bride and groom standing on a doorstep, attendants stand either side, ushers with one foot raised onto the step. Arrange the poses of junior attendants. A page might pose with his hand in his belt, cap in hand, or hold his hat under his arm.

Indoors to avoid red eyes under flashlight have another light source from windows or turn on more lights. The subjects should not all stare at the camera. The bride and groom can look at each other.

Prevent flashlight whitening the faces by keeping about five feet distant. Check your camera instruction book and practise in advance.

If the photos are not successful you may be able to photograph the bride and bridesmaids in bridal clothes a few days later. If hired clothes must be returned photograph the bride with a veil or flowers in her hair alongside the groom, or alone beside a lighted candle or candelabra.

Sit elegantly, either ankles crossed and toes together, or knees together and ankles to one side, or knees, ankles and toes together in front of you. Sit up straight. Don't block the view of the person behind or hide behind the person in front. Don't look worried. Smile and try not to spread your mouth in a false artificial grin showing lots of teeth with unsmiling eyes.

CHECKLIST: at the church

☆ While you wait at the church before the ceremony keep neat and tidy and occupy other bridesmaids during the wait for the bride outside the church.

☆ Go to the toilet with junior bridesmaids. (Send pageboys under age of seven to toilet with an usher.)

☆ Comb hair. Check shoes and clothes.

☆ Blow noses of small bridesmaids and pageboys.

☆ Pay compliments to other bridesmaids, especially juniors.

☆ Point out the exit door and where you will stand for photographs afterwards.

☆ Supervise younger bridesmaids.

☆ In the procession walk ahead of the bride behind younger bridesmaids.

☆ Take the bouquet from the bride at the start of the ceremony.

☆ Sign the register as witness.

☆ Return the bouquet after the signing of the register/ after the ceremony.

☆ In the recession walk with the best man behind the bride.

☆ Travel ahead of the bride to the reception and arrange her dress for photographs.

☆ At most church weddings the organist strikes up with Here Comes The Bride or other music to warn the congregation of the bride's arrival. For a grand effect a trumpet fanfare announces her arrival so that those seated in the congregation stand up.

THE MARRIAGE

The maid of honour or chief bridesmaid stands behind the bride holding bouquet and prayerbook, and wearing the bride's engagement ring unless the bride wears it on her right hand. The ring can be returned after signing the register out of sight or just before entering the reception.

The junior bridesmaid could hold the bride's gloves during the ceremony and in a two-ring ceremony the groom's ring. If the bride has gloves without fingers or has made a slit in the seams of the glove's ring finger this will not be necessary.

In an Anglican church the best man hands the ring to the vicar who blesses it and then gives it to the groom. The best man signals with a slight wave of his hand to the chief bridesmaid that she can retire and she enters the pew to sit down. Move small bridesmaids ahead into the pew so they don't skip down the aisle to join their mother.

SIGNING THE REGISTER

If the chief bridesmaid is a witness she follows the bride into the vestry and returns the bouquet to the bride in the vestry after the bride has signed the register. Otherwise she stays where she is, and organizes her colleagues for the recession.

To arrange the train for the recession, the bridesmaid may have to place her own bouquet on the table, hand it to the bride's mother, or put it on the floor and retrieve it later.

While the congregation waits, often music plays, a choir sings, and the entire congregation joins in the hymns.

THE RECESSION

Don't tread on the bride's train or dress. Watch that the bride doesn't twirl around a corner, toss her head and catch her long veil on a post, as one bride did. The bridesmaid saved the day by reaching forward, and disentangled it so quickly that the bride never noticed. You really have to stay alert!

AFTERWARDS

Ask in advance if the bride wants confetti so she isn't disappointed by its absence. If it rains she might prefer not to risk getting coloured patches on her white dress. When guests throw confetti, rice or birdseed you may have as much confetti thrown over you as over the bride. When pelted by rice which is quite hard you have to shake it out of your dress.

The flower girl might also present a posy to the bride just before her departure.

At the reception venue, the chief bridesmaid goes with the bride to the bedroom suite or changing room and has a comb for the bride, lipstick, and hanky, then helps the bride downstairs to join the receiving line.

SECOND MARRIAGE

Plan food, entertainment and babysitting afterwards even for granny's small wedding. One elderly couple went back to their family's house and ended up babysitting both sets of grandchildren while the children went shopping.

HANDICAPPED PARTICIPANTS

You may be involved in helping any handicapped people in various ways on the big day – this can add a satisfying new dimension to the joyous celebrations as you help them share the event.

BLIND BRIDAL PARTY

A blind or partially sighted bride may need help from the bridesmaid when dressing, but she may have many clever ideas such as putting string through the zip, enabling her to zip her own dress up. Visually impaired bridesmaids may also require extra assistance with dressing.

The blind bride will be on her father's arm and groom's arm so the ceremony will present few difficulties except with steps on entering the building. Check whether buildings such as the reception venue and/or the hotel have special provisions and advise the bride. Some hotels have lifts with floor numbers marked in braille and bedroom doors with braille numbers.

The majority of blind people are over 65 so you are more likely to be helping the bride's grandmother and older relatives than the bride herself. Few people who become partially sighted in later life can read braille and

large print invitations are more useful. Arrange to meet
them outside buildings to help them enter. Show them to
the bathroom on the way in.

At home clear overhanging branches from paths.
Indoors move toys and obstacles off the floor and keep
doors shut or wide open. At a buffet reception collect
food and drink for blind and partially-sighted people.
Introduce them to others at standing room only receptions, and locate relatives they want to meet and cannot
see.

DEAF PARTICIPANTS

Even if you know sign language, it is a good idea to have
an interpreter translating into sign language at the speed
of speech. The interpreter should attend the practice or
wedding rehearsal and go to pre-wedding consultations
to get everything agreed by the vicar or priest. A vicar
who won't normally allow video-recording might make
an exception after realizing how much the deaf miss
without aural memory of hymns, songs and speech.

You might like to make a detailed order of service
including the words of hymns, timing from the entry of
the bride onwards, name the bridal march which deaf
people won't hear and identify, and mention that an
interpreter will be signing. One bride whose groom was
deaf used sign language when making her vows.

Hearing bridesmaids chosen from the family of the
deaf bride or groom can be very helpful. The bride may
have her veil lifted by her father so her lips can be seen
so the deaf groom and guests can see her and lipread.

In a large church the interpreter should stand high up
so the signing can be seen by deaf people at the back. At
one wedding where half the guests had hearing difficulties
most of the deaf people sat on the side of the church
facing the interpreter while all the hearing people sat the
other side. The interpreter followed the photographer to

summon deaf people to be photographed and instructed them how to be grouped and when to smile.

The bride's family usually choose their family church for the wedding, unless a church for the deaf is nearby, although several special churches for the deaf exist.

Churches for the deaf are smaller so that everyone can see, and have fewer pillars obscuring vision, front-facing seats, and soundproofing to reduce traffic noise and echoes from people walking up the aisle. The vicar and staff may be deaf and can use sign language. The standard choir is often supplemented by a group using sign language.

You could make a special effort to teach ushers the fingerspell alphabet so that they can give the bride's and groom's names, 'Jane, or John?' when asking guests where they want to sit.

To help others lipread face them and speak clearly keeping your head still. When you are not understood don't shout which distorts your face but try again using different words.

In restaurants deaf people can communicate by pointing at the menu and carrying a card which says, 'I am deaf but can lipread. Please stand facing the light and don't have the light behind you.' This is useful when making introductions at the wedding reception.

WHEELCHAIR USERS

Access causes the most difficulties for wheelchair users – especially steps. Brief two ushers to help in getting wheelchairs inside buildings. Order one of the modern taxis which are adapted with space on the left beside the driver to allow room for a wheelchair.

Many hotels have adapted ground floor bedrooms where you can stay overnight or use bathroom facilities during the reception and ramps into dining rooms. At a buffet be on hand to delegate someone else to supply food to guests who cannot move about. Make sure that wheelchairs can be fitted under the reception tables. Have photographs taken of the bride and bridesmaids seated with wheelchair-bound guests behind the table so that they are not obviously different nor seated while others stand towering above.

The video can be shown to the wheelchair-bound guests afterwards so they can see what went on in parts of the building such as the garden where they could not go.

At church help family members using crutches to the front pew in advance, even the bride's mother who normally enters last. Check whether nearer side doors are open.

TROUBLESHOOTING GUIDANCE

Your jobs include asking about possible problems and having backup plans, finding missing items or supplying duplicates, opening bottles and locks, repairing and mending, fetching and returning items, and sending thanks. Stock a bag containing: pen, notebook, glue, scissors, coins for phone boxes, phonecard, paper tissues, spare tights, taxi phone number, nail varnish and remover, comb, lipstick, handcream, spotcover, perfume, disposable toothbrush and toothpaste, pocket clothes brush or lint remover, Swiss army knife containing bottle-opener, nailfile, mini-scissors and tweezers, camera film, batteries, non-aspirin painkiller, elastoplast/band-aid, attendants' medication, sanitary towels, spare car keys, dictionary, diary, address-telephone book containing phone numbers of nearest doctor, airport, and railway station, cards with your business, home and hotel addresses for guests to contact you afterwards, hair rollers, hair drier, travel iron, moisturizer, Waspeze, zinc ointment, first aid kit, shoe-cleaning wipes, suntan oil and sunburn lotion (in hot countries).

This bag can be left in the changing room provided by the church or hotel, or in the boot of a car for which you have keys.

When the bride spills red wine on her dress and is about to burst into tears what will you do? Ask dress suppliers about stain removal in advance. If the dress is home-made or custom-made take a spare piece of material and try dropping red and white wine on it and test the action of stain removers. Carry notes on removing confetti and wine stains.

Swap dresses if the vicar won't marry the bride in her red dress or a miniskirt. Or drive home for a long skirt or coat. Make friends of hotel staff in advance. In hotels catering disasters such as sinking cakes, food shortages, and guests on diets, can be sorted out by hotel staff. Avoid drinking too much, and convert to low alcohol after your third drink or add more mixers each time. Watch known alcoholics and ask waiters not to keep refilling their glasses with neat alcohol.

Repair tears in wedding dress or clothing. For needles and cotton try the staffed ladies cloakroom, housekeeping department, guest relations, reception, and if no luck phone the hotel manager. If the groom dances on the bride's dress and splits the skirt and she says he is a 'clumsy, careless ...' and the groom retorts that she has chosen a stupid impractical dress and they are about to have a row, you can save the day. Try joking, 'Now, now, children. He's made sure you won't be able to wear that again,' separation and distraction, 'John, your mother wants to see you ...' and, 'Never mind, Anne. Come upstairs and I'll sew on some spare ribbon.

When disaster strikes, *e.g.* the cake collapses, take a picture so you can help the bride get compensation as consolation and don't despair, laugh about it afterwards.

THE RECEPTION

At the reception make sure you arrive ahead of the bride to await her arrival and arrange her train. If no usher is available alert a porter to open the door for the bride. If no-one else is available you open doors for the bride.

THE RECEIVING LINE

At very traditional English weddings the bridesmaids do not stand in the receiving line, which is essentially the hosts receiving the guests, thus the mother of the bride, as hostess, her husband, the bride and groom, the groom's parents. When a matron of honour hosts the reception at her house in lieu of the bride's deceased, sick, or absent mother, she heads the line.

Slightly less formal UK and Roman Catholic weddings and American weddings (which are less traditional) often include bridesmaids in the receiving line, but this is not the case at UK Jewish weddings.

WELCOME ROOM

If you are invited to join the line, listen out for introductions so that you know who people are. Shake hands or accept a kiss on the cheek as appropriate, and say a few words – but do not enter long conversations as you will hold up proceedings.

If the receiving line is at the front door, gate or path, and assuming she is not officially part of it, the chief bridesmaid could still stand at the end of the line and point the way to the welcome room, or greet guests entering the welcome room.

At larger formal receptions the toastmaster announces guests approaching the receiving line. Listen for the name and use it when greeting guests coming off the line and directing them to drinks or making introductions. Copy formal titles. 'Your Grace . . .', though you can lapse into familiarity with friends. Introduce yourself to strangers saying your name distinctly, 'I'm the bride's sister, Anne,' then clearly and enthusiastically introduce the other bridesmaids, especially juniors, 'and this is our youngest sister, Susan'.

Tiny children do not stand in the receiving line because they are not hosts and it would tire them. A bridesmaid might sit at a table where guests sign the visitors' book and direct them to the rail where their clothes are put on hangers by a younger bridesmaid or pageboy if the reception venue staff cannot do this.

Another bridesmaid could then direct ladies to the bathroom and mirrors. An usher usually takes the men's clothes. Alternatively a bridesmaid keeps each group's coats together, issuing one coat ticket to the head of the family.

A third bridesmaid might point the way to the garden or lounge where drinks are being served, or the marquee.

The ushers may stand singly along a roped path or canopy leading to a marquee, or the ushers and bridesmaids could stand paired as in church.

THE DINING/BANQUETING HALL

The master of ceremonies may announce, 'Ladies and gentlemen, please stand to welcome the bride and groom', and sometimes the wedding march is played, the lights are dimmed and the bride and groom enter, perhaps with spotlights on them, or the lights come on again as they enter. For a theatrical effect common at Greek or Italian weddings the happy couple step through a curtain which draws back on the stage where the band plays and the bride and groom descend an arched stairway, possibly in the same order as the recession, preceded by the pageboy, ring-bearer and flower girl, followed by the bridesmaids. On reaching a flowered arch the bride and groom stop with a ribbon across their path, tied to the sides of the arch.

Or they might enter on a pathway of red carpet between the guests, with bridesmaids and ushers forming an arch of flowers by holding up long-stemmed carnations. The bride and groom walk to the end of the archway where their progress is stopped by a ribbon held by the pageboy and youngest usher. Then the master of ceremonies announces, 'To mark the beginning of your married life together, David and Sandra, will you please untie the ribbon.' The bride and groom pull both ends of the bow in the centre of the ribbon. Or the master of ceremonies asks the groom to cut the ribbon and a member of staff steps forward with a pair of scissors on a tray.

TAKING SEATS AT THE TABLE

The bride and groom walk around the top table, sometimes separately, bride to the right, groom left, guided by the restaurant staff. The bridesmaid does not usually need to hold the bride's train, as this should be done by banqueting staff who see that the bride is seated. Or the bride arrives with the train looped over her (left) arm as she will be holding it later when dancing.

The bride and groom sit down first and only when they are seated do you sit down. You may need to wait for the minister to say grace before you start eating.

The paired pageboy and flower girl could go up to the top table to make a presentation to the bride at this point.

BRIDESMAIDS' GIFTS

The bridegroom might hand over wrapped gifts to the bridesmaids privately after the ceremony, and before the guests gather at the receiving line at the reception, or alternatively he might hand over the gifts after or during his speech when he toasts the bridesmaids.

For a theatrical effect the gifts may be presented after the cake-cutting. The band plays a few bars of music, a drum roll or clash of cymbals to get attention, the lights dim or flash on and off, and the restaurant staff wheel in the presents on a trolley, or bring them forward one by one on a circular silver tray, from which the gift is lifted by the bride or groom.

The bride hands the first present to the best man who shakes hands and waits. The groom hands the second present to the chief bridesmaid and kisses her. (The bride also thanks the bridesmaid and kisses her. Sometimes the bride instead of the groom hands the present to the bridesmaid.)

The chief bridesmaid should turn to face the camera while holding onto the present which the donor does not necessarily release. The photographer snaps the bride, groom, best man and bridesmaid with the presents held prominently. The bridesmaid holds her gift at waist level or jointly with the donor.

The best man and chief bridesmaid sit down and other bridesmaids and ushers get ready to stand up and go forward. Another pair follow in the same order as the recession. A gift is handed by the bride to the chief usher, and so on, until lastly the pageboy and flower girl are called. On each occasion a photo is often taken of the two recipients with the bride and groom.

You may be at a loss for words when others have already said what you wanted to say when you are presented with a gift. Some phrases to keep in mind are, 'It is so pretty, suits me . . . goes beautifully with the dress. It's just what I've always wanted. How thoughtful of you. I shall treasure it. I can wear it at my . . . You're a darling, an angel.' Finally say, 'Thank you!' hug the donor and give her a kiss. If the gift can be worn, put it on. Don't say, 'You shouldn't have spent so much'. You don't want her to regret it and feel badly, do you? Say something complimentary such as, 'That's really generous of you.'

If the donor says, 'I hope you haven't already got one,' don't reveal that you have by saying, 'I have – but it doesn't matter'.

When shown someone else's gift say, 'It's gorgeous . . . looks terrific on you . . . what a lovely present'.

ARRANGING INTRODUCTIONS

You could ask the bride beforehand to show you a list of the guests and a table plan. Find out which guests have something in common and ask the bride who should meet whom. When making introductions first tell the important person who the less important one is. The order is VIPs such as titled people first, the married before the unmarried, and those senior in position or age before younger ones. Great-aunt is told the name of the five-year old. The woman is the person to whom the man must be introduced, 'Anne, may I introduce Philip.' Then make the introduction the other way round so that both people hear the other's name again. 'Philip, this is Anne'.

Add facts you know about them to get their conversation started, their relationship to the bride or groom, homeland, hobbies, and employment. This gets shy boys talking and saves luckless girls from asking, 'What do you do?' and getting the conversation-stopping reply, 'As little as possible.'

SMALLER RECEPTIONS

When twenty of the fifty guests are family the numbers on the top table would dominate the room, with only three tables of ten guests. So instead of one top table the family is divided with bridesmaids on the bride's youngsters' table and older relatives on her parents' table.

The bride and groom sit at a top table with their attendants facing into the room. The bridesmaid's bouquets are placed on the table in front of them as decoration. The bride's parents sit with the groom's parents and the minister and his wife, any grandparents, the sisters and brothers of the parents or other older folk.

SUPERVISING CHILDREN

During the ceremony and at the reception buffet or pre-dinner drinks the older bridesmaid stands behind or beside the younger one, talks to her, if necessary takes her to the toilet, reminds her to smile, says 'hush' subtly by holding a finger to her lips or says 'whisper to me'.

Place a napkin on her lap when she is eating or wash her hands so she does not get sticky fingers on her dress. Stop her sitting down on the dirty floor when she gets tired; say, 'come and sit on my lap'. The younger one may go home early before the evening celebrations. At some weddings there is a party bus which parks outside.

Children eat inside the decorated coach during speeches, and play games related to weddings. A boy of about 12 can be dressed up as a bride and told to speak with a falsetto voice. A girl is dressed as a groom and prompted to propose, 'Will you marry me?'. The answer is 'not likely'. The prompt suggests, 'Ask "Is she rich?" ' which becomes, 'Have you got any money?'

Pass the Parcel can be played as Pass the Ring. Each player takes the ring off the hand of the person on his left, places it on his own finger, and is out if wearing it when the music stops. Prizes are given to all children by the end of the party. Such games can be more fun for children than boring wedding dinners. At large weddings such as Greek or Asian there are sometimes sufficient children to occupy a separate party room.

AFTER THE MEAL

Arrange for the master of ceremonies to allow you time after eating to retire with the bride to her changing room and reapply her lipstick and yours. He announces to guests that you have a five minute break. Help the bride remove a removable train, bodice or bolero for dancing. However, make sure you are present when a minister is called upon to say grace at the end of the meal before smoking is permitted, and of course everyone must return in time to hear speeches, toasts and telemessages.

CUTTING THE CAKE

The most common wedding disaster is the toppling cake. If you see it leaning or the icing cracking summon the banqueting manager. At home if icing on the lower level isn't solid you must dismantle the cake and reassemble it just for the cake cutting. The 'cement' cake which cannot be cut bends or breaks the knife. Stab the cake through the centre to get it started. Cut it and fill the cut with butter icing.

DANCING

The master of ceremonies might call the bride and groom onto the dance floor, then after they have circled the floor once he calls the best man and chief bridesmaid by name, 'Please welcome Peter and Belinda'. The audience applauds as they walk onto the dance floor. After a few moments' dancing the other bridesmaids and ushers are called in pairs, often after the bride's parents, and the groom's parents, until the top table is empty. The photographer photographs the bride dancing and bridesmaids dancing with ushers.

The chief bridesmaid or bride might hint that ushers invite the younger bridesmaids and single ladies lacking partners to dance. Bridesmaids could dance with each other but it is better to provide partners.

DISTRIBUTING SUGARED ALMOND FAVOURS

You may be asked to distribute cake and favours such as *bonbonnières* (sugared almonds in coloured lace) unless the bride wants to take the favours. Keep extras for later arrivals, particularly children, so no-one feels neglected. If there are insufficient favours handy don't keep a disappointed child waiting: donate your own and seek a replacement.

CATCHING THE BOUQUET

When the bride throws the bouquet she symbolizes the marital status passing from the bride to whoever catches the bouquet. The bride may throw her bouquet from the top of the stairs to the bridesmaids below. When there are no stairs she can throw the bouquet over her shoulder on the dance floor to the bridesmaids lined up behind her. If there is only one bridesmaid the master of ceremonies calls all the single women for this event.

Who should catch it? In theory there is a contest. In practice it should be a girl eligible to marry. However, a good-natured older bridesmaid who sets no store by such superstition might let her younger sister catch it, or catch it and hand it to her.

The bouquet is not always thrown. The bride may wish to keep it or give it to a sick relative or charity. A florist collecting the bouquet to preserve it for the bride can supply an identical bouquet for throwing.

THROWING THE GARTER

The bride's garter is usually thrown to the ushers or to the single men. Alternatively throwing the garter to the girls supposedly transfers some of the bride's sexual power to the bridesmaid who captures it. Putting your piece of cake under your pillow is also supposed to inspire you to dream of a future husband.

THE COUPLE'S DEPARTURE

The chief bridesmaid helps the bride change. When the bride and groom are both dressed ready to leave, call the bride's parents for a private hug, goodwill message and farewell kiss. Remind the bride to say goodbye privately to her in-laws too. Check that the hire car or vehicle has arrived and is decorated (ask the best man or second bridesmaid to tell you) before letting the bridal couple exit.

The photographer may want to snap the bride and groom getting into the car alone, without crowds of arms and legs obscuring it, then a picture of bride and groom leaving in it with guests throwing rice.

CHECKLIST: at the reception

Sit at the top table or a table near the bride.
If required assist with catering.
Catch the bouquet.
Help the bride change into her going-away outfit.
Return the bride's dress.
Reception location: Name, address, phone ....
    date .... time ....
Bandleader's Name ....
Master of Ceremonies' name ....
Banqueting manager's name ....
Names of VIP relatives ....
Names of VIP guests ....
Guest departure time ....

DECORATING THE CAR

Hire cars arrive decorated with a white ribbon. A borrowed car must be cleaned. Cover seats with white sheets to protect dresses. Decorate a red car with white ribbon, and a white car with white plus perhaps a colour such as pink to match dresses. Place flowers on the back shelf. The car colour should not clash with bridesmaids' dresses.

The bridesmaids may be asked to help ushers decorate the going-away car using flowers and ribbons. Flowers on wire from bouquets can create artistic effects. Balloons decorating the hall can be re-used to decorate the car. A Just Married sign looks neater when made in advance. Write messages or the first names of the couple with shaving cream (messy but easily removed) or lipstick (hard to remove). Confetti can be sprinkled in the car or on the back parcel shelf. A music cassette might be supplied for a long journey.

Thoughtless ushers sometimes plan silly tricks. The bridesmaid who suspects that this may happen should ensure no harm is done. While the chief bridesmaid helps the bride change another bridesmaid could 'help' the groomsmen with decoration and say, 'That's enough!' if things get out of hand. She might bring a neatly written card and discuss early on with the groomsmen how to attach it, so establishing their plans.

What is excessive? I saw a car completely covered with white shaving foam so it was impossible to drive. Don't obscure windows or otherwise delay the getaway, especially if the bride and groom have to catch a plane.

A simple countryside pony and trap can be kitted out prettily with white reins and white roses in the lamps.

Tin cans are often tied on the back of the car. A more elegant music effect is obtained by attaching jingle bells. Ring cowbells and handbells, bang gongs and clack castanets, or you could even serenade the couple with ethnic music using guitars and accordions as they drive off!

Stationers sell balloons with the words Just Married. Helium-filled balloons with the same wording are sold by balloon specialists. Guests might throw confetti, rose petals, or rice after the car.

CHECKLIST: decorating the car

Decorating the Car

Umbrellas supplied by .... colour ....
    ribbons supplied by .... colour ....

Balloons .... colour ....
Flowers for parcel shelf ....
   flower on internal mirror support?
   ribbons on left and right internal doorpost straps?
Do confer with the best man and ushers about type of
   decorations
Do make decorations pretty not messy (finger messages
   in foam look untidy on a smart car)
Do make conventional Just Married sign in advance
Do plan who will hide it
Do plan an extra personalised slogan or pretty surprise
Do rehearse the decorating once – perhaps on the best
   man's car – to check how long it takes
Do check how the decorations can be safely removed and
   supply any required cloth in the glovebox
Do clear front windows by using the windscreen wipers
Don't obscure windows
Don't let balloons fall inside the pedal area

Don't make the car undrivable

Do advise bride and groom to threaten to daub pranksters' cars Not Married

Don't use lipsticks or other items which might stain clothes and damage cars

Don't forget a pre-arranged signal so the decorators know when they can start in secret

Don't forget a pre-arranged signal to tell whoever is helping the bride change that they have finished

Don't forget your camera to photograph the going-away car

HIRED CARS

Don't expect to decorate a hired car

Do check if the going-away car is hired (the chauffeur won't allow daubing)

Do check whether the hired car company can supply a Just Married sign and ask what else they can supply

Do check on the internal flower decorations. Add your posy if the hire car decorations are not sufficient.

AFTER THE RECEPTION PARTY

You may be asked to distribute flowers from tables to the hosts or guests according to the bride's wishes. Clear up the catering, helping the bride's mother pack and carry the cake tier she's saving.

You can store bouquets wrapped in the fridge as instructed until the florist collects, or next day deliver bouquets to be pressed. As the bride will be away now, take her and your dresses to the cleaners as soon as possible before stains have time to set. Return hired clothes to the shop or send the bride's dress to her home if she left in going-away clothes. Professional cleaning and packing services are offered for dresses.

You may be able to help by attaching cards to cake boxes sent to guests unable to attend. Send wedding announcements and photos of the bride and groom to friends abroad who were not invited.

Some bridesmaids who are close friends, acknowledge safe arrival of presents explaining that the bride will shortly reply personally after her honeymoon.

WHILE THEY'RE AWAY

Department stores can be instructed not to send gifts while the bride and groom are away on honeymoon. Printed cards are impersonal as the sole acknowledgement of a gift. However, the bridesmaid can add a handwritten line that the bride will be writing in person on her return.

While the bride and groom are away put leftover food from the wedding reception in their freezer. If you live near their new home, move letters, parcels, newspapers, dustbins and telltale signs that the house is empty to prevent burglary. Water new plants. Write a note of what has been done, reminders of calls to be returned, and a welcome home message. Leave fresh flowers, fruit, bread, biscuits, milk, coffee and wine or arrange a welcome home party.

HONEYMOON NIGHT AT HOME

In the old days the bridesmaids would help the bride prepare for bed, help her remove the wedding gown, hang up her clothes, prepare a scented bath or bowl of hot water, let down her hair and comb it out, help her put on her nightdress and turn down the bed for her.

If the couple are spending their first night at home near the reception you can send one of the bridesmaids to decorate the bedroom after the bride has left for the wedding, perhaps during the evening dancing, as a surprise. The Greeks and Romans used red satin sheets. The Chinese hung red paper over the bed. You need to keep the items for decoration somewhere handy, watch the time, and make sure the girls doing the decorating have transport and a spare door key.

For a happy 'your family loves you' effect, have a new welcome mat or a banner in the hall visible as they open the front door saying, 'Welcome to your new Home', or 'Hello Mr and Mrs Montagu', and in the bedroom balloons from the reception and a congratulations card.

Make the home like a luxurious, romantic hotel honeymoon suite with fresh flowers, fresh fruit by the bed, a small tin of biscuits, a bottle of mineral water and glasses on a tray, fresh perfumed soap and toiletries in the bathroom, embroidered his and hers towels, curtains drawn, sheets turned down on both sides with a flower as decoration or a chocolate, bedside lights switched on and mood music playing.

For fun you could have jokey pillows saying YES on one side and NO on the other turned to the YES side. Pink and blue crackers could be saved from the reception (one of each) with a small gift for him in the blue cracker, a small gift for her in the pink cracker. Wedding dolls could be placed on the bed, or teddy bears in bride and groom outfits. Overnight place signs outside on the gate and garden wall and against the front door saying, 'JUST MARRIED. DO NOT DISTURB'. If you are living or staying in the same house and rise earlier it would make a lovely surprise to place a tray with croissants and orange juice on a table outside the door with a note.

ANNIVERSARIES

The bride may invite her former bridesmaids to a christening or the anniversary party when the upper tier of the wedding cake is served. If you are invited, take along the wedding photographs. Some couples simply have wedding anniversary cards and a quiet candle-lit dinner for two. Remember to send a card.

If the bride isn't planning a party you could invite the bridal couple to dinner at an unspecified restaurant but drive them to your home where the bridesmaids are wearing bridesmaids' dresses for a surprise anniversary party! For a party at home buy from stationers balloons with the words Happy Anniversary. Play *The Anniversary Waltz*. The groom buys the bride major presents such as diamonds for the diamond wedding anniversary. Other guests buy smaller gifts, trinkets and cards reflecting the theme. If you want to buy a party gift see the list on page 263 for the traditional anniversaries and their modern alternatives.

COMPLETE WEDDING CHECKLIST

Bride's name, home address and phone ....
Rendez-vous date .... time ....
Bride's parents' names, home address and phone ....
Groom's name, home address and phone ....
Groom's parents' names, address and phone numbers ....
Children's names ....
Nanny's/au pair's/childminder's/babysitter's name ....
Bride's grandparents' names ....
Groom's grandparents' names ....
Best Man's name, home address and phone ....
Matron of Honour's name, address and phone ....
Chief bridesmaid's name, address and phone ....
Clothes suppliers' names, address and phone ....
Delivery date and time ....
Hairdresser's name, address and phone ....
Appointment date and time ...... Assistant ....
Taxi company name, address and phone ....
Arrival date and time ....
Doctor's name, address and phone ....

Dentist's name, address and phone ....

Minister's name, address and phone ....

Minister's wife's name ....

Bandleader's name ....

Master of Ceremonies' name ....

Banqueting manager's name ....

Names of VIP relatives ....

Names of VIP guests ....

Engagement party location: Name, address, phone ....

contact .... date .... time ....

Hen party location: Name, address, phone ....

date .... time ....

Stag party/Bachelor dinner location:

Name, address, phone ....

date .... time ....

Shower party host's name, address and phone ....

date .... time ....

Out of town guests' party:

Host's name, address and phone ....

date .... time ....

Rehearsal party location:

Name, address, phone ....

date .... time ....

Department store with wedding list:

Name, address, phone ....

Wedding ceremony location name,

address, phone ....

date .... time ....

Reception location:

Name, address, phone ....

date .... time ....

Honeymoon location:

Name, address, phone ....

Travel agent's name, address, phone ....

Airline name, address, reservations phone number ....

Airport's airline flight departure/arrival enquiry number .

Hotel name, address, phone number, fax number ....

Railway station address, phone ....
Bridesmaids' return train/flight/taxi from:
Location address and phone ....
date .... time ....
Newspaper name, address, phone ....
Photographer's name, address, phone ....
Film printing and developing company name, address,
phone ....
Bride and groom's return from honeymoon:
date .... time .... tour operator ....
airport .... airline .... flight number ....
Flight arrivals information phone number: ....
Airport taxi phone number: ....
Train station ....
Bride and groom's new name, address and phone ....
Dog kennel/petminder's name, address and phone ....
Collection date and time ....

BUDGET WEDDINGS

The chief bridesmaid is likely to be much more involved in the practicalities of the day at a budget wedding and she can help in many ways from cooking to helping serve the drinks.

DRESSES

When budgets are tight, you can make your own dresses or have them made by your mother, the bride's mother or a seamstress. Pattern books can be obtained from libraries. Second-hand dresses can sometimes be bought from the shops or from individuals through advertisements in local newspapers.

If you plan to use a white or pastel dress, blouse or jumper you can decorate the neckline, sleeves or cuffs with ribbon roses bought from department store sewing sections. The same ribbon roses can be sewn onto a handbag or purse made from material cut off the dress hem, or attached to an Alice band or hair ribbon, and sewn or pinned to your shoes. You could also try to find period dresses and shawls, evening bags, buttons and beads at jumble sales, markets, or by asking older relatives.

PLANNING FOOD

List the number of guests and calculate how many the house and garden or nearby hall accommodate and decide whether to entertain everyone together, or older relatives to a sit-down lunch and younger people to an evening buffet party and disco.

After tasting samples of fruit cakes at bakeries or bridal shows, if you think you can make a better cake, you could still have your home-made cake decorated by a bakery. A cake covered with marzipan, plain white icing and a simple border can supplement pieces distributed from the bottom layer of the elaborate cake. If the bride and groom or guests do not all like heavy fruit cake, the top layer of the cake can be sponge, the bottom layer fruit cake.

Make a test cake in advance. Recipes for wedding cakes are available from bridal magazines, women's magazines, manufacturers of cake ingredients, sugar, icing sugar, flour and dried fruit, and suppliers of icing, marzipan and decoration kits. Visit kitchen shops which supply sets of cake tins in different sizes, solid white or transparent columns, and bride and groom cake decorations. Other symbols include bells, horseshoes or miniature silver car numberplates with the letters of the bride's and groom's names.

Library books on catering for large numbers can be supplemented by asking home economics teachers at the bridesmaids' schools for buffet recipes and advice. Bridesmaids may need to loan space in their fridges and transport food at the last moment.

SIMPLE FOOD

To minimize cooking and preparation on the day prepare cold foods such as quiches and meringues in advance. A simple menu is melon, then cold meats, fresh or smoked fish, cheeses, an easy to prepare filling savoury like smoked salmon and cream cheese on bagels, or sandwiches made from pre-cut loaves sliced horizontally. The simplest dessert is strawberries and cream. Have net covers or a supply of plastic film to keep off insects.

If the weather is unpredictable and might be chilly, plan an easily prepared hot dish such as soup. For a hot day have a good supply of ice for drinks or as a bed to keep trays of food cool. Slices of fruit can be arranged prettily in fans and circles on ice, but it is worth planning an elaborate centrepiece of either food or flowers. If you run out of food for guests who stay on all evening phone for pizzas to be delivered, some vegetarian, some meat.

You could also make your own wedding favours for each guest. Wrap five sugared almonds in a piece of white net tied with a peice of white ribbon.

DRINK

Prepare a tray of drinks, jugs of cold juice, decorated with slices of lemon, a whole strawberry with a cut half way across, balanced on the side of the glass, or sprig of mint, and red or other coloured straws.

Make mint tea from mint tea bags. Or use ordinary tea bags plus chopped mint which you remove using a tea strainer before serving. Place washed fresh mint from your garden in each glass. Serve hot or cold as iced tea.

Champagne cocktail is cheaper than neat champagne or you could use sparkling wines. For a pink party have lots of rose wines or pink champagne.

Find out if you can get reductions by buying wine by the case. If not you can please and amuse your guests by having a greater variety of drink than you would have at a banquet where only one type of table wine was allocated. Stock spirits and beers, both light and dark, if your guests require these.

BEFOREHAND

What does the house look like when people arrive? Perhaps you could help out by cleaning the windows and windowsills, mowing the lawn, or steam-clean the carpets, curtains and upholstery (borrowing a machine from a hire shop or relatives) and wash the net curtains. Ushers or children can vacuum carpets, water plants and cut off dead leaves, empty wastebins and do the dusting.

Check the numbers of guests who have replied and count the chairs, tables, crockery, cutlery and glasses available at the house that is to hold the reception. Arrange for extras required to be bought or borrowed and decide who will transport bulky items such as chairs. Try out the table for the wedding cake and the tablecloth. Leave room for the bride and groom to stand behind to cut the cake. If using a small rickety cardtable, make sure it is not going to collapse.

PREPARATION FOR THE DAY

Non-cooks can make fruit salad and sandwiches, or stick sausages and cubes of cheese on cocktail sticks. Ask the other bridesmaids and their mothers to hunt through their kitchens for gadgets which cut tomatoes and fruit into fancy shapes. Ask friends who have worked in a bar, restaurant or hotel to demonstrate fancy or fast ways of preparing food. Call the ushers and delegate them to collect wines and glasses from the wineshop. For champagne the tall glass flute with narrow brim is more correct because you lose the bubbles from wide brim glasses. Make a punch, lay out bottles and glasses in groups of triangular or diamond patterns, locate bottle openers and move furniture.

One of the bridesmaids can take the small pageboy or flower girl out of the way for the morning to a park or take them to a video hire shop and then sit with the children while they watch a video. Someone who hates cooking but likes cleaning can tidy the cloakroom, clean the toilets and basins, buy and put out fresh soap, and install full toilet rolls. Clear the hall cupboard or have the best bedroom tidied ready for guests to lay their coats on the beds. Get the ushers and children to make a sign saying 'coats'. The ushers can cut a large piece of white card and draw pencil lines. The children can draw round alphabet letters and colour them in. To guide younger children colour the letter outlines with a broad line first.

DECORATION

Alternatively keep children usefully occupied with an uncle or friend who blows up balloons while others tie balloons onto strings and ribbons. Children can help decide where to attach balloons and fix them on in the agreed designated places. For a unified effect choose a colour theme co-ordinating the surroundings, the table-ware, and the bridesmaids' dresses. If the bride's family has insufficient flowers for decorating the tables and your garden is full of blossoms, take some with you.

LAYING TABLES

Keep a list of things to do on the larder or kitchen cupboard or kitchen door. Establish what help is available, if any, for preparing, serving and clearing up. When laying tables never place your fingers inside the wineglass: hold it by the stem; and never place your fingers inside a soup or cereal plate: use the handles or place your hands under the bowl. For a grand effect which costs nothing place saucers or plates under bowls.

ON THE DAY

SERVING FOOD

Stationers sell paper plates which save on washing up and matching partyware such as paper cups and streamers. The bride can economize by having homemade food served by hired staff, or professionally made food which you lay out on a buffet and let guests help themselves. Handing around plates of food is a good way to meet all the guests and gives you a conversation opener.

ENTERTAINMENT

If the groom is to serenade the bride on a guitar, take your photos afterwards, not while he is singing. Perhaps you and the best man can organize and lead a sing-song. You could borrow songbooks from libraries. Practise the songs until you know them by heart. Write out or duplicate the words on paper sheets for guests.

SERVING FOOD AND DRINKS

After cake-cutting carry plates with pieces of cake to the guests. If you are not giving each guest a plate take a pile of paper serviettes. Before serving tea and coffee, place sugar and milk on each table. Offer second cups of tea before spiriting away the crockery. Collect dirty cups and saucers afterwards to minimize accidents and make the place look tidy.

PART 5

WEDDING SPEECHES

ETIQUETTE

The purpose of etiquette is to provide an easy set of rules which can be followed when you are in a hurry and want to make sure that you do not give offence to anybody. For example, you would not wish to neglect to thank the hosts, or fail to recognize the presence and importance of an honoured guest. The rules are most useful on formal occasions like weddings, and particularly when they happen only once in a lifetime. But because lifestyles are changing constantly the rules of etiquette are changing too – a little slower than lifestyles perhaps, but still changing.

Social occasions are now more flexible, so that the bride or bride's mother can speak if she so wishes, and sometimes the best man can be a best girl! The bride may also be given away by her mother.

THE TIMING OF SPEECHES

Circumstances and ideas vary in different countries and the rules of speechmaking differ for different religions. When speeches are made after seated dinners at lengthy, formal wedding receptions, they begin after all eating at the formal meal has finished, and are preceded by the announcement from the toastmaster, 'Ladies and Gentlemen, you may now smoke.' If the meal finishes with tea or coffee and wedding cake, speeches will be made after the cutting of the cake. There is a natural tendency to call for speeches after the bride and groom have stood behind the cake to be photographed. It is easier to hold the attention of the diners at the end of the meal while they are seated, and still too full to want to get up and start dancing.

However, if the celebration is to continue all evening and the tea and coffee and wedding cake are to be served later, it is possible to delay the cutting of the cake until after the speeches which conclude the meal. Whatever the wedding organizers decide, it is important to let the toastmaster and the speechmakers know, so that they are prepared and do not disappear at the vital moment.

Let us suppose you have late guests arriving after the wedding meal. What do you do? At seated dinners the number of guests invited to the meal may be limited by the cost or the size of the hall. Sometimes the seated guests are just the closest family and friends, while other friends, children, neighbours and colleagues from work are invited for the dancing and party later in the day. A few guests who are invited to a midweek ceremony may not be able to leave work early, are delayed by rush hour traffic, or have to return home to change their clothes, and therefore they reach the reception after it has started.

Guests should not enter during speeches, distracting the audience and disconcerting the speakers. But it is also necessary to avoid keeping them standing outside in the rain, or waiting in draughty corridors feeling unwanted while the meal finishes or the speeches are in progress. The hotel or hall staff can arrange chairs, drinks, and someone to direct and greet the late arrivals, who can then view the wedding presents, or be introduced to each other until a suitable moment arrives for them to enter the dining hall. They should then not be left standing if other guests are seated, but shown to chairs on one side of the hall, or be directed to the seating plans so that they can fill the places kept for them, or go to seats left empty by 'no-shows' such as anyone taken ill at the last minute. You may wish to time the cake-cutting and speeches so that later arrivals can enjoy them. The printed invitation can make any such timing clear.

WHAT TO DO AT BUFFETS AND INFORMAL WEDDINGS

At a buffet you ensure that elderly and infirm guests, and those who have travelled long distances, have seats near the buffet table so that they are not obliged to stand for a long period. If there is no toastmaster, the best man, or woman, calls the attention of the guests to the start of the cake-cutting ceremony. The bride and groom pose for photographs to be taken by the official photographer and relatives who have brought their cameras. The chief bridesmaid, if she is not making a speech, can then lead the call for a speech.

THE TOASTMASTER

The first question you need to ask yourself is do you need a toastmaster? At a large wedding it is useful to have a toastmaster to announce guests on the receiving line. He will know the traditional way to announce titles, that Mr and Mrs John Smith are husband and wife, Mrs John Smith is without her husband John who is away on business, Mrs Anne Smith is a widow, or that Mr John Smith and Mrs Anne Smith are the elderly aunt and uncle, brother and sister, not married to each other. The toastmaster opens the proceedings and keeps them flowing smoothly. In his absence the task would fall to the best man.

There are other benefits from employing a toastmaster. Since one essential quality of a good toastmaster is a loud voice, (which often goes with an imposing, extrovert personality) they will get attention faster than you can (an alternative way to get the attention of the audience is to ask the band, if you have one, to do a drum roll for you). However, to ensure that proceedings go as you would wish, give the toastmaster instructions in advance, rather than piecemeal later.

If a toastmaster attends, he will begin his duties by announcing the names of guests stepping forward to shake hands with the bridal party on the receiving line. Afterwards he will raise his voice and holler loud enough to be heard by the whole roomful of guests milling around chatting, perhaps talking excitedly with drinks in their hands, 'LADIES and GENTLEMEN! Pray be seated. DINNER is now being served!' When everyone has found their places he stands by the microphone at the top table, hammers on the table with a gavel, and announces loudly, 'Ladies and Gentlemen, Pray SILENCE for the Reverend John Smith, who will now say grace.'

If there is no toastmaster, the best man may introduce the minister more simply, 'Ladies and Gentlemen, Reverend John Smith will now say grace.' The best man should check in advance the correct title and form of address for the minister, Archbishop, Chief Rabbi, or whoever will be attending. Is it Reverend, the Reverend, Mr, Mrs, or what?

THE WHO AND WHEN OF SPEECHMAKING

The traditional order of toasts has a certain logic. The first speech leads up to a toast to bride and groom, the most important people of the day. In effect at a traditional first wedding they are the honoured guests of the hosts, her parents. But while as host her father can make a speech or toast to his new son-in-law, it would be a bit immodest for him to sing the praises of his own daughter, so often a friend of the family is chosen to make a speech and toast to both bride and groom, particularly if the father is going to speak later. The honour of making the first speech may go to the best speaker or the best friend, providing your choice keeps as many people as possible happy!

It falls to the groom to reply to the first speech on behalf of himself and his bride. Whom should he thank? Both his in-laws, especially if they've paid for or organized the wedding, and especially his mother-in-law. Who else has helped? Presumably the bridesmaids. So he ends with a toast to the bridesmaids and/or Matron of Honour.

The bride, however, may speak instead of her husband or as well as him. If there are no bridesmaids the groom can make a toast to his bride, who can speak next in reply. The bride can propose a toast to the bridegroom if the first toast was to her alone, or to the bridesmaids or Matron of Honour. Alternatively she can propose a toast to the family of the bridegroom, or if they are not present, to the guests.

The best man replies on behalf of the helpers (the bridesmaids). If there are no bridesmaids he does not have to speak, though he may wish to do so. The best man or the groom can end his speech with a toast to the hosts, and the bride's father or mother, or both, can reply.

An optional final toast to HM the Queen is made at most Jewish weddings in the UK. Lastly the best man or the toastmaster reads the telemessages in full if there are only a few, or reads the wittiest and then just gives the names of the senders of the others if there are many.

Variations to these customs can be made when there are no bridesmaids, or parents, or for a second marriage where the couple are paying for their own wedding.

When you have decided who is speaking, tell them all how many speakers there are and in which order they are speaking. Also check whom they will be toasting.

SURPRISE ANNOUNCEMENTS

The surprise delivery of a large gift, or the surprise arrival of a friend or relative from overseas, can be great fun. However, the best man or chief bridesmaid will have to take responsibility for the announcement, and the safekeeping of any gift. Most gifts are sent to the bride's mother's home in advance. That way the donor's cards are not muddled in the confusion of the day, and presents are kept safely and not left in hotels or halls where they might go astray.

It is the bride's day, and surprise announcements of the engagements and forthcoming weddings of other guests might cause illwill. They could deflect attention from the bride. The announcement of the bride's sister's engagement would be acceptable, but only if the bride herself knows in advance and gladly agrees to the public announcement being made at her wedding.

LANGUAGE BARRIERS

It can be a problem if, for example, the groom speaks no English: either he, or the bride and her family, may feel he ought to have the opportunity to speak at his own wedding, or that he has a duty to honour his hosts by thanking them publicly.

There are two solutions. Either he speaks in his own language and an interpreter delivers a translation; the translator can be the bride or another person. Or he can remain silent except for nodding, smiling and lifting his glass, allowing the bride to speak on their behalf, making due reference to him – my husband has asked me, etc.

The same system will be adopted if you have two receptions, one in each country. The speakers just have to do everything twice, taking note of which family is playing host.

INFORMAL RECEPTIONS

If your wedding guests are not seated in a reception hall but milling around a hotel or house your problem is to ensure that everyone is gathered in the right place at the right time to hear the speeches. You may have to tell guests in advance, 'We're cutting the cake and having the speeches in the dining room at half past,' then send the chief bridesmaid into the garden if it is a fine day, and the other bridesmaids around the house, to inform stragglers that the speeches are about to be made.

Don't start the proceedings until you are sure that the speakers themselves are present as well as the hosts or anyone else who will be thanked or mentioned in the speeches. Keep the speeches short because one third of the audience can't see, one third can't hear, and one third are trying to locate a seat so that they will not drop their handbag, glass, or plate, when they clap you.

Even if you decide to dispense with speeches altogether, you may find that after the cake is cut the crowd of well-wishers start chanting, 'Speech! Speech!', so that at least the groom has to give a speech. Somebody will then decide to give an impromptu reply if the best man doesn't, which makes him feel he should have spoken. So if you are the best man, you might as well prepare a few words. You might then find that having gone to the trouble of preparing a good speech and a joke just in case, you decide that you might as well give the speech anyway!

AFTER THE PARTY

Souvenirs of the wedding may include photographs of the speakers delivering speeches, the guests standing around the happy couple with glasses raised, typed copies of the speeches to go in the wedding album, or video recordings of the occasion.

When the party is over, members of the bridal party, and guests, may want to go up to the speakers and personally thank them, complimenting them on a good, amusing speech. In addition the bride and groom or hosts could express thanks in the form of a short note and accompanying photo or small gift.

Following the honeymoon, a party is often held to show the family photos of the trip. At the same time if a video has been taken of the wedding the speakers will want to see themselves. Should they have made any small mistakes they will laugh and learn to improve next time, and if their performance was perfect they will be absolutely delighted.

PREPARING THE SPEECH

When first sitting down to write your speech it may be a good idea to ask yourself why you have been asked to speak? Is it because you are expected to express good wishes or thanks, or because you are old and wise and expected to give advice, or because you are an extrovert and known for being humorous, because you are closely related to the other members of the family, or because you are a friend who has known the bride and groom for many years? The answer to this question may suggest to you what sort of speech to give.

PLANNING YOUR SPEECH

It is imporant to leave yourself enough time before the wedding in order to give much consideration as to what you would like to say, to do any research necessary, as well as to write your speech and to perform any last minute pruning. Remember, a few scribbled notes will not suffice.

LENGTH OF SPEECH

It is important to decide the length of your speech before beginning to research and write it. Too short and it may seem rude, too long and it may bore the guests and dampen the proceedings. If you really *can't* decide, settle on about five minutes. As a rule of thumb, if the occasion is a very formal one it will demand a longer speech; an informal occasion is more flexible. Remember, your speech will reflect not only on those you are speaking about but upon yourself.

GATHERING INFORMATION

Before even attempting to write your speech, take stock of the information you have to hand and see where the gaps occur. Only then should you set about researching in order to fill your speech out, make it interesting, witty, or whatever style of speech you would like to make. Beware, however, of drowning yourself in pages of notes. Panic will not be too far away if having collected all your information you have only a little time to write the speech.

Begin your research by looking for ideas on which you can expound and expand. For instance, the theme of marriage itself is always popular. You could research ideas on the history of marriage and interesting marriage customs both here and abroad.

In addition you could ask the parents of the bride and groom about their marriages. Did the marriage take place in wartime? Wearing similar clothes? With hundreds of guests? Enquire about the cake, photographer, transport, food, music, dancing, honeymoon destination, and first home. The living grandparents, uncles and aunts, may also have interesting stories about their weddings and marriages of friends, brothers, sisters and other relatives which took place in unusual or typically different circumstances in earlier days.

The best time to get people to talk about themselves is when you are sitting around the table over a meal or having tea, and when they are relaxed and are not likely to be diverted by other activities. Remember here that some people do not like seeing you write down their words for it interrupts their flow of thought. If you have a poor memory you could slip away for a moment and write yourself a quick note. Alternatively use a small tape recorder so that you can join in the conversation without notetaking. Reactions to tape recording differ. While a few people do not like tape recorders, others love to have what they said played back at a family party, and then argue and correct each other and make interesting extra comments.

From the family history you can learn about the family's ancestors, where they have lived and worked, where they met, their education, work skills, achievements, hobbies, and character. Personal anecdotes can be added. You will need to strike a balance between personal and general remarks. It would be unfortunate if you generalized a great deal and delivered a speech which could have been given at anybody's wedding, when the bride and groom have fascinating family histories.

So make sure you persist even if your first enquiry produces no immediate result. You may find that the bride says, 'Don't bother to say anything about where I went to school and where we met. It's not really interesting.' If one of your subjects doesn't provide you with information, ask another. You might discover that someone else such as the bride's mother has really interesting revelations about the bride. Maybe despite or because of failing 'O' levels she went on to become the first woman engineer at her college because her earlier setbacks had made her determined to prove that she could succeed.

Make enquiries from both sides of the family. The discovery of the meaning of the family name may be news to the other side. And the countries all the grandparents came from could be quite interesting. But so is the fact that one or both families have lived in the same area for four generations. This is not the sort of news which would make the front pages of newspapers, but you can assume that on the day everyone will be interested in the bride and groom and their respective families.

The profession of the bride or groom may provide speech matter. If your subject has academic qualifications you could ask such questions as, 'How long did it take you to get your degree?'; 'What subject is your PhD in?'; 'How long have you been a member of the Architect's Association?'; 'Where did you study for the bar?'; 'How does the FBOA differ from the FSMC?'.

If the bride or groom or their families or ancestors are famous, it might be worth your while looking them up in *Who's Who*, and similar reference works, of which there are many editions covering authors, scientists, theatrical personages, and royalty.

COMPOSING AND PRUNING YOUR SPEECH

WORK OUT THE STRUCTURE

Prune your notes if necessary and arrange them in the order in which you would like to use them. List the essentials to be included such as thanks and the toast. Only then should you consider your opening remarks.

Avoid stereotyped ideas if possible. Have you talked only about the bride cooking for the bridegroom when you know she is a career girl and a women's libber, and if *she* is not some of the audience will be?

Delete anything in dubious taste. If in doubt, leave it out. Avoid negatives, regrets, criticisms of others, making the families appear foolish, making yourself appear foolish, and anything vague.

Remove rude jokes and deliberate sexual innuendos,

and also watch out for unintended double entendres which might make inebriated members of the audience laugh when you are being serious and sincere. You can cause hysterics all round with such apparently innocent remarks as the bride's father saying, 'I didn't expect to enjoy myself so much. You don't enjoy things so much when you get older.'

READING YOUR SPEECH ALOUD

Read the speech aloud to yourself first to be sure the sentences are not too long and you are not stumbling over them. It must sound like something you would say spontaneously. Later when you are satisfied, you might read it to a limited number of people – just one or two. You don't want all the wedding party to have heard the speech in advance of the wedding.

IMPROVING THE STYLE

Change words or phrases you have repeated. Enliven cliches by subtly altering them if possible. Explain jargon and foreign phrases.

Change repetitions by looking for new words with the same meaning in Roget's *Thesaurus*. Paperback copies are available from bookshops. A dictionary of synonyms and antonyms might also be useful. And if you intend to compose your own poems, limericks or verses, a songwriter's rhyming dictionary would be invaluable.

For an ordinary wedding a colloquial way of speaking will be suitable. However, should you be called upon to speak at a grand, formal wedding you may feel that a more erudite speech is required. Forms of address and titles for important personages can be found in reference books.

To eliminate or locate colloquial words there are dictionaries of slang. For the transatlantic marriages, several dictionaries of American expressions are available, enabling you to eliminate Americanisms, explain yourself to American listeners, or make jokes about the differences between Americanisms and conventional English language.

ANTICIPATING LITTLE PROBLEMS

Try to anticipate any controversial subjects and disasters you might have to mention, or avoid mentioning, in the course of your speech.

Make yourself a troubleshooter's checklist. What would I say if: her Dad died; his parents couldn't attend; her parents didn't attend; the best man didn't arrive because his plane from India was delayed; it turned out to be the groom's second wedding, although it is her first; the Matron of Honour didn't turn up because she was ill; the groom dried up and forgot to compliment the bridesmaids so I couldn't thank him?

You may also have to state facts which are obvious to you, but not to cousins who have not seen the family for several years. You might also have to avoid stating the obvious.

FINAL CHECK

Finally, check that your speech fits in with the speeches and toasts given by others. Be sure that you know the name of the previous speaker so that you can say, 'Thank you, George,' confident that his name is not James. And if your friend, the bridegroom, or the bride's father-in-law or another old man is usually called 'Al', on this occasion should you be calling him by his full name, (and if so, is that short for Albert, Alfred, Ali, Alexis, Alexander), or, even more formally, Mr Smith?

DELIVERING THE SPEECH

Perhaps the most important rule to follow when delivering your speech is to make sure that you are relaxed right from the start. With this in mind take a few relaxing deep breaths before you stand to speak and then make sure you are standing comfortably. Above all, if you are well prepared you will be more relaxed.

IMPORTANT TECHNIQUES

BEING HEARD

Being audible depends on your ability to project your voice and correctly using a microphone if one is available. To begin, take a deep breath before you start so that you don't run out of breath in the middle of the sentence. Do not lose interest and let the end of a sentence fade away as you scan your notes for the next remark. Throughout the speech you must speak loudly, aiming to be heard by the person at the far end of the room.

Keep your head up. Don't talk to your tie or your shoes. Don't mumble. If you have an audience of about a hundred people at least one will have hearing problems, difficulty understanding English, or difficulty understanding your accent. That is another reason for keeping your head up, so that such people can see your lips moving as well as hearing what you are saying. If they have to turn to their neighbour and ask for a repetition of what you just said, the resulting muttering will also prevent other members of the audience from hearing what you say next. If you know in advance that some people are hard of hearing you can seat them accordingly.

You must get the attention of your audience right at the start of the speech – then hold the audience's attention during the speech. Their attention will wander if you pause to look at your notes, and again the muttering of some will prevent others from hearing. However, you should pause after jokes for two reasons. Firstly, so that those who are slow know when the joke ends, or can have a moment to reflect and catch the subtleties of any double entendre. Secondly, if the joke is so successful that it gets a lot of laughter you do not want to rush on so fast that your next words cannot be heard.

USING A MICROPHONE

When you arrive at the reception check whether a microphone will be available. But be prepared and able to speak without it just in case it is not available or an electrical fault develops.

At a seated dinner the speakers are usually at the top table and the microphone is nearby and can be handed to each speaker. But if the first speaker is not seated at the top table there may be a pause while he walks to the microphone. If a delay occurs between one speaker and the next the audience may start talking so that the next speaker will have to recapture their attention. A toast-master has his own techniques. He may bang on the table with a mallet and then shout, 'Pray silence for THE BRIDEGROOM!'

The first speaker should not be the one who discovers whether the microphone is working at all. Perhaps the best man could take on the responsibility of arriving before the guests and checking the microphone. However, the best man is sometimes asked to stay behind at the church, organizing transport and ensuring that the last guest does not get stranded when all the cars have departed. In this case another usher or bridesmaid could take over the duty of checking the microphone.

The usual technique for checking that the microphone is set to the correct level after the audience arrives is to call, 'Can you all hear me?' Since those at the front shout loudly, you won't necessarily know that those at the back can't. A more interesting variation would be, 'Hello, I'm going to check that the microphone works before I start. Could those on the back table shout, "Hello".' Another variation would be, 'Hello, I just want to check you all got here all right. Did the relatives from Manchester arrive?' (Check the table plan in advance to see who is on the back table or tables.) 'Yes? Good. Now I can start.'

Microphones can make high-pitched screaming noises called 'howl', and they are due to feedback. The cure is to move the microphone or to move the loudspeakers, which is not always practical, or adjust the microphone volume to a lower level. The adjusting device is located on the amplifier that the microphone is plugged into. If you cannot correct it, anyone experienced in public speaking, such as the toastmaster, should be able to remedy the problem. Sophisticated systems do not present this problem at all.

When you are testing the microphone, start softly and then speak louder. You don't want to start by bellowing so loudly that people shrink in alarm. If you see the audience cowering back, you are too loud. Alternatively, see if they are straining to hear you. Some experienced speakers ask a friend to stand against the back wall and signal with hands facing forward by their ears if you need to speak louder, and with hands horizontal if you should speak more softly.

Ensure that you are not so near the microphone that it picks up every sound including heavy breathing and muttered asides. Neither stand so far away that it cannot pick up your voice. The other thing to avoid is swaying backward and forward so that you are alternately bellowing and whispering, fading out or disappearing entirely at intervals like a badly tuned radio station!

Don't be frightened by hearing the sound of your own voice magnified. Everybody wants to hear you because they are your friends, or because they are friends of the happy couple and want to hear what you have to say about them. If you practise listening to yourself speaking on tape, you will be used to the timbre or magnification of your voice.

EMPHASIS AND SPEED

The pace of your delivery is important. Don't gallop through your speech as if you can't wait to finish it and get away. Vary the pace and speed; if the sentences are varied in length this helps. If you are inclined to race along like a commentator at a horse race try to slow down and introduce a pause or two. But if you have a slow, sad delivery, try to talk faster, and reach a climax at the end of one or two sentences, at least as you reach the end of the speech.

Introduce some changes in emotion: gratitude, surprise, amusement, and seriousness. This will be partly dictated by the text. But if you have practised on a tape recorder and you discover that you are talking in a monotonous, even tone, try reading the speech putting emphasis on certain words. Decide which is the most important word in the sentence. Should the sentence, 'I have never seen such a beautiful bride' be read as, 'I have NEVER seen such a beautiful bride', or 'I have never seen such as BEAUTIFUL bride'? Or even, ' "I" have never seen such a beautiful bride'. You could even underline key phrases or words in your speech notes. Your facial expressions can help to emphasize parts of your speech too: try smiling, scowling, or raising your eyebrows.

You will find that ease of emphasis comes more readily if you are not standing stiffly to attention while delivering your speech. A rehearsal plot used by actors may be useful here. Stand and rehearse in front of a full length mirror, checking that you are smiling and making the right gestures, including lifting your glass sufficiently high and forward when proposing the toast so that you convey enthusiasm.

CONFIDENCE

If you are lacking in confidence ask yourself what most frightens you. If it is finding a good speech to interest and amuse the audience, then with preparation you should have solved that problem already. Is it having people looking at you or having to speak to a large crowd when you have never done that before? Perhaps you think that some of the more important people present will think your speech is not good enough. If you are afraid of talking to a crowd, remember that this is not a crowd of strangers, but a crowd of friends. Your audience is not critical. They want you to succeed. They are out to have a good time. They are expecting you to say something nice. You can rely on their goodwill.

Where you look when making your speech can be a help. Start by concentrating on one person, perhaps addressing your mother or your best friend and then, when you see them smiling back and you gather confidence, turn to the rest of the audience. In fact, to get confidence when rehearsing your speech, read it to the person who is most likely to be encouraging.

Again it will be your posture that will help you and give an impression of confidence, or lack of it, to your audience. Walk tall if you have to walk towards the microphone. Don't sink into your shoulders as if one of the chandeliers is about to descend and hit you on the head. Stretch up as if you are trying to reach something on the top shelf of the kitchen at home and you know you are going to succeed.

Try not to look anxious and afraid. Smile. If you smile, other people will smile back. Look at people as you pass them and you will see that they are smiling at you. This is a happy occasion and a party occasion so almost certainly they will be smiling!

CONQUERING NERVES

There are many techniques you can use beforehand to help you relax. It could be having a good night's sleep the night before, playing tennis or taking a sauna, losing weight or having a stiff drink just before you begin. For those who know how, doing yoga for half an hour in the morning, or meditating in a darkened room for ten minutes just before giving the speech will assist, or perhaps it will require nothing more than taking a deep breath before you speak.

PRACTISING PUBLIC SPEAKING

If you have never stood up in front of other people and given a speech, you could take a course in public speaking, or buy a book on the subject and go through the techniques they practise. This may seem rather excessive just for giving one speech, but if this is your first and you speak well, you may well be asked to give speeches later at other weddings and functions. And if you enjoy it you may even volunteer to do so. A public speaking course may be very useful for your career, and will give you confidence in general, but if you have no spare cash or time for a course because the wedding is approaching, you might try practising public speaking by yourself.

Since general public speaking courses are not preparing you to give a particular speech, but to give speeches in general, the first task is simply to get you to stand up in a room full of people and ask you to speak about anything you like for three minutes. You could try this with several subjects. Pick three subjects you know well, such as your hobby, your job, and your mother. For example, 'Ladies and Gentlemen, I am very glad to have this opportunity of telling you about my magnificent stamp collection. I have been collecting stamps of the world since I was eight-years-old and specialize in, etc.' Or, 'Ladies and Gentlemen, I am delighted to be invited to tell you about the amusing experiences I have had while travelling/teaching as a, etc.' Perhaps, 'Ladies and Gentlemen, everybody thinks their own mother is something special and I am no exception. My mother . . .' You can either record this and play it back or stand in front of a friend and let them criticize and make helpful suggestions.

REHEARSING IN THE RECEPTION HALL

Most people are slightly nervous in unfamiliar situations ranging from opening the door into a strange room to having a job interview. If being in unfamiliar places worries you, you might find it helpful to visit the reception hall in advance and even to stand where you will be standing to give the speech and rehearse the opening sentence.

PRE-WEDDING SPEECHES

Various kinds of engagement and pre-wedding parties can be held. An engagement party can be arranged to introduce families and friends to the other families, and inform everyone that the young couple are now attached. If the engagement period is to be protracted because the couple are young or studying, there may be a big party not unlike a small-scale version of the wedding at which the future bride has a chance to display her ring to well-wishers and acquire presents for the new home, for which the guests must be thanked.

More than one bride's father has been heard to say that he did not want to have a large engagement party if the wedding was to follow within a year because that would involve him in the organization and expense of 'two weddings'. That is why the bridegroom's family hosts the engagement party.

An engagement party is traditionally held by the future bridegroom's parents, but there is no reason why one should not be held by the bride's family, or by both families in their own home or elsewhere, particularly if the two families live in different areas.

Unlike wedding reception speeches the engagement party speeches are usually very short, merely introducing the young couple, expressing pleasure at the engagement, and wishing them happiness. A parent of the bride or groom speaks or, if there are no parents present, another older relative playing host can make the speech.

ENGAGEMENT PARTY SPEECHES

TO THE HAPPY COUPLE BY THE GROOM'S FATHER/MOTHER (OR THE BRIDE'S)

I am delighted to welcome you to meet Steven's fiancée Annabelle and her family (or Annabelle's fiancé Steven and his family). They hope to marry next June, or sooner if they find a house. It is lovely to see you all, and so many friends from their old school and college and Steven's office (or from Annabelle's old school). Thank you so much for your good wishes. I hope everybody's got a glass of champagne – Have you? Good! Because I would like you to join me in wishing every happiness to Annabelle and Steven.

To Annabelle and Steven.

REPLY AND THANKS TO THE HOST AND GUESTS BY BRIDE/GROOM AND TOAST TO THE OTHER FAMILY

I want to thank Mum and Dad for throwing this lovely party so that you could meet Annabelle and her family (or Steven and his family). Thank you all for coming this evening, and for bringing such generous presents. I'd like you to drink a toast to Annabelle's parents Betty and Jim (or Steven's parents John and Clare).

To Betty and Jim (or John and Clare).

THANKS AND TOAST TO HOSTS BY THE OTHER FAMILY

I'd like to thank Betty and Jim for organizing this wonderful party to give both of our families the ideal opportunity to get to know each other. And thank you everyone for the lovely presents for our new home. Please join me in wishing good health to Betty and Jim.

To Betty and Jim.

BACHELOR PARTIES

Stag parties and hen parties used to be held the night before the wedding, the last opportunity for the girls and boys to go out, or stay at home, with friends of their own sex. The timing of these parties, and their occasionally unfortunate results have made it very unpopular to hold them immediately before the wedding.

An innocuous bachelor party can be held either at a respectable restaurant where food is served along with drink, or with food and family present at home. The entertainment is the pleasure of reminiscing with one's friends and making a couple of witty speeches. If this is thought too tame, a lively and amusing party can be held at home or in a room at a sports club along the lines of a fancy dress party, again with humorous speeches.

The responsibility of the brother, sister, or best friend who organizes the bachelor party is to ensure that it is a happy event for the guest of honour, and that the jokes, entertainment and gifts do not embarrass those present or absent who will hear about the party later, or imperil the relationship between the engaged couple. To organize the event successfully, make an amusing speech, and get the right balance between outrageous fun and good taste, will indicate to the bride or groom that you can be relied upon to perform well as best man or bridesmaid at the subsequent wedding.

BACHELOR PARTY SPEECHES

SPEECH BY BEST FRIEND TO BRIDEGROOM-TO-BE

We are here to say goodbye to our brother, Steven, who is departing for the land of the married. We all knew that

Steven was regarded as an eligible bachelor, but we didn't think that marriage was what he was eligible for. We tried to dissuade Steven from marrying, but alas to no avail. We warned him that a husband is a glorified handyman, that he will be spending his weekends painting, decorating, gardening, and maintaining the car. He will be abandoning happy Saturday afternoons spent watching football, and instead spend them shopping, spending money. If he cannot afford a dishwasher he will be a dishwasher. Sundays will no longer be a day of rest spent playing cricket or sailing, but devoted to visiting in-laws. Evenings at the pub or the bar will have to be abandoned and he will stay at home, opening bottles for others to drink. To all this, he said, and I quote, 'Rubbish.' So you see, his vocabulary has changed already! He continued, 'You are not married. How do you know?'

So we sought wiser men than ourselves who have trodden the same path he proposes to take. W. C. Fields said that women are like elephants, very nice to look at, but he wouldn't want to own one. A look at our former friends who have married will show that marriages are made in heaven, to make life hell below.

(Alternatively choose a quotation from the selection in the chapter entitled Quotations.)

Many young ladies will mourn Steven's departure. He was all things to all young women. Sometimes they were queuing to telephone him. In fact a lady who looked like Mae West was hiding in the phone box at the car park waiting to see him as we came along tonight. She is still waiting, alas in vain.

We, too, have failed. He remains unconvinced. To him an evening with one woman is worth an evening with ten of us. She must be a truly wonderful girl. We shall never know. So we have gathered here this evening to spend a last evening telling jokes with our friend, who is unfettered by responsibilities. We decided to present him with a small token which he can take to his new life, and keep in memory of his bachelor days and the friends he has left behind. Unfortunately when we went into the shop to buy his gift we met a couple of his ex-girlfriends who insisted on coming along to remind him of the girls he is leaving behind, and to present him with a small, but wonderfully-packaged gift, a token of our friendship. Steven – Here they are!

Two male friends dressed in drag appear, possibly as twin brides, preferably in long dresses or other outfits that keep them well covered to prevent any incidents among their own group or from outsiders. They present the gift. It should be something useful for setting up home, if only a rather expensive bottle-opener, possibly with other small mementoes of his favourite bachelor activities or sport such as golf balls, presented inside something amusing and clearly feminine but not in bad taste, such as a pair of stockings, with a blue garter for him to give to his bride for the wedding so that she can wear 'something borrowed, something blue'.

An alternative would be a huge gift, something large which the drag brides have difficulty getting through the door, such as a golfing umbrella, or a garden umbrella if the couple hope to move from bachelor flats into a house. It could be extended to look even longer, and presented with the words that we wanted to give you 'a small gift' or a gift 'big enough for two'. The jokes which this will certainly provoke can be left to the inspiration of the moment.

SPEECH OF REPLY BY THE BACHELOR BOY

Dear Friends. I appreciate your concern for me. I, too, am concerned for you. Your gifts are very welcome and will be appreciated by Annabelle as well as myself. Boys/ Guys/Mates, you don't know what you are missing. While I am tucked up by my warm fire being waited on hand and foot, you will be out in your cars touring the streets with nowhere to go, wishing in vain for a lovely girl to console you and end your loneliness.

How can a football or a golfball be compared to a girl? Those of you who still do not know the difference, I hope will one day find out the good news, and meet the girl of their dreams. In only five weeks I shall be getting married to Annabelle. We look forward to seeing you all at our wedding, and later to welcoming you to dinner in our new home. Who knows, at the wedding or at our place you may meet the girl who may change your mind about the joys of remaining a bachelor. Annabelle and I have 'got a little list' of eligible bachelors, and you are all on it. We bachelors have had many good times together, and we shall have more. They are not over. I am not halving my friends, but doubling them. Please raise your glass and drink a toast to Alan who has organized this party for me. May he enjoy happy bachelor days, but not too many, before he realizes the error of his ways and is claimed by one of the angels on Earth. To Alan. (An alternative toast could be to friendships which endure forever.)

SPEECH BY BEST FRIEND TO BRIDE-TO-BE

We tried to dissuade Annabelle from marrying, but alas to no avail. We warned her that a wife's work is never done. She is chained to the kitchen sink and washing socks. Unpaid secretary, social organizer, babysitter, cook, etcetera. When we told her this she said, and I quote, 'Phooey!'

There are many young men who will mourn her departure from the ranks of the available, ah (sigh), some of whom had fond memories of her, others, merely hopes. She was a very popular girl. Men flocked into her office. We realized why when we called. She had taken the sign MEN from the Gents, and put it on her office door.

But now that Steven has claimed her, those days are

gone. Her parents and flatmates look forward to the recovery of their telephones and bathrooms.

We must admit that it looks to us like a very good match, and it is only because she is marrying Steven that she has such an idealized view of what men and marriage are really like. Does she not know the truth, that after marriage, life changes. Men can be late. Women cannot. We are duty bound to warn her of what others who married have said. But since we have failed to persuade her to stay single, we can only wish her well, and give her this small token of our good wishes for her future, in memory of our happy bachelor days together.

The girls bringing in the parcel should dress up like the bridegroom-to-be, taking his work or hobby as the theme, or like any male characters such as footballers, policemen or policewomen wearing sunglasses, gorillas with cigars, city gents in bowler hats, or a spoof pop group of boys in short trousers and caps singing, 'Will you still need me when I'm sixty-four?'. The parcel presented should be amusing, either an unusual shape, or several boxes inside each other so that the gift takes a while to find. The gift presented should be one of value and usefulness for setting up home (so that she is not disappointed), perhaps with a memento of her bachelor days, such as a cassette by her favourite pop singers, but inside a container gift which is a joke, e.g. a silver cake slice, or selection of kitchen implements, or telephone address book, plus cassettes in a pair of large man's football socks (the correct size to fit her husband to be), or a pair of pillowcases embroidered 'his' and 'hers'. There should be a card signed by all the friends.

SPEECH OF REPLY BY BACHELOR GIRL

Dear Friends. I appreciate your message of goodwill, and your charming gifts. Don't you dare tell Steven that you found this pair of red socks under my bed! I shall always remember you, the way you look tonight! We have had a lot of fun together and we still shall. You'll all be at my wedding in six weeks'/six months' time, and frequent guests at my house, and in my garden. I shall throw my bouquet to one of you at the wedding and who knows, there might be another wedding in the not too distant future for somebody. My mother says, there's one for everyone. Let's all have a drink together, I hope all my girlfriends will meet steady boyfriends, but as Helen organized this party and is going to be my chief bridesmaid, I'd like to wish happiness to Helen. To Helen. (An alternative toast would be, 'To friendship. May good friends stay together forever'.)

WEDDING SPEECHES

The following sample speeches are to suit different situations and speakers. Choose the most appropriate speech and substitute your own details. Alternatively pick up a pen and a piece of paper and compose your own speech immediately after reading all these suggestions for inspiration.

TOAST TO THE BRIDE AND GROOM

(Brief toast at an informal wedding party.)

I would like to propose a toast to Annabelle and Steven, wishing them much joy and happiness for their future together. May all their troubles be little ones. To Annabelle and Steven.

TOAST TO THE BRIDE AND GROOM

(A brief, simple, direct speech for the bride's father.)

Reverend Brown, Ladies and Gentlemen, all my guests, I cannot tell you how pleased I am today to see my daughter Annabelle looking so radiantly happy, as she begins life as the wife of Steven. My wife and I do not feel that we are losing Annabelle, but entrusting her to

Steven's good care. During the last few months as we have got to know him better, he has shown himself to be exactly the sort of person we had hoped Annabelle would marry – charming, sincere, reliable – with a clear idea of what he wants from life and how to achieve it. I know that his many friends and family, as well as those who have only recently met him, think that this must be one of those marriages that are made in heaven, and will want to join me in wishing Steven and Annabelle a long and happy married life together. So please stand and raise your glasses, and drink to the health and happiness of Annabelle and Steven. (Pause.)

To Annabelle and Steven.

TOAST TO THE BRIDE AND GROOM

(Longer, personalized speech by old friend or relative when bride's father is present but does not make a speech.)

Annabelle's father, George, and her mother, Martha, have done me the honour of offering me the opportunity to make a speech on this wonderful occasion and propose a toast to Annabelle and Steven. When I asked why they chose me, George said, because you are the President of the Oxford Drama Club/my bank manager/my oldest friend/the boss/have known us for twenty-five years/you are the tallest/you have the loudest voice/, and Martha said, because you have known Annabelle since she was fourteen/a baby/a child/all her life/at school/at college/ you tell the best jokes. I have seen Annabelle acting in school plays/at the drama club on many occasions but today she doesn't need to act, she has a starring role.

Seriously, over the years I have seen Annabelle develop many talents and accomplishments. She has won prizes for (drama/music/essay-writing/cookery/coming top of her class in school, been awarded the first grade in music/drama, studied nursing/teaching/ballet/ice-skating/French and management/interviewing/accounting, learned how to drive/ski/sail/swim/dance/surf/, followed her interests in travelling/bridge-playing/opera/the orchestra/film and reading science fiction/historical novels/biographies, as well as finding time to raise money for charity/do voluntary work with handicapped children/attend church functions regularly/design clothes/paint/draw and to help in her family's shop/business/company/restaurant.

It was while she was at school/college/work, that she met Steven who was studying/working/travelling.

Though Steven has not yet qualified as a doctor/passed his A levels/opened his restaurant/learned to tell the difference between a gasket and a sprocket, it was obvious that they had much in common. (*Or*: At first it didn't look as if they had much in common.) But as they got to know each other Annabelle discovered that Steven liked the arts as much as the sciences/hiking as well as driving/driving cars as well as repairing them. And Steven learned that Annabelle could pilot a plane/ice a cake/run a playgroup/speak fluent French. And when Steven learned that Annabelle/Annabelle's father/mother/brother was an MP/barrister/had the best collection of Beatles records, that clinched it.

These young people have a bright future ahead of them, a wonderful career/job/home planned in London/New York/Sydney. And I am sure you will want to join me in wishing them every success and happiness in their new venture and marriage. Please raise your glasses and drink to the health and prosperity of Annabelle and Steven. (Pause.)

To Annabelle and Steven.

TOAST TO THE BRIDE AND GROOM

(Relative/friend's speech when the bride's family is recently deceased.)

It is my great pleasure to be here with you on this happy occasion and to help Annabelle and Steven celebrate their marriage. I have known Annabelle and her parents for many years, since I/we/they came to live in London/Glasgow/Cardiff.

Annabelle's late father, George, used to enjoy a game of football/a game of golf/fixing the car on Saturday afternoons, and we spent many happy hours together sailing/relaxing often accompanied by Steven. I remember George saying that Steven seemed to be a very pleasant/good-natured/hard-working/ambitious/talented young man. I know George and Steven got on well and George would have been delighted to have seen this happy day. Although we miss George's presence, and his unfailing good humour, we know that he was looking forward to this wedding and we have fulfilled his hopes and wishes, and in a sense he is with us here today in our memories of him.

He would have been very satisfied to know what a comfort Steven has been to our family, how understanding, how supportive a friend in time of need, a valuable help to us in everything from fixing the car, taking over day to day decisions affecting the business/work/Annabelle's job, to just being there when we wanted advice and assistance. The wedding was postponed, but Annabelle is a girl well worth waiting for. Doesn't she look a picture today? George would have been proud of her, as I am sure Steven is. And it is with every confidence that I tell you I am sure that this young couple will have a very happy marriage, and I would ask you to join me in wishing them both a long, happy, and prosperous future together. Please stand and lift your glasses. I propose a toast – to Annabelle and Steven. (Lift glass in air and wait for everybody to stand and raise glasses.)

To Annabelle and Steven.

TOAST TO THE BRIDE AND GROOM

(Suitable for an older man addressing a large, distinguished audience.)

Ladies and Gentlemen, it is always a pleasure to attend a wedding. They say that the world loves a lover and I think this is true. Marriage is the expression of love, and also the start of a lifelong adventure. Plato said, 'The beginning is the most important part of the work'. If that is the case, then Annabelle and Steven have been fortunate in enjoying the most wonderful beginning. They already have most of the good gifts one would wish upon a young couple. Annabelle is a beautiful bride, Steven is a handsome husband, and both come from secure family homes where their parents have set examples of what a good marriage should be.

A good marriage is not something you can create on your own without help from your partner. It is a joint venture. Marriage is like a journey in a boat. You cannot drill a hole in the boat and when water floods in say to your companion, 'It's nothing to do with you, the water is coming in on my side of the boat.' You must row in the same direction. In fact love has been defined as not looking at each other, but looking in the same direction.

If marriage is a boat, then many of us are in the same boat! Annabelle and Steven, you are embarking on a wonderful journey, and you have many friends who will support you, and help you, and wish you well. I would now like to ask everyone in this room to stand with me, and raise their glasses. (Pause briefly until noise of moving chairs ceases.) I propose a toast to the long life, health, wealth, and happy marriage, of Annabelle and Steven.

To Annabelle and Steven!

TOAST TO THE BRIDE AND GROOM

(By the best man or best girl.)
It gives me special pleasure to be present at the wedding of my good friends Annabelle and Steven, because I introduced them at the Dashing Disco/Royal Hotel/ Country Club and because I have known both of them for many years at school/the tennis club. May their lives continue with equal joy and may they share many happy occasions and reunions such as this with our families and friends. Here's to Annabelle and Steven.

BEST MAN'S TOAST TO BRIDE AND GROOM

('Impromptu' speech at a very small wedding without bridesmaids.)
This is a lovely small, intimate gathering of friends, which is just the way Annabelle and Steven wanted it to be. And we appreciate how honoured we are to be among the select few whom they chose to share this very special occasion with them. Everyone here is a close friend or relative and we all have personal knowledge of Annabelle's unique qualities, her kindness, her gift for creating a happy atmosphere and her loyal friendship. And we are delighted that she is marrying Steven, who is so loved/admired by his family and close friends and is respected by all of us for his hard work/talents/skills/zest for life. He shares many of her good qualities and they both deserve all the good things in life. So let's wish them

both a very happy married life together. Has everyone got a drink? Good.

To Annabelle and Steven.

TOAST TO THE BRIDE'S PARENTS

(Groom's speech, replying to first toast to bride and groom, a longer, humorous speech.)

Reverend Brown, Ladies and Gentlemen, (Pause). Thank you very much, George, for those kind words. It goes almost without saying how pleased I am to be here today. In order not to dull your pleasure I intend to only speak for a few minutes in case we all get snowed in/melt away in the heat! We couldn't have wished for better weather – perfect sunshine, just the right start for a wedding day and honeymoon/the most beautiful, romantic white Christmas.

As you all know Annabelle has been a much sought after girl/woman, but I'm pleased to announce the winner of the competition, me. There are no runners up, or associated prizes.

My new mother-in-law, Martha, has worked long and hard for many months to prepare this wonderful occasion, all the little details such as these beautiful flower/cake decorations were planned by her, and my father-in-law has taken on his second mortgage without complaint, like the good-natured man he is. I am very pleased to be part of the same family and to know that my parents feel the same.

Speaking of whom, today represents a great occasion for both my parents, being the culmination of many years of planning of a different sort. They have prepared me well, supported me through university, taught me the difference between right and wrong, so that I know which I am enjoying at any given time!

Annabelle is beautiful, intelligent, and hard working. The list of her good qualities is extremely long. Unfortunately I cannot read her handwriting.

I would like to thank you all for your presence – in both senses of the word, but especially for the smiling faces I see in front of me. I am particularly pleased that Aunt Alice managed to make the long journey down to Surrey from Aberdeen for this occasion, and we are all delighted that Annabelle's sister, Sharon, flew all the way from Australia to join us and be such a charming bridesmaid. Of course she had a 'little help' – quite a big help, actually, from Tracey, who looked so sweet holding Annabelle's train.

My best man, Alan, has made everything go smoothly, and made his contribution to what has seemed the perfect day.

(Alternative ending: Finally, I must pay tribute to the bridesmaids Sharon, Natalie, Margaret and Sue whose invaluable support has helped to make this day so successful.)

If there are no bridesmaids, the toast is to his parents-in-law as follows:

In conclusion, thank you, everybody, for listening, and I hope you are having a wonderful afternoon/evening and are all as happy as we are today. Would you kindly stand and raise your glasses and drink a toast to the health of your hosts, two wonderful people, George and Martha. (Pause.)

To George and Martha!

TOAST TO BRIDEGROOM AND BOTH FAMILIES

(Informal toast by the bride.)

I'd like to propose a toast to the most wonderful man

in the world, my new husband, Steven. I'd also like to thank his parents for what they have contributed over the years to make him the person he is, supporting him through college, and also for making me such a welcome member of their family. I must also thank my parents for everything they have done for me and especially this wonderful event, my wedding to Steven. May we all meet on many more happy occasions.

To Steven.

TOAST TO THE BRIDESMAIDS

(Bridegroom's speech in reply to toast to the bride and groom, a brief but sincere speech.)

My wife and I (pause for laughter), thank you for your kind words. It is wonderful to be surrounded by so many friends and good wishes. We have been overwhelmed by the kindness and help we have received, the generous gifts, and the people who have made extra contributions on this, our special day. I must mention the bridesmaids who have done so much to help my wife, and added glamour to the photographs which will remind us of this very happy occasion.

To the bridesmaids!

TOAST TO GROOM'S FAMILY

(By the bride's father, replying to the groom's toast to the bride's parents who are hosts, giving personal family marriage details.)

Thank you, Steven. As you know Annabelle is our only daughter, so this will be our only chance to stage such a lovely wedding. And we did not want to miss the opportunity of having such a wonderful day, complete with the white wedding car. When my parents' generation were marrying back in the 1950s not everyone had cars and the best man's responsibility was to organize transport for all the guests. After the ceremony the bridal couple rushed to the photographer's studio to have their portrait taken, before joining their guests who were waiting for the wedding meal. For each generation the circumstances are different. Now we can have a photographer visiting us to make a video, so that we can remember this magical day for the rest of our lives.

Martha and I married during the Second World War, as did Steven's parents, when wedding couples needed clothing coupons from all their relatives to make the wedding dress and wedding suits, which had to be of sensible material so that they could be worn again. Everybody saved all their food coupons for the wedding cake. Since you could not go abroad you honeymooned on the south coast at resorts such as Bournemouth where there was barbed wire on the beaches. Despite that, Martha and I had a wonderful wedding, and were very grateful that when other families were separated, we had the opportunity to be together. But I think you will understand why we do not regret staging a grand wedding for Annabelle and Steven.

For us this has been a second chance, our only chance, to enjoy a wedding with all the luxuries and trimmings, and all our family around us. We want Annabelle and Steven to enjoy the things we never had, not to take them for granted, but to appreciate how lucky they are to be able to celebrate like this surrounded by their families and friends.

I know that Steven's parents understand how glad we are to do whatever we can for our daughter, and their son. We are very pleased to have Gregory and Gillian and their family here to celebrate with us. Their generous support and presence, joining in enthusiastically with everything we planned, has enabled us to truly enjoy this day. So please join me in drinking a toast to the health of my son-in-law's parents, Gregory and Gillian.

To Gregory and Gillian.

On a second or subsequent marriage it is frequently said that a wedding speech should make no reference to previous spouses, nor children of earlier marriages unless they are junior pages and need to be acknowledged and welcomed, or even the fact that either party has been married before. In theory you can use the usual wedding speeches, simply omitting any references to white weddings. However, rather than having the guests whispering conspiratorially amongst themselves the unmentionable secret that this is a second marriage, some speakers prefer a more direct and honest approach. This particularly applies where there is no question of a divorced previous spouse. It may be felt desirable to inform guests that one party was previously a devoted husband or wife, a widow or widower, who after years of loneliness should be congratulated on at last having found happiness again.

TOAST TO BRIDE AND GROOM (SECOND MARRIAGE)

(Short, happy, slightly humorous speech for a bride enjoying her first marriage to a divorced man.)

Annabelle, for you this is a first marriage and a time of excitement and hope. For Steven it is a second marriage. He liked marriage so much that despite all the difficulties of his first attempt, when he met you he decided to try it again.

Annabelle, you may not realize it, but you are gaining the advantage of marrying a man who has had the sharp corners rubbed off him. A mature specimen. A vintage blend.

We hope that you will always enjoy life together, a very long and happy life together, and that you will always retain the enthusiasm of this new start, and remember the joy and delight of finding each other, which is so evident today. So we will all raise our glasses to you and toast your future.

To Annabelle and Steven.

TOAST TO BRIDE AND GROOM

(Short, happy, slightly humorous speech when the groom is marrying for the first time to a divorced woman.)

Steven, for you this is a first marriage and a time of expectation and hope. For Annabelle it is a second marriage. You must be especially proud today, because she liked you so much that despite all the difficulties of her first marriage, when she met you she decided to try it again. What an honour!

Annabelle, you have the advantage of experience. Steven, you may not realize it, but you are gaining many advantages by marrying a mature woman. Vintage. We hope that both of you will always enjoy married life, a very long and happy life together. And that you will always retain the enthusiasm of this new start, and remember the joy and delight of finding each other, which is so evident today. So we will all raise our glasses to you and toast your future.

To Annabelle and Steven.

TOAST TO BRIDE AND GROOM

(Sincere speech by a friend on the occasion of a second or third marriage where both parties have been divorced or widowed at least once. Select part, or all, of the following paragraphs, according to whether the parties have been recently widowed/divorced or alone for many years.)

All marriages are special occasions but a second marriage is a doubly precious time because you do not take everything for granted. You realize how very lucky you are to be given another chance to be happy, and appreciate the blessing you have received in finding a soulmate and companion you can trust. It is a time of renewed hope.

I know that the two of you who are getting married today feel it is wonderful to be with so many good friends, and in particular one good friend, who understands your heartaches as well as your joys. That is so important.

It is a pleasure for you to experience an end to loneliness and sadness, and a joy for us to be witnesses and share this beginning with you. When you have experienced past disappointments, hardship and disillusionment, you know you have been up and down on life's waves. And when you are in the troughs of those waves, you sometimes wonder when you will ever come up again. Yet there is always a chance anew, an opportunity to feel love for someone, just like the first time. The past does not burden the present – but you learn by it, and do not repeat your mistakes. You have an opportunity through experience for knowing better than anyone else what is at stake and how much effort it takes, and what a loss it is if you don't do everything you can to make your partner contented. How fortunate you are to have found yet another chance at happiness together, with a better understanding than most people of what you should do to make a successful marriage, and how much you will gain.

It is difficult late in life to put away the past, and start again, but you have all the means at your disposal to make a success of the venture. Everyone has the right to happiness, and you should have the chance to find happiness, whether you are someone young starting life again, or a grandmother, why not?

We are confident that you will now receive the joy you deserve, and we are really happy for you. I speak for everyone here when I say we wish you all the best, and hope that for you (pause) 'the best is yet to come'. So, Annabelle and Steven, we would like to drink a toast to your happy future together. (Raise glass.)

To Annabelle and Steven.

SPEECHES TO AVOID

OVER-APOLOGETIC SPEECH

I don't know why anyone picked me to give a speech. I've never given a speech in my life before. And I'm sure you don't want a long speech but I've tried to prepare something, and I hope it's all right. Anyway, all I can say is, I did make some notes somewhere, I think I put them in my pocket, or maybe (silence). Well, I can't find them, but (pause), oh, here it is. I've got a joke! 'As I was on my way to the wedding' (pause). Oh, I've dropped it! Can you move your chair? No, don't bother. It's not really funny, and you've probably heard it anyway. Most of you don't know Alf, but I expect you'll want to wish him, and the bride of course, a happy, er, future.

NEGATIVE SPEECH – AND RATHER TOO REVEALING!

I don't like speeches and I didn't want to give a speech, but Martha insisted I should. I suppose there was nobody else. I'm not a good speaker so I'm not going to bore you by making a long speech.

Anne's a nice girl. I went out with Anne for a long time before she decided to marry Alfred, or he decided to marry her. So I suppose it's what she wanted and she's done the right thing. Anyway, they know each other pretty well, having been living together for two years now. They wouldn't have got married if she hadn't been pregnant, so the baby has done something good. I know her Mum's pleased. The baby's going to be a big change. Everyone says, 'May all your troubles be little ones'. Apart from that I don't suppose they'll have any troubles. Marriage won't be a big change for them as they'll be living in the same place, you know. So everything is going to be all right, more or less.

Er – what else am I supposed to say? If you haven't got a drink the bar's still open. Prices are a bit steep but you don't go to weddings every day. We're going to pass the hat round later, buy some beer and go back to their place. Anne's shaking her head. What's the matter? Don't you want us to? Alfred says it's all right. Anyway, if you can't afford the whisky and you haven't got any beer left, grab a glass of water. To Anne and Alf! Can I sit down now?

EXTREMELY BRIEF REPLY FROM THE BRIDEGROOM

Thank you.

DEPRESSING SPEECH

Relatives and friends, the one person missing here today is of course, Anne's father, and no day can be really happy without him with us. Though I have tried to take his place, it is mere formality. No-one can take his place. Our happiness would have been complete if he had been here. Alas he is not. We miss his help and his advice, as a husband to Martha, and father to Anne. He made so many plans for this wedding. If only he could have seen Anne today . . . (breaks off). Has somebody got a handkerchief to give to Anne?'

RELUCTANT FATHER-IN-LAW'S SPEECH

We're very pleased to see Anne getting married, at last. When I first met Alfred I didn't like him very much, because of his hair and his clothes and the fact that he didn't have a steady job, but now I've got to know him he doesn't seem too bad. All these are things which can be changed. I'm sure Anne could change him if she wanted to, but she seems to like him the way he is. We're sorry that his Mum, what's her name?, died, and that his Dad didn't come along with his new stepmother, but perhaps it's just as well. Anyway, um, where was I? Well, er, I think that's everything. Let's all have a drink. Was I supposed to toast somebody?

GUSHING SPEECH

I am deeply honoured to be invited to this momentous and lavish occasion by my esteemed friends, Martha and George. It is a privilege to pay them this small token of respect. I am sure Martha will forgive me for saying that her very presence excites envy from others. Martha has always been admired for her brilliant elegance, the epitome of good taste. The evidence before our eyes is her faultless attention to detail in these exquisite flower decorations. It has been a day which commenced so stunningly with the horse and carriage procession, swept forward with the harmonious, soaring, musical arrangements at the wedding ceremony, and has culminated in the utter perfection of the gourmet dinner, all in keeping with what we have come to expect from the organizational abilities of one of the world's paragons. No woman on earth could have been a more devoted, exacting, wife and mother, and Annabelle has admirably folowed her mother's fine example, having inherited flawless covergirl looks, and demonstrating impeccable good manners. You will, I am quite sure, agree with me totally when I say, our beautiful, delectable, Annabelle is irreplaceable, and we shall miss her dreadfully, when she departs across the skies to the beautiful tropical paradise which she will enhance immeasurably . . .

LONG POMPOUS SPEECH

Your Royal Highness, ladies and gentlemen, as a minister, judge and professor, I feel I am in a good position to speak about the history of marriage, its importance in society, and the duties of the married couple to each other and the wider community. First, the history of marriage (continues) . . .

Now, we shall continue with the sayings of the numerous venerable sages (continues) . . .

. . . Well, I agreed not to speak more than half an hour, but I see that I have been speaking for a little longer than forty-five minutes. I could continue considerably longer on this fascinating subject, in fact I have several pages of notes here if anybody wishes to come and ask me any questions. Unfortunately I am obliged to terminate at this stage, because someone has just passed me a note saying that the band has to depart at 11 pm, and it is now 10.30. So I will conclude by saying that (continues) . . .

JOKES, COMIC STORIES & ANECDOTES

On a happy occasion such as a wedding, jokes and comic stories are welcome and make a particularly good ending for a speech. If you cannot tell long jokes without getting lost, stick to one-liners. Try out each of your jokes on someone who will not be at the wedding to see if it sounds funny the way you tell it.

FINDING A JOKE

Books of quotations and joke books provide sources. Humorous books related to your subjects are also useful.

Turn for advice to witty friends, those who are often invited to give speeches, or to professional speech writers. When constructing a funny story remember that one of the elements of humour in the punchline is surprise, going suddenly from the sublime to the ridiculous, from exhilaration to despair, from discovery of a tragedy to self-centred concern about some minor problem.

CHANGING CLICHES

Two dangers with clichés such as 'May all their troubles be little ones' are that older members of the audience have heard them before and that the previous speaker may use the same joke or saying. To create a more original effect well-known phrases and sayings can be contrasted with others which contradict them. To be sure of surprise and originality adapt the joke to a new locality or profession, or better still find a funny story based on a situation taken from real life.

AVOIDING UNSUITABLE SUBJECT MATTER

The Victorians said that at the dinner table you should not discuss sex, politics, or religion. Similarly in a wedding speech statements about religion or politics might result in a quarrel or give offence by causing people with opposing views to disagree, insult each other, or try to convert each other. Sexual references might give offence, as can double entendres. As a general rule you should avoid unintentionally offending friends or potential friends, but instead flatter or compliment them.

If your audience is Irish, even if you are Irish, you do not want a joke which makes Irish people appear stupid, but clever instead. The same applies to Jews or any other national or religious group. Remember, that unless you have inspected the wedding list and know everybody on both sides of the family you can never be sure who is in a large audience.

ADAPTING JOKES

Jokes have a vogue. The same jokes are told about foreigners in different countries. The jokes told about the Irish in England are told about the Belgians in France. They are really stock jokes, and often have little reference to the nationalities mentioned.

If the most amusing anecdote you can find is one which is rather negative, tell it and then dissociate yourself from the views it expresses. For example, supposing you want to refer to the fact that the groom is a medical student and you have a story about a king dying in the Middle Ages who says the physician has killed him, tell this story but end it, 'Of course medicine has come a long way since those days'.

Another way to tell a joke without directing it against your subject is to refer it to other people. For example, if you wanted to use the line that, 'Doctors bury their mistakes' without appearing to criticize the bridegroom who is a medical student or doctor, you could say that 'other doctors' bury their mistakes.

In addition to deleting anything in bad or questionable taste, you might like to add a national, regional or personal dimension to a good joke. Jokes can become more amusing if you can perfect the appropriate accent, or introduce local placenames and references. So if you find a good Irish joke and want to tell it about another local or ethnic group you could do so. To perfect the accent you could obtain one of many BBC records of stories told in various accents. Alternatively if you are trying to use an accent because some members of the wedding party speak like that, get one of them to record a short passage for you on tape and play it over until you have perfected their accent.

A SHORT COMPENDIUM OF JOKE THEMES

ACTORS

I come not to bury Caesar but to praise (bridegroom's

name). When an accomplished actor like (bridegroom's name) realizes he is going to have a speaking part in the wedding ceremony he jumps at the opportunity. Alas, being the best man at an actor's wedding is like trying to direct an actor who wants to direct. At the wedding rehearsal we got the video camera out and (bridegroom's name) said, 'To do or not to do . . .' Then he asked who was the understudy.

As an actor myself, I wanted a part, too, but there isn't a speaking part for the best man at a wedding ceremony. So (bridegroom's name) very kindly invited me to give a speech. I was a trifle nervous when I remembered all the films I'd seen about weddings. There's Jane Eyre where the wedding is interrupted by someone who says the groom is already married. When we did the rehearsal again and Steven got it right I asked myself, has he played this scene before? Worse still, on the day, how could I be sure, with so many actors around, that the bridesmaids wouldn't turn out to be actors in drag? You can imagine my relief now that it's all over, and that it has turned out to be such a beautiful, conventional, dream wedding. They played their parts perfectly.

BUILDERS/DECORATORS

It is harder to build than to destroy.

CINEMA/THEATRE/WEDDING USHERS/USHERETTES

A woman in the audience/church left in the middle of the performance/wedding and as she left she trod on the foot of the man at the end of the row. When she returned she said, 'Did I tread on your foot on the way out?'

'Yes, he replied.'

'Good!' she said, 'Then this is my row.'

COMMITTEES/OFFICE WORKERS

A camel is a horse which got designed by a committee.

COMPUTER OPERATORS

President Kennedy said to an astronaut, 'Man is still the most extraordinary computer of all.'

To err is human. To really foul things up requires a computer.

Always check computerized bills. When we had just married our only gas consumption was the cooker, but we had a bill which would have enabled us to have cooked meals for the whole of Harrow.

CRAFTSPERSON

I asked (bride's/bridegroom's name) what he/she did and he/she said, 'I'm a craftsperson.'
   'Ah, I said, crafty, eh?'

CRICKET

Foreigners often ask me to explain the rules of cricket. A cricket game lasts up to five days. There are eleven players in each team. We do not follow the decimal system. That's 'not cricket'. We do not follow the British system of counting in dozens. That is not cricket. We count in elevenses. That is cricket. Three important words are in and out and over. In cricket there is a wicket. One man stands near the wicket and bats and another bowls. The batsman is in. If he knocks down the wicket with his own leg, he is out. If he hits the ball he runs. There's another batsman who runs too, in the opposite direction. Every six balls they change the bowler. That's called an over. But the game isn't over. Not until they're all out. That's not the end of the game either, just the end of that innings. Now you know all the ins and outs of cricket. Simple, isn't it!

DANCING

We had to ask the bridesmaids not to pirouette in the aisle.

The bride was going to get married in a tutu but we persuaded her against it.

DENTISTS/DENTAL TECHNICIANS

What makes you nervous about them is that when you go to dinner with them, they pump up the chair.

DOCTORS/NURSES/MEDICAL

In the dress rehearsal when she held out her finger for the ring he took her pulse./In the dress rehearsal when he held out the ring to her she took his pulse.

We have three empty seats today. One of these was for a doctor who has gone to the Middlesex Hospital. The other seats were for a couple who didn't know their way to this hall and decided to follow *his* car. We just had a call from them. They're at the Middlesex Hospital. They want to know the way back.

Most doctors have three things on their mind, ill, pill and bill. But he's/she's such a successful doctor he/she can afford to tell the patients when there's nothing wrong with them.

Good doctors aim to add life to your years, not just years to your life.

DRINKING A TOAST

A glass of wine/whisky/champagne is said to cure all sorts of ills such as the common cold. All you need is a candle and a glass of wine/whisky/champagne. Light the candle, drink the first glass and wait five minutes. Drink another glass and wait, still watching the candle. Keep drinking until you see three candles, then snuff out the middle one and go to sleep.

DRIVERS (OF BUSES, TAXIS, CARS, LORRIES)

The French chauffeurs/Israeli motorists/Glasgow/Dublin drivers/East End taxi drivers/bus drivers, like (bridegroom's name) and his Dad are skilful, safe drivers. I was in a car/taxi/bus once which shot through a red light. At the next crossing it shot through another red light. The third light was green and it skidded to a halt. 'Why did you do that?' I asked.

He (bridegroom's name) said, 'You can't be too careful. There could have been another car/coach/taxi coming the other way!'

FARMERS AND FOOTBALLERS

Football coach, Bear Bryant, is also a farmhand and in the old days farmhands used to guide a team of animals in front of the plough, encouraging them and making sure they all pulled together. But he also coaches a football team and his secret for teamwork is this. What he says is that if anything goes badly, he tells the team, 'I did it'. If anything goes reasonably well, he says, 'We did it!' But when everything goes really well, he says to them, 'You did it!' Marriage is not a game: it is a team.

FINANCE

Charles Dickens had some advice on budgeting. The

character Mr Micawber was based on Dickens' father and according to Dickens, Mr Micawber said, 'Annual income twenty pounds, annual expenditure nineteen and sixpence, result happiness. Annual income twenty pounds, annual expenditure twenty pounds and sixpence, result misery.' (Pause.) Mr Micawber's problem was he didn't have an account at (name bride's or bridegroom's bank/business).

Jane Austen said, 'It is a truth universally acknowledged, that a single man in possession of a good fortune must be in want of a wife.' She must have been thinking of Steven (bridegroom's name). However, she must also have been thinking of Annabelle (bride's name) when she added, 'She was of course only too good for him: but as nobody minds what is too good for them, he was very steadily earnest in pursuit of the blessing.'

FOOD INDUSTRY WORKER/WAITERS/WAITRESSES

It is said that Colman's Mustard made their money from the amount of mustard left on the plate.

A customer asked (bridegroom's name) if the fruit salad was fresh. 'Yes,' he said, 'fresh last week!'

A diner called over Annabelle/Steven and said, 'Waiter, waiter . . ./Waitress, waitress, there's a . . .'

GOLFERS

Golf has been defined as a good walk spoilt.

All is fair in love and golf.

One thing you should remember: when he says, 'I just made a hole in one,' don't say, 'I didn't see you. Do it again, dear'.

You've all heard of golf widows. Golfers have all sorts of excuses about why they get home late. There was one who told his wife, 'The reason I'm late is that Harry died at the third hole, so we had to go all the way round the other fifteen holes on the course, dragging Harry.'

GARDENERS/GROCERS/GREENGROCERS

George has the best fruit/fruit trees. One day a little boy was standing looking at his apples/apple trees. George (name of bridegroom, father-in-law) said, 'Were you trying to take an apple?'

The little boy answered, 'No. I was trying not to take an apple.'

GREEK LANGUAGE LESSON

Steven's (groom's name) language is Greek and the Greek alphabet may be all Greek to you but it is surprising how much Greek we all use. A popular Greek saying is 'Know Thyself', which dates back to the ancient Greeks. Everybody has heard of Socrates and Plato. At college we did a philosophy course and we were very impressed to see a student reading Plato in the original Greek. Then we discovered the student was Greek! (Bridegroom's name) explained to me the Greek alphabet which is really very familiar. It goes from alpha to omega, beginning Alpha, beta, gamma, delta. From these we get out word alphabet, delta, and gamma which gives us gamma rays. And iota means very little. I asked (bridegroom's name) what the Greek for 'I' is. 'Ego' is I. Everybody here has an ego. You can tell that (bridegroom's name) is a good teacher. He makes it all sound so easy.

JOURNALISTS/PRINTERS/NEWSAGENTS

A journalist is someone who hears shouts from a river, rushes up and asks, 'Are you all right?' When the man shouts back, 'I'm drowning,' the journalist replies, 'You're out of luck. You've missed the evening edition. But we can give you a paragraph in the morning edition.'

Adapt this by inserting bride's or groom's name; e.g. 'When Steven/Annabelle was a young reporter he/she heard a shout from someone drowning in a river . . .'

A journalist tries to get into places other people are trying to get out of.

Some journalists work for the paper read by the people who run the country (The Times). Some journalists work for the paper read by the people who think they run the country (The Telegraph). Some journalists work for the paper read by the people who want to run the country (The Mail/The Express). Some journalists work for the paper whose readers don't care who runs the country so long as the girl on page three is well endowed (The Sun).

(Adapt this by finishing with appropriate newspaper or magazine, e.g. 'But (bridegroom's name) works for the paper read by the people who want to buy a Ford Granada for fourpence/by twenty stone women who want to be as slim as Twiggy by Tuesday/Saturday (day of wedding)' etc. This can be equally adapted to American or other foreign newspapers.)

LAWYERS, JUDGES, AND SOLICITORS

A jury consists of twelve persons chosen to decide who has the better lawyer.

(Robert Frost)

MANAGERS

The secret of good management is, never put off until tomorrow what you can get someone else to do today, especially if you want it done yesterday.

MUSICIANS/SINGERS

As a keen musician and clarinet player (name your own musical instrument or say 'As one who appreciates music but cannot play anything more difficult than a gramophone record, I was very impressed to learn) I was delighted to learn that Annabelle's uncle plays for the BBC orchestra (or pop group, etc.), on the violin (or drums). He has played us excerpts from Wagner's Ring Cycle. We managed to persuade him not to perform the whole work during the wedding ceremony.

PHILOSOPHY TEACHERS

A philosopher is a man who, when you ask how his wife is, replies, 'In relation to whom?'

POLITICIANS

Politics it not a bad profession. If you succeed there are many rewards. If you disgrace yourself you can always write a book.

(*Ronald Reagan*)

POST OFFICE WORKERS

They deliver letters everywhere, even the cemetery – Dead Letters.

PSYCHIATRISTS AND PSYCHOLOGISTS

I am often asked the difference between a psychologist

and a psychiatrist. I say that a psychologist deals with the things normal people say and do, while a psychiatrist deals with the things dotty people say and do. When two psychologists are in a lift and a man gets into the lift and says hello, one psychologist turns to another and asks, 'What do you think he meant by that?'

SECOND MARRIAGES

I'm not so old, and not so plain,
And I'm quite prepared to marry again.

(W. S. Gilbert)

SHOPKEEPERS

The following type of story might be told by the best man, a friend, or groom who works in the bride's family business:

Annabelle's family have owned their furniture shop for over 100 years and it is easy to see why they are a success if you have had the privilege of actually working for them, as I have. When customers buy on sunny days and then change their minds when the goods are delivered the next day, a rainy day, goods are returned frequently in wet plastic sheets. Annabelle's father insists that any furniture order is delivered the same day, even if it means driving fifty miles and doing the driving and shifting himself. That means the customer gets the goods while still enthusiastic – and is very satisfied.

SOCIAL WORKERS/PRISON VISITORS

When Pope John XXIII visited prison he said to the inmates 'You could not come to see me so I have come to see you.'

Steven/Annabelle went to visit a woman in prison who was accused of poisoning a relative/colleague. Now it isn't easy to deal with this sort of situation. But Annabelle/Steven won the woman's confidence. The woman showed her appreciation by baking Annabelle/Steven a cake.

SPORT

Wellington said that the Battle of Waterloo was won on the playing fields of Eton.

STATISTICIANS

Everybody asks me what a statistician does. This story will explain it. A treasury statistician came down the steps of the ministry and met a beggar who held out his hand and said, 'Spare a shilling, mister? I haven't eaten for a week!'

The statistician replied, 'Really? And how does that compare with the same period last year?'

TEACHERS

One of the most difficult tasks of a teacher is to tell a father that his son can't cope with the new maths. But you can soften the blow by telling his Dad that none of the other dads can do it either.

TELEVISION

Buckminster Fuller said television is the third parent.

On television, detective series end at just the right moment, after the criminal has been caught and before the courts turn him loose.

TENNIS PLAYERS

Annabelle (bride's name) and Steven (groom's name) are both tennis players – the perfect match.

VETS/PET LOVERS

Vets have very strange conversations on the phone. Sometimes we are on call at someone else's house, and a call is referred from a dog-owner and a relative hears us saying, 'And how is his third leg?'

In America the pet department at Macy's stocks dresses and bows for the best-dressed poodle. We did think of bringing a pooch along to follow the bride, dressed as a bridesmaid.

Other sources of ideas can be found in the books of the well-known author-vet James Herriot and humorous poems on cats and dogs can be found in the collected works of T. S. Eliot.

WEDDING CUSTOMS

The French have some amusing wedding customs. When the dance music starts they play games. The first time the music stops every man gives his right shoe to his partner. Then he turns and dances with the woman behind. Next time the music stops he gives away his left shoe and again takes the partner behind. Then the woman gives away her right shoe, then her left shoe, then the man removes his jacket, then his tie. After the music stops for the last time the first man to return the ladies' shoes and collect up all his clothing is allowed to kiss every woman in the room!

WORK

Some people like to rest. 'I like work. I can enjoy watching it for hours.' Others are workaholics who cannot stop working. Pius XII said to doctors who told him to cut down on his work schedule, 'I shall be able to rest one minute after I die.'

Of every 100 people in this country 55 per cent are of working age. At any one time fifteen per cent are unemployed, that leaves 40 per cent. Of these, five per cent are sick, leaving 35 per cent. Of these, five per cent are on strike, leaving 30 per cent. At this time of year 20 per cent are on holiday, leaving 10 per cent. And of these, 8 per cent are looking after children or relatives. That leaves you and me. That means all the work has to be done by Annabelle (bride's name) and me (groom's name).

One hundred people said they would help Matilda (insert bride's mother's name) organize the wedding. Of these fifty-five were at work. Five were looking for work. Five were away on business. One was minding the shop/on night duty/taking exams. (Continue as above.)

That left only Annabelle and me to help with the washing up. But we are going away on our honeymoon. Now you appreciate how much work and effort and thought Matilda (bride's mother's name) has put into organizing this wonderful wedding.

WRITERS

When Agatha Christie was asked where she got her plots she replied, 'Harrods'.

ANECDOTES

Other humorous and serious anecdotes can be obtained by speaking to the subjects of your speech or their families and colleagues. Ask them: What was the most surprising thing that happened to you when you started working on the buses/in the shop/in the hospital/in the school? Have there been any funny customers/patients/pupils/incidents? Who was your best pupil/patient? What was the most useful thing you learnt when you started working/teaching? Did you have any disasters at the beginning? What was your greatest success?

There are many ready-made collections of anecdotes available in book form. Try browsing along the reference shelves of your local library, or the humour section of the local bookshop.

QUOTATIONS

Add spice to your speech and toast by inserting an amusing, interesting or relevant quotation. This chapter includes a selection of quotations for the most common subjects you are likely to want to cover: love, marriage, weddings, family, work and hobbies and so on. Libraries and bookshops stock treasuries of quotations.

OCCUPATIONAL HEROES AND HAZARDS

If the bride's or groom's family is in the entertainment professions it is easy to produce a humorous quotation from an actor, singer, movie star, television personality, songwriter, or playwright. These suit numerous ancillary professions, such as TV company employees, where the fun can be enjoyed by rival organizations. Statesmen and politicians in the family offer equally numerous opportunities for choosing quotations from famous world leaders.

For relevant quotations for other occupations, look in trade journals and magazines.

RELIGIOUS AND INSPIRATIONAL SUBJECTS

For locating religious quotations, concordances to the

Bible will direct you to quotations in the Old and New Testament. Many religious organizations keep stocks of books in their bookshops or libraries. If you are getting married at a particular church or synagogue you may be granted access to a library not normally opened to the public. The priest, minister, rabbi, or other community leader probably knows sources and will most likely quote them to you from memory if you telephone or approach him or her after a service. If you cannot find help from the nearest religious Catholic, Protestant, Methodist, Hindu, Muslim, Buddhist, or Jewish organization, try the history or language departments of colleges – Hebrew Studies, Arabic Studies, Modern Languages for French and Spanish Language & Literature, Oriental Studies, or Asian Languages.

WITTY QUOTATIONS

Well-known humorous writers include James Thurber, Charles Dickens, Mark Twain, Jane Austen, Oscar Wilde, George Bernard Shaw and of course William Shakespeare. There are concordances to Shakespeare and a *Who's Who in Dickens*.

Songwriters are another good source of quotable lines. You can track down the words of songwrwiters from books of librettos, record sleeves, or by playing their records or cassettes if you have a lot of time to spare. Try W. S. Gilbert, Sammy Cahn, and Noel Coward or a dictionary of popular music.

AMERICAN AND CANADIAN QUOTATIONS

American quotations can be found among the sayings of

every past President from Washington, Jefferson, Lincoln, Roosevelt, and Kennedy to Reagan. Politics, business, morality, and determination to win against the odds are popular subjects. *The Oxford Companion to American Literature* will help to locate American novels, plays and other books.

Depending on the language spoken and preferred by Canadians in your audience, you can quote from either English or French authors, or both, as well as modern Canadian authors, or traditional favourites such as L. M. Montgomery who wrote the ever-popular *Anne of Green Gables* and Mazo de la Roche who wrote the *Jalna* series.

FINDING POEMS

Unless you are a great actor or orator avoid any verse over four lines long. Five-line limericks, however, add humour, but be sure that are in good taste. Your local library should have a variety of poetry anthologies for your reference.

ADAPTING QUOTATIONS

The more you can relate your quotations to your audience and the people you are praising in your speech, the more interested and flattered they will feel. If the only quotation you can find is not very relevant or complimentary, adapt it. For example, when the subject of your speech is a soldier you could start, 'According to the British Grenadiers, "Some talk of Alexander, and some of Hercules, and others of Lysander and such great names as these." But I would rather talk about Captain (bride-groom's name).'

A SELECTION OF QUOTATIONS

To make the following quotations more suitable for delivery in a speech, those using old-fashioned language have been updated.

QUOTATIONS

It is a good thing for an uneducated man to read books of quotations.

(*Winston Churchill*)

ADVICE

In giving advice I advise you, be short.

(*Horace*)

Don't give a woman advice; one should never give a woman anything she can't wear in the evening.

(*Oscar Wilde*)

Tact is the art of making a point without making an enemy. The most difficult thing in the world is to know how to do a thing and to watch someone else doing it wrong and keep quiet.

Live within your means, even if you have to borrow money to do it.

God helps them that helps themselves.

(*Benjamin Franklin*)

Forgive one another, as God forgives you.

(*New Testament*)

No act of kindness, no matter how small, is ever wasted.

(*Aesop*)

AGE

Age brings wisdom. American millionaire, Bernard Baruch, said that, 'an elder statesman is somebody old enough to know his mind – and keep quiet about it'.

You're only young once, and if you work it right, once is enough.

(*Joe E. Lewis*)

Wrinkles should merely indicate where smiles have been.

(*Mark Twain*)

Grow old along with me!
The best is yet to be.

(*Robert Browning*)

BLESSINGS, THANKS, PRAYERS AND HOPES

The Lord is my shepherd; I shall not want. . . .
Surely goodness and mercy shall follow me all the days of my life.

(*Psalm 23. A Psalm of David*)

God bless us and cause his face to shine upon us.

(*Psalm 67*)

CHILDREN

Children are your heritage, like arrows in the hand of a mighty man. Happy is the man who has his quiver full of them.

(*Adapted from Psalm 127*)

May your wife be like a fruitful vine growing by the side of your house, and your children like olive plants round about your table.

(*Adapted from Psalm 128*)

DRINKING AND TOASTS

Drink to me only with thine eyes,
And I will pledge with mine;
Or leave a kiss within the cup,
And I'll not look for wine.

(*Ben Jonson*)

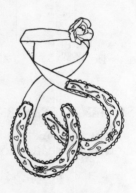

FAMILIES

Important families are like potatoes. The best parts are underground.

He that hath a wife and children hath given hostages to fortune.

(*Francis Bacon*)

The apple does not fall far from the tree.

(*Proverb*)

Everyone is the son of his own works.

(Don Quixote, *Miguel de Cervantes*)

The child is the father of the man.

(William Wordsworth)

Winston Churchill said, a family starts 'with a young man falling in love with a girl. No superior alternative has been found.'

A man must first govern himself ere he is fit to govern a family.

(Sir Walter Raleigh)

FATHER

A father of the fatherless is God.

(Psalm 68)

Honour thy father and thy mother.

(Old Testament)

FRIENDSHIP

No man is useless while he has a friend.

(Robert Louis Stevenson)

One man in a thousand, Solomon says,
Will stick more close than a brother.
But the thousandth Man will stand by your side
To the gallows-foot – and after!

(Rudyard Kipling)

A faithful friend is the medicine of life.

(Ecclesiasticus)

Happiness consists not in the multitude of friends but in their worth and choice.

(Ben Jonson)

(The only way) to have a friend is to be one.
                              (*Ralph Waldo Emerson*)

GUESTS

Too late I stayed, – forgive the crime;
Unheeded flew the hours.
How noiseless falls the foot of time,
That only treads on flowers!
                  (*Hon. William Robert Spencer*)

Laugh and be merry together, like brothers akin,
Guesting awhile in the room of a beautiful inn.
Glad till the dancing stops, and the lilt of the music
    ends.
Laugh till the game is played; and be you merry my
    friends.
          (*John Masefield – from* Laugh and be Merry)

HAPPINESS

The greatest happiness of the greatest number.
                              (*Jeremy Bentham*)

HEALTH AND WEALTH

If you enjoy good health, you are rich.

Early to bed and early to rise makes a man healthy,
wealthy and wise.

I wish you health; I wish you wealth; I wish you gold in
store; I wish you heaven when you die; what could I wish
you more?

HOME AND AWAY

East, west, home's best.

There is no place like home after the other places close.

> If solid happiness we prize,
> Within our breast this jewel lies;
> And they are fools who roam;
> The world has nothing to bestow;
> From our own selves our joys must flow,
> And that dear place – our home.
>
> *(Nathaniel Cotton)*

> Wherever I roam, whatever realms I see,
> My heart untravelled fondly turns to thee.
>
> *(Oliver Goldsmith)*

> 't is distance leads enchantment to the view,
> And robes the mountain in its azure hue.
>
> *(Thomas Campbell)*

HONEYMOON

Ten years ago the moon was source of inspiration for lovers. In ten years time it will be just another airport.

> *(Emmanuel G. Mesthene – adapted)*

HOUSE

> I often wish that I had clear,
> For life, six hundred pounds a year,
> A handsome house to lodge a friend,
> A river at my garden's end.
>
> *(Jonathan Swift)*

HUSBANDS

American women expect to find in their husbands a perfection that English women only hope to find in their butlers.

Being a husband is a whole time job.

(Arnold Bennett)

Husbands love your wives and do not be bitter against them.

(New Testament, Colossians)

LOVE

Whatever you do ... love those who love you.

(Voltaire)

Love and marriage go together like a horse and carriage.

(Sammy Cahn – song)

Whoever loved that loved not at first sight?

(Christopher Marlowe)

And to his eye
There was but one beloved face on earth
And that was shining on him.

(Lord Byron)

A thing of beauty is a joy forever.

(John Keats)

Love conquers all.

(Virgil)

None but the brave deserve the fair.

(Dryden)

He will hold thee, when his passion shall have spent its
   novel force,
Something better than his dog, a little dearer than his
   horse.

(Alfred Lord Tennyson)

The meeting of two personalities is like the contact of two
chemical substances; if there is any reaction, both are
transformed.

(Carl Jung)

The course of true love never did run smooth.

(William Shakespeare)

Love does not consist in gazing at each other, but in
looking outward in the same direction.

(Antoine de Saint-Exupery)

MARRIAGE

Here's to marriage, that happy estate that resembles a
pair of scissors: 'So joined that they cannot be separated,
often moving in opposite directions, yet punishing
anyone who comes between them.'

(Sydney Smith)

Marriage is a bargain and somebody has to get the worst
of a bargain.

(Helen Rowland)

Let me not to the marriage of true minds
Admit impediments.

(William Shakespeare)

Happiness in marriage is entirely a matter of chance.

(Jane Austen)

It is a woman's business to get married as soon as possible and a man's to keep unmarried as long as he can.

(*George Bernard Shaw*)

Marriage is popular because it combines the maximum of temptation with the maximum of opportunity.

(*George Bernard Shaw*)

Marriage is like a cage; one sees the birds outside desperate to get in; and those inside desperate to get out.

(*Montaigne*)

SECOND MARRIAGE

To lose one husband is a misfortune. To lose two looks like carelessness.

(*Jane Austen*)

The triumph of hope over experience.

(*Dr Samuel Johnson*)

'Tis better to have loved and lost than never to have loved at all.

(*Alfred Lord Tennyson*)

We're number two. We try harder.

(*Avis Car Rental advertisement*)

When I lost my wife every family in town offered me another.

(*Proverb*)

And on her lover's arm she leant,
And round her waist she felt it fold,
And far across the hills they went
In that new world which is the old.

(*Alfred Lord Tennyson*)

I chose my wife, as she did her wedding gown, for qualities that would wear well.

(*Oliver Goldsmith*)

When widows exclaim loudly against second marriages, I would always lay a wager, that the man, if not the wedding-day, is absolutely fixed on.

(*Henry Fielding*)

... speak of one that loved not wisely but too well; of one not easily jealous, but being wrong perplex'd in the extreme.

(*William Shakespeare*)

MEN AND CHARACTER

The test of a man or woman's breeding is how they behave in a quarrel.

(*George Bernard Shaw*)

MEN AND WOMEN

Men have sight, women insight.

(*Victor Hugo*)

MONEY

Money is like a sixth sense without which you cannot make use of the other five.

(*W. Somerset Maugham*)

Get money; still get money, boy;
No matter by what means.

(*Ben Jonson*)

MOTHERS

A mother is a mother still,
The holiest thing alive.

(Samuel Taylor Coleridge)

For a wife take the daughter of a good mother.

(Thomas Fuller)

Lincoln said, All that I am, or hope to be, I owe to my angel mother.

A mother's love endures through all; in good repute, in bad repute, in the face of the world's condemnation, a mother still loves on, and still hopes that her child may turn from his evil ways, and repent; she . . . remembers the infant smiles . . . the joyful shout of childhood, and the . . . promise of his youth; and she can never be brought to think him all unworthy.

(Washington Irving)

The hand that rocks the cradle . . . rules the world.

(William Ross Wallace)

MUSIC

If music be the food of love, play on.

(William Shakespeare)

Music hath charms to soothe a savage breast.

(William Congreve)

SPEECHES

It usually takes me more than three weeks to prepare a good impromptu speech.

(Mark Twain)

TRAVEL

I know where I'm going and I know who's going with me
(Anon)

WELCOME AND FRIENDSHIP

This land is your land.

(Woody Guthrie)

Will ye no come back again?

(Scottish)

Whither thou goest I will go.

(Book of Ruth, Old Testament)

WOMEN

The great question which I have never been able to answer is, 'What does a woman want?'

(Freud)

If men knew what women really think, they'd be ten times more daring.

(Alphonse Karr)

It is assumed that the woman must wait, motionless, until she is wooed. That is how the spider waits for the fly.

(George Bernard Shaw)

First, then, a woman will, or won't, – depend on it;
If she will do it, she will; and there's the end of it.

(Aaron Hill)

HOW TO INTRODUCE QUOTATIONS AND ANECDOTES INTO YOUR SPEECH

A slightly cumbersome but straightforward method is to begin, 'When I knew I was going to have to mention sailing, because that is Peter's great interest, I thought I would look up what great writers and poets of the past have said about sailing. The poet John Masefield said, "..."' If the quotation is a common one you could acknowledge this fact but turn it into a plus, 'We all know the lovely poem by John Masefield, which you can never tire of hearing, (Pause) "I must go down to the seas ..."'

If you happen to know your bride or bridegroom's tastes you could say, 'I would like to read you just the first verse/first two lines/last two lines of one of Sharon's favourite poems about the sea. It was written by John Masefield, and the title is Sea Fever.'

You may prefer to follow this by a lesser known quotation from another author. You could then relate their interest in the sea to what the bride and groom will have in common, 'I hope they will have many happy voyages/sailing trips together,' and finally relate your subject to the wider issue of marriage, 'and enjoy the voyage of life together'.

The symbolism of the sea has often been used by writers and speakers, but a similar ploy can be used relating to other professions, hobbies and subjects ranging from football to plane travel with original effect.

Make all your points positive ones. If your audience includes members who speak different languages or hold different religious views make sure that they can enjoy the quotations too and feel that you are addressing them as well as appreciate their point of view. For example, you might say, 'Whatever your religious background, you can appreciate the beautiful poetry of the psalms.'

ON THE DAY

IS THERE ANYBODY THERE?

Make sure you have your audience's attention from the moment you stand up. It is disconcerting to try to talk to a group of people who are clearly not listening. Stand up and wait for silence. If necessary, tap a glass for attention before starting to speak. A few well-aimed, well-considered words above the hubbub may well do the trick. The first paragraph of your speech after the preamble should be designed to hold everyone's attention.

It is also worth remembering that the way to hold someone's attention is to look at them. You lose their attention if you keep staring down at the papers in your hand. Look around at the whole audience, those at the front, the left, the right, and the back. When you raise your head and look at them they will be able to see you clearly too.

The sound of somebody's name attracts their attention. You will not want to reprove any children for talking during your speech. But if the pageboy William is talking, making noises, or turning paper napkins into darts, you could say, 'All the children have been as good as they could be, even little William!' This should momentarily distract William from whatever he is doing and raise a laugh from neighbouring tables.

YOUR PROPS

YOUR SPEECH OR SPEECH NOTES

Whether you have chosen to write out a full speech or to use comprehensive, ordered notes, there will be your main prop. Where should you keep them handily? Select a place where they are easy to reach, and keep them there all the time so that you do not have to hunt for them. Women have no difficulty – the handbag is the obvious choice. For men, if you are right-handed your right-hand outside pocket would be a good place; if you are left-handed, your left-hand pocket. A rented suit will be collected from a hire firm on the day before the wedding so make yourself a checklist which includes, 'Put speech notes in jacket pocket. Notes are now in desk.' If you are nervous or accident-prone, give a second copy to the best man or chief bridesmaid to guard against loss.

Handwritten notes may be hard to read when you are flustered, inebriated or reading in a dim light. It is also particularly difficult to discover your place in a speech after you have been looking up at the audience. Get the notes typewritten using a new ribbon, or copy them out in black felt tip pen in large capital letters. Write out large headings so that if possible you just need to glance at the headings to remind you of what to say.

Flimsy paper will rattle if your hands are shaking, betraying your nerves to the audience, and possibly making sounds over the microphone or on tape. So use card. If your pockets are small you may have to use index cards. Your speech may run over several cards. You want to avoid getting them in the wrong order or dropping them, so number them in the top corner, and link them together with a tag.

A GLASS OF WINE

You need a glass of wine to raise at the end of your speech if you are going to propose a toast. You may also want to have a tumbler of alcohol to sip to relax beforehand. But don't get so tiddly that you keep hiccoughing, or giggle all the way through, especially at your own jokes before you reach the punchline. And don't get so drunk that you can't stand up and have to sit down in the middle or, worse still, cannot speak at all. A glass of water is an ideal prop.

ADDITIONAL PROPS

Unless you are in the entertainment world you will find that dressing up in conventional wedding clothes is quite time-consuming. For the bride there is the challenge of walking and dancing in a full length dress, and perhaps not getting tangled in the microphone cable. For the ushers wearing grey morning suits, tails and bow ties, and dancing in them, is quite enough excitement, not to mention keeping track of where you left the top hat. You will not want to perform a dance on the table, or change twenty costumes for non-stop comedy routines. However, just one prop such as a funny hat, or a quick joke about how to get a grey top hat to fit, using a spare outsize one which comes right down over your eyes, can make the speech unusual. This could be effective at a wedding where grey top hats are worn, or even funnier at an informal wedding as part of a speech, showing why they decided NOT to have a formal wedding!

WHAT TO AVOID

The first essential is to be there. Don't disappear into the loo at the vital moment.

If you are prone to stammering or stuttering you may prefer not to speak, although if you are the bridegroom others will probably insist upon it. Winston Churchill became a famous speaker even though he stuttered, because what he said was so interesting, and he persisted in public speaking. King George VI stammered but everyone was so sympathetic that his first radio broadcast on Christmas Day in wartime established the popular tradition of the royal Christmas Day speech.

Decide whether drink will make the problem worse or better. Eliminate from your speech any words containing awkward letters or multiple syllables. Many people stammer or stutter because they are nervous; but with sufficient determination you can carry this off with aplomb and turn it to your advantage by laughing at yourself, 'I am so hap–p–p ... I'll try that again. Hap ... No, I'm not going to get it right. I'm going to keep on being hap hap happy for the rest of my life!'

Avoid distracting mannerisms such as jingling keys and coins in your pocket. These sounds wil be magnified by the microphone. Don't keep coughing, sniffing, and saying er, um, or 'you know'. Don't twiddle your hair, pull your ears, scratch your face, nor rub your nose or chin. Don't clench your fists tensely, or get so enthusiastic about what you are saying that you wave your arms about and knock over the wine. You may not knock over the wine, but the person sitting next to you and other members of the audience won't listen to your words. Your dramatic gestures will certainly mesmerize them, but they will be staring apprehensively at the glass, or laughing hysterically waiting for it to fall!

In order to cover up a faux pas do not look disconcerted but look pleased and pretend that the action was deliberate. For example, if somebody in the distant kitchen drops a tray with a clatter in the middle of your speech you could say, 'Applause at the end please!'

If there is a minor mishap you can make a joke of it. List all the worse mishaps which could have happened. These include the best man losing the ring, or going to the wrong church, and the groom finding the wrong woman when he lifts the veil. At one wedding the bridegroom and best man were standing in the wrong place, with the best man prompting a tongue-tied groom in a stage whisper. After the ceremony they really did discover that the minister had married the bride to the best man!

When latecomers appear through doors which slam noisily behind them and creep across the room in front of you, do not try to continue by raising your voice while your audience turn to look at the newcomers. There is a danger that the newcomers will dodge about trying to find somewhere to sit, and then whisper apologies to those near them, while you and your audience lose track of what you were saying. Instead you should pause, welcome them, and direct them to their seats: 'Aunt Mathilda, take a seat at the table. We're so glad you could make it. You're just in time for the toast to Annabelle. I was telling everyone how Annabelle met Steven in Kenya when they were on a safari holiday and . . .'

HOW TO AD LIB

You must be prepared to reply to an unexpected remark or joke by the previous speaker. You will probably find that this comes naturally and that you are happier and more confident than you thought you would be. But don't be overconfident about what others will understand when making off the cuff remarks to those you know well. Leave out obscure remarks, jargon, and private jokes, otherwise you'll have to keep explaining them to people all evening.

You may find that you are subject to some good-natured heckling from the audience. Think of two or three things that might be called out and invent some amusing replies. If several remarks are shouted at you, your replies will fit one of them. Nobody will remember what you did not say. You will get credit for the quick-thinking repartee of your one success.

The names of those attending the wedding are usually known in advance but if not you may be able to look at the seating plan or guest list on the day and make some joke about the names, picking out amusing surnames such as, 'In this room we have a Black but no White, two Browns, some Blues, and a Green, but no 'reds'. 'I'm glad to see that Annabelle's family includes several Golds, a lot of Silver, two Smiths, and a Cook. Steven's family, I'm afraid, has no Silver at all, but they are very practical. They have a lot of Smiths. And a Baker.'

First names and family names offer other possibilities, if there are several Johns, Josephs, Marias, Mohammeds, or Joneses, Cohens, Singhs, or Patels. 'Annabelle told me to look out for her brother John. But when I found John he knew nothing about car maintenance. He was a musician.' Name something connected with the first John's job or home area. You then continue by naming the professions, the towns of origin, or the streets where the other Johns live. End, 'She didn't tell me there were fifteen Johns/Joneses/Patels in the family.'

The clothes of those attending can also be referred to, especially if you can introduce them into a joke. You say that the chief character in your joke or story was wearing such and such a hat or pair of shoes. You progress slowly, gradually adding more details. The suspense and amusement increases as more and more people realize you are referring to the bride's father, or the bridegroom's mother, or the person sitting on your right. Lastly the audience laughs as the person being described realizes it.

If it still goes wrong on the day, never mind. You can console yourself with the thought that you did your best.

Don't worry too much about giving a good speech. This is a happy occasion and people aren't going to mind. Your effort has not been wasted. From now on you will listen with increased appreciation to the speeches of others. And whether you made mistakes or did well, you will be able to do better next time. Even if you only get married once, there will be more speeches to give or hear, at the weddings of your friends or your children. So enjoy yourself on the day. I am sure you will. Good luck!

INDEX